THE LIFE OF
ST. DOMINIC

"Preach the word: be instant in season, out of season: reprove, entreat, rebuke in all patience and doctrine. For there shall be a time, when they will not endure sound doctrine; but, according to their own desires, they will heap to themselves teachers, having itching ears: And will indeed turn away their hearing from the truth, but will be turned unto fables."
—2 Timothy 4:2-4

The trial by fire: the writings of the Albigenses are consumed in the flames, while St. Dominic's book on the Flesh of Christ is miraculously borne safely away in the presence of the whole assembly. (See pages 18 and 236.) In this book St. Dominic affirmed the Immaculate Conception of the Blessed Virgin Mary.

THE LIFE OF
ST. DOMINIC

by

Augusta Theodosia Drane
(Mother Frances Raphael)

SIXTH EDITION

Pie Pater Dominice,
Tuorum memor operum,
Sta coram summo Judice,
Pro tuo coetu pauperum.

O Venerable Father Dominic,
Mindful of thy works
(We beseech thee to) stand before
   the Supreme Judge
On behalf of the throngs of
   thy poor.

TAN BOOKS AND PUBLISHERS, INC.
Rockford, Illinois 61105

The Life of St. Dominic by Augusta Theodosia Drane (1823-1894) was first published in 1857 in London. The present edition is retypeset from the first part of a two-part work entitled *The Life of St. Dominic, with a Sketch of the Dominican Order* published by Burns, Oates & Washbourne Ltd., London, c. 1890.

Retypeset and published in 1988 by TAN Books and Publishers, Inc.

Library of Congress Catalog Card No.: 88-50268

ISBN: 0-89555-336-8

Printed and bound in the United States of America.

TAN BOOKS AND PUBLISHERS, INC.
P.O. Box 424
Rockford, Illinois 61105

1988

" 'And how shall they hear, without a preacher? And how shall they preach unless they be sent, as it is written: *How beautiful are the feet of them that preach the gospel of peace, of them that bring glad tidings of good things!* . . .Yes, verily, *their sound hath gone forth into all the earth, and their words unto the ends of the whole world.*"

—*Romans* 10:14-15, 18

CONTENTS

vii

PREFACE

A few words of explanation may seem required as an apology for presenting the public with a new biography of St. Dominic. The beautiful life of the Saint by Père Lacordaire seemed to have furnished everything that could be desired in clothing the legendary story of his great patriarch in a modern dress. But although there can certainly be no temptation to pretend to anything like a rivalry with that eloquent writer, there are some reasons which appear to make a fresh biography desirable for those among ourselves who wish to form a more familiar acquaintance with St. Dominic than is furnished in the brief notices given in English collections of the lives of the Saints. It is true Père Lacordaire's life has for some time been translated into our own language; but the very beauty of its style is so essentially French that no translation can preserve its peculiar charm, or render it as popular as it deserves to be. But it is French in something more than idiom: It was written with the avowed object of advancing the Order in France, and a prominence is therefore given to the Gallican associations of the Order of Preachers which, by readers of another nation, is felt to be undue.

In the following pages, the course of the Saint's life has been followed with no view save that of giving his character in its true historical light; and for this end, the simple narrative of facts, without comment or explanation, has been felt to be sufficient. We are much mistaken if the best defense that can be offered of St. Dominic's character, so long the subject of the strangest misrepresentation, be not to be found in the unvarnished story of his life, drawn from the testimony of those who saw him face to face, and whose writings form the principal material from which the following pages have been compiled.

There are some subjects which our readers may be disappointed in finding so briefly touched upon in a life of St. Dominic. But we have felt that several of the disputed points, commonly discussed by his biographers, have little real interest to the student of his character. We have not, therefore, entered at length into the history of the Albigensian war, or of the foundation of the Inquisition, preferring to leave the doubts arising out of these subjects to be resolved by others whose object is the critical examination of historical questions. Our only task has been to lay before our readers the personal portrait of one whose influence in the Church of Christ must endure so long as the religious and apostolic life shall be found within her bosom.

The authorities from which we have drawn our sketch have been chiefly Mamachi's Annals, with the ancient chronicles and memoirs reprinted in that work, including the Acts of Bologna, the memoir of Sister Cecilia, and that of blessed Humbert; Polidori's life, which follows the facts, and in many places the text, of Blessed Jordan; Ferdinand Castiglio's history of the Order, and the life of St. Dominic by Touron; whilst in the account of the early Fathers of the Order, great use has been made of F. Michel Pio's work entitled *Progenie dell' Ordine in Italia* (which collects all the particulars given by Gerard de Frachet and the old writers), and of the biographical sketches of F. Marchese in his *Diario Domenicano.*

The summary of the history of the Friars Preachers subsequent to the death of St. Dominic has been chiefly taken from Touron's great work on *The Illustrious Men of the Order.* In selecting a few out of the many names that called for notice, we have necessarily omitted a number that will readily suggest themselves to our readers; but our object has been to avoid wearying them with a mere enumeration of authors and learned works, and, without attempting such a complete sketch as our limited space rendered impossible, to suggest something of the general features of the Order as illustrated by the lives of its greatest men.

THE LIFE OF
ST. DOMINIC

"To me, the least of all the saints, is given this grace, to preach among the Gentiles, the unsearchable riches of Christ."

—Ephesians 3:8

CHAPTER 1

The birth of Dominic. His youth and university life.

It was in the year 1170, during the pontificate of Alexander III, that Dominic Guzman, the founder of the Order of Friars Preachers, was born at his father's castle of Calaroga, in Old Castile. The history of a genealogy, however illustrious, seems scarcely to find its place in the biography of a saint; though indeed few families can boast of one more honorable than that of the Castilian Guzmans. But if their long line of chivalrous ancestors, and the royal privileges granted to them by the kings of Spain, have no claim to be noticed here, the immediate ancestors of St. Dominic possessed at least one distinction which had a more powerful influence on his life. They were a family of saints.

The household of his father, Don Felix Guzman, was so remarkable for the religious character of its inmates that it was said to resemble rather a monastery than a knightly castle. His mother, Joanna of Aza, after being constantly held in popular veneration, has, almost within our own time, received the solemn beatification of the Church. The same testimony has been borne to the heroic sanctity of Manez, her second son; and though Antonio, the eldest of the three brothers, has not indeed received similar honors, yet was he no unworthy member of his illustrious family. We read of him that he became a secular priest, in which position he might have aspired to the highest ecclesiastical distinctions; but, enamored of holy poverty, he distributed his patrimony to the poor and retired to a hospital where he spent the remainder of his days in humbly ministering to the sick.

The future greatness of her younger son was announced to Joanna even before his birth. The mysterious vision of

1

a dog, bearing in his mouth a lighted torch which set fire to the world, appeared to indicate the power of that doctrine which should kindle and illuminate men's hearts through the ministry of his words. The noble lady who held him at the font saw, as the water was poured on his head, a brilliant star shining on the infant's forehead; and this circumstance, which is mentioned in the earliest life which we have of the saint (that of Blessed Jordan), bears a singular connection with the beautiful description of his appearance in after-life, left by his spiritual daughter, the Blessed Cecilia; in which she says, among other things, that "from his forehead, and between his brows, there shone forth a kind of radiant light, which filled men with respect and love."

Nor were the expectations which were excited by these prodigies in any way diminished by the promises of his childhood. His early years were passed in a holy household, and his first impressions were received from the all-powerful influence of a saintly mother. Amid the associations of a Christian family, his mind was molded into a religious shape even from his cradle; and the effect of this training is to be traced in the character of his maturer sanctity.

From first to last we admire the same profound and unruffled tranquillity of soul. So far as his interior life is revealed to us, he seems to have known nothing of those storms and agitations through which the human mind so often works its way to God; nothing seems to have interrupted the upward growth of his soul; and even the tales of his combats with the powers of evil give us more the idea of triumphs achieved, than of temptations suffered and overcome.

When seven years old, he was committed to the charge of his uncle, the arch-priest of Gumiel di Izan, a town not far from Calaroga. Here he grew up in the service of the altar, finding his pleasure in frequenting the churches and learning to recite the Divine Office, in singing hymns, and serving at Mass and other public ceremonies, and in all those numberless little devout offices which make the life of so many Catholic boys much like that of the child Samuel in the Temple. To Dominic they were all labors of love; and his biographers dwell on the devotion kindled in the hearts of those who saw the grave and reverent manner with which he bore himself in the presence of the Most Holy Sacrament, or busied himself in the cleaning and adorning of the altar. At fourteen he was sent to the University of Palencia, then one of the most celebrated in Spain. He was but young to be suddenly removed from so retired and sheltered a home into intercourse with a world of which, as yet, he knew nothing. With how many would such a change have brought only the rapid loss of all which had hitherto rendered his life so innocent and happy. But to Dominic it did but give room for larger growth in holiness.

During the ten years of his residence at Palencia, he was equally distinguished for his application to study, and for the angelic purity of his life. Worldly pleasures afforded no seductions to one who from his very birth had received an attraction to the things of God. Even human science failed to satisfy his desires, and he hastened to apply himself to the study of theology, as to the only fountain whose limpid waters were capable of quenching the thirst of his soul after the highest truth. He spent four years in the most profound application to philosophy and sacred letters, often spending his nights as well as his days over his books; and, convinced that Divine Science can only be acquired by a mind that has learned to subjugate the flesh, he practiced a rigid austerity, and for ten years never broke the rule he imposed on himself at the commencement of his studies to abstain entirely from wine.

The influence of a holy life is never unfelt by those who would be the last to imitate its example. Dominic's companions bore witness, by their respect, to the sublimity of a virtue far above the standard of their own lives. Boy as he was, none ever spoke with him without going away the better for his words, and feeling the charm of that Divine grace which shone even in his exterior gestures. "It was a thing most marvelous and lovely to behold," says Theodoric of Apoldia; "this

man, a boy in years, but a sage in wisdom; superior to the
pleasures of his age, he thirsted only after justice; and not
to lose time, he preferred the bosom of his mother the Church
to the aimless and objectless life of the foolish world around
him. The sacred repose of her tabernacles was his resting
place; all his time was equally divided between prayer and
study; and God rewarded the fervent love with which he kept
His Commandments by bestowing on him such a spirit of
wisdom and understanding as made it easy for him to resolve the most deep and difficult questions."

Before we quit his university life, two circumstances must
be recorded which happened during its course and illustrate the peculiar gentleness and tenderness of his character. Such terms may seem strange to a Protestant reader,
for there is, as it were, a traditional portrait of St. Dominic,
handed down from one age to another by means of epithets,
which writers are content to repeat and readers to receive,
without a thought of inquiry as to their justice. We can
scarcely open a book which professes to give the history
of the thirteenth century and its religious features without
finding something about "the cruel and bloodthirsty
Dominic," or the "gloomy founder of the Inquisition"; and
under this popular idea the imagination depicts him as a
dark-browed, mysterious zealot, without a touch of human
tenderness, remorselessly handing over to the flames the victims of his morose fanaticism. The author of the well-known
Handbook, from which so many English travellers gather
their little stock of knowledge on Italian matters, finds something of an almost providential significancy in the fact that
the tree planted by the father of the Friars Preachers in
his convent garden at Bologna should be the "dark and melancholy cypress." And all the while the true tradition of
his character is one preeminently of joy and gentleness. With
his fair auburn hair and beaming smile, he does not present
in his exterior a more perfect contrast to the received notion
of the Spanish Inquisitor than may be found in the tales
of tender-hearted compassion, which are almost all we know

of him during the first twenty years of his life.

We find him, in the midst of the famine which then desolated Spain, so sensibly touched with the sufferings of the people that not only did he give all he had, in alms, selling his very clothes to feed the poor—but he set a yet nobler example of charity to his fellow students by a sacrifice which may well be believed to have been a hard one. His dear and precious books were all that remained to give; and even those he parted with, that their price might be distributed to the starving multitudes. To estimate the cost of such an act, we must remember the rarity and costliness of manuscripts in those days, many having probably been laboriously copied out by his own hands. Yet when one of his companions expressed astonishment that he should deprive himself of the means of pursuing his studies, he replied, in words preserved by Theodoric of Apoldia and treasured by after-writers as the first which have come down to posterity, "Would you have me study off those dead parchments, when there were men dying of hunger?" This example roused the charity of the professors and students of the university, and an effort was soon made which relieved the sufferers from their most urgent wants.

On another occasion, finding a poor woman in great distress on account of the captivity of her only son, who had been taken by the Moors, Dominic—having no money to offer for his ransom—desired her to take him and sell him, and release her son with his price; and though this was not permitted to be done, yet the fact exhibits him to us under a character which is strangely opposed to the vulgar tradition of his severity and gloom.

It is said by some authors that his early desires led him to form plans for the foundation of an order for the Redemption of Captives, similar to that afterwards established by St. John of Matha; but of this we find no authoritative mention in the writers of his own order; and it is probable that the idea arose from the fact to which allusion has just been made.

CHAPTER 2

Dominic is appointed canon of Osma. His mission to the north in company with Diego of Azevedo.

It was not until his 25th year that Dominic was called to the ecclesiastical state. Until that time the designs of God regarding him had not been clearly manifested; but some important changes which took place in the diocese of Osma were the means of bringing him into a position where the latent powers of his soul were displayed before the eyes of the world. Martin de Bazan at that time ruled the Church of Osma—a man of eminent holiness, and most zealous for the restoration of Church discipline. Following the plan then generally adopted in most of the countries of Europe, he had engaged in the difficult but important task of converting the canons of his cathedral into canons regular, an arrangement by which they became subject to stricter ecclesiastical discipline and community life. In this labor he had been greatly assisted by a man whose name will ever have a peculiar interest to all the children of St. Dominic—Don Diego de Azevedo, the first prior of the new community, and afterwards successor to Martin in the episcopal see.

The name of Dominic, and the reputation of his singular holiness no less than of his learning, had already reached the ears of both; and they determined, if possible, to secure him as a member of the chapter, not doubting but the influence of his example and doctrine would greatly assist their designs of reform. In his 25th year, therefore, he received the habit of the Canons Regular, and the influence of his character was so soon felt and appreciated by his brethren that he was shortly afterwards chosen sub-prior, in spite

6

of his being the youngest of the whole body of canons.

Nine years were thus spent at Osma, during which time God was doubtless gradually training and preparing his soul for the great work of his future life. Jordan of Saxony has left us a beautiful sketch of his manner of life at this period. "Now it was," he says, "that he began to appear among his brethren like a bright burning torch, the first in holiness, the last in humility, spreading about him an odor of life which gave life, and a perfume like the sweetness of summer days. Day and night he was in the church, praying as it were without ceasing. God gave him the grace to weep for sinners and for the afflicted; he bore their sorrows in an inner sanctuary of holy compassion, and so this loving compassion which pressed on his heart flowed out and escaped in tears. It was his custom to spend the night in prayer, and to speak to God with his door shut. But often there might be heard the voice of his groans and sighs, which burst from him against his will. His one constant petition to God was for the gift of a true charity; for he was persuaded that he could not be truly a member of Christ unless he consecrated himself wholly to the work of gaining souls, following the example of Him who sacrificed Himself without reserve for our redemption."

It is interesting, among the very scanty details left us of Dominic's early years, to find two books mentioned, the study of which seem to have had an extraordinary influence in forming and directing his mind. The one was the *Dialogues of Cassian*, and the other, the *Epistles of St. Paul*. In after-years he always carried a copy of the *Epistles* about his person, and he seems to have shaped his whole idea of an apostolic life after the model of this great master. In 1201, Don Diego de Azevedo succeeded to the bishopric of Osma, and two years afterwards was appointed by Alfonso VIII, the king of Castile, to negotiate a marriage between his eldest son and a princess of Denmark. He accordingly set out for the north, taking Dominic as his companion; and it was on the occasion of this journey that, as they passed through the south of France, the frightful character and extent of the Albigensian heresy, which then infected the whole of the southern provinces, first came under their notice. Though they were not then able to commence the apostolic labors for which they saw there was so urgent a demand, yet an impression was left on the hearts of both which was never effaced; and Dominic felt that his life, which had hitherto seemed without any determinate call or destiny, had been, as it were, reserved for a work which he now saw clear before him. Probably this feeling was strengthened by a circumstance which occurred at Toulouse, where they stopped for a night on their journey. The house where they lodged was kept by a man who belonged to the sect of the Albigenses, and when Dominic became aware of the fact, he resolved to attempt at least to gain this one soul back to the Faith. The time was short, but the dispute was prolonged during the whole night; and in the morning the eloquence and fervor of his unknown guest had conquered the obduracy of the heretic. Before they left the house he made his submission, and was received back into the bosom of the Church.

The effect of this first conquest on Dominic's mind was a feeling of unspeakable gratitude and a determination, so soon as he should be free to act, to found an order for the express purpose of preaching the Faith. Castiglio, in his history of the Order, tells us that the embassy on which Diego and Dominic were employed was not to Denmark, but to the court of France—and that it was on this occasion that, finding Queen Blanche in much affliction on account of her being without children, Dominic recommended to her the use of the Rosary.

The queen, he adds, not only adopted the devotion herself, but propagated it among her people and distributed rosaries amongst them, engaging them to join their prayers to hers, that her desire might be granted; and the son whom God gave in answer to these prayers was no other than the great St. Louis. This is the first direct mention of the devotion

of the Rosary which we find in St. Dominic's life; it is probable, from the date of St. Louis' birth, which is generally
given in 1215, that the circumstances referred to—if they
ever really took place—occurred at some later visit to the
French court. But though there is evidently some confusion
in the time, we do not like altogether to abandon the story
as without foundation; for there is always a peculiar charm
in the little links which unite the lives of two great saints
together, and those who claim any interest in the Order
of St. Dominic may feel a pleasure in thinking of St. Louis
as a child of the Rosary.

CHAPTER 3

The death of the princess whose marriage they were negotiating whilst engaged in a second embassy at her father's court, having relieved Diego and Dominic from their charge in this affair, they determined to take the occasion of their absence from the diocese to visit Rome on pilgrimage before returning to Spain. Many motives concurred in inducing them to undertake this journey; but with Diego the most powerful one was the desire to obtain permission from Pope Innocent III to resign his bishopric and undertake the labors of an apostolic missionary life among the Cuman Tartars, who were then ravaging the fold of Christ in Hungary and the surrounding countries.

It would seem as if the impressions made on the minds of these two great men by what they had witnessed of the sufferings of the Church in their journey through Europe had been of that kind which is never effaced, and which, whenever it touches the soul, is to it the commencement of a new life. In them it had kindled the desire to devote themselves to a far wider field of labor than the limits of one diocese: they had both received the heroic call of the apostolate. The state of the Church at that time was one which might well make such an appeal to hearts ready to receive it. "Without were fightings, within were fears." Whilst hordes of savage and heathen enemies were pressing hard on the outworks of Christendom and watering the ground with the blood of unnumbered martyrs, heresy, as we have seen, was at work within the fold; and during this memorable year, Diego and Dominic had in some degree been eyewitnesses of both these evils. We know in what manner they had been thrown among the Albigenses of France, and it is at least probable that in the course of their Danish journey they had become in some way more vividly aware of the dangers to which the northern nations were exposed. Pope Innocent, however, knew the value of Diego too well to grant him the permission he sought, and exhorted him not to abandon that charge which God had given him in his Church, but to reassume the care of his diocese; and after a short residence in Rome, the two friends accordingly prepared to return to Spain, it being then March of the year 1205.

They had come to Rome as pilgrims, and it was in the same spirit that on their journey home they turned from the direct road in order to visit the celebrated Abbey of Citeaux, which the fame of St. Bernard had made illustrious throughout Europe. The charm of its religious character and associations captivated the heart of Diego; doubtless the failure of his deeply cherished plan had been no little pain to him, and his return to Osma was a hard obedience. He was suffering under that strange thirst to strip himself of the world which sometimes attacks the soul at the very time when it bows to the law that forces it back to the world's duties. Very willingly would he have remained at Citeaux and commenced his novitiate in that school of holy living; but as this could not be, he contented himself with taking the habit of the Order and soliciting that he might carry some of the religious back with him to Spain, to learn from them their rule and manner of life.

It is interesting to us to know that he was probably moved to this by the example of our own St. Thomas of Canterbury who, several years before, had received the religious habit at the same monastery whilst in exile from his diocese, and whose popularity as a saint was just at that time at its greatest height. After this he no longer delayed his homeward journey; but accompanied by Dominic and some of the Cistercian brethren, he set out for Spain and soon arrived in the neighborhood of Montpellier.

And here, if we may so speak, the will of God awaited
them. Those inward stirrings which both had felt, yet had
not fully comprehended, had truly been the whisperings of
the Divine voice; and dimly feeling in the dark, in obedience
to the hand that was beckoning them on, the dream of a
martyr's crown among the Cumans or a monk's cowl at
Citeaux had, as it were, been two false guesses as to what
that whisper meant. This feature in what we may call the
vocation of St. Dominic is worthy of notice because, whilst
we are often inclined to regret that more details of his personal life have not been preserved, there is a peculiarity in
this early portion of it, not without its interest.

His call was not sudden, or miraculous, or even extraordinary; it was that which is the likeliest to come to men
like ourselves; particular impressions of mind were given
just at the time when circumstances combined together
gradually to develop the way in which those impressions
could be carried out. He was always being led forward,
not knowing whither he went. As sub-prior of Osma he probably saw nothing before him but the ordinary community
life of the cathedral chapter. Then came the journey to Denmark, on a mission whose ostensible object was a failure,
but whose real end in the designs of God was accomplished
when it brought him into the presence of the heresy which
it was his destiny to destroy. Yet though we have reason
to believe that from the time of his first collision with the
Albigenses a very clear and distinct idea was formed in his
mind of some future apostolate of preaching, it is evident
that he had no equally clear and determinate view in what
direction he was to work; and it hung on circumstances
alone and on the will of another to decide whether or not
he were to end his days as a nameless missioner among the
Tartars.

He was on the road back to his old home, preparing to
take up again the old duties and the old life which had
been interrupted by two years, rich with new thoughts and
hopes now, as it seemed, to be forever abandoned; and then,

when he had made what was probably a painful sacrifice of great desires, those mysterious orderings of Providence which we call chance and coincidence had prepared for him, under the walls of Montpellier, a combination of events which was to make all clear.

The alarming progress and character of the Albigensian heresy had at length determined the Roman Pontiff on active measures for its suppression. A commission had been appointed for that purpose, the most distinguished members of which were Arnold, Abbot of Citeaux, and Rudolph and Peter de Castelnau, the papal legates. These were, all three, Cistercian monks, and with them were associated several other abbots of the same order. They found their task a difficult one, for the country was entirely in the power of Count Raymond of Toulouse, the avowed protector of the Albigenses; and unhappily the bishops and clergy, by their coldness and indifference, too often even by yet more culpable irregularities, were themselves the chief causes of the spread of the evil.

Innocent III, in a letter to his legates, speaks in bitter and yet in touching terms of this degeneracy of those who should have been foremost in the ranks. "The pastor," he says, "has become a hireling; he no longer feeds the flock, but himself; wolves enter the fold, and he is not there to oppose himself as a wall against the enemies of God's house." This scandal was of course the great weapon used by the heretics in all their conferences with the legates. It was a short and triumphant argument to quote the words of the Gospel, "By their fruits shall ye know them"; and then to point at the careless and worldly character of the priesthood.

Baffled and confounded in all their efforts, the Catholic leaders had met to consult together in the neighborhood of Montpellier; and it was whilst discussing the gloomy prospects of their commission that they heard of the arrival of the two travellers. Their reputation and the interest they had shown in the state of the distracted province on the occasion of their former visit were well known, and the legates sent them an invitation to assist at the conference. It was accepted, and the disappointments and perplexities of the whole case were laid before them.

The chief difficulty in their way was the impossibility of convincing the heretics that the truth of the Christian Faith depended, not on the good or bad example of individuals, but on the sure and infallible word of God made known to them through the Church. Diego inquired very particularly concerning the mode of life adopted by the legates and their opponents, and gave it as his opinion that the great obstacle which had hindered the work of souls had been the neglect of evangelical poverty among the Catholic missioners. For "he remarked," says Blessed Jordan, "that the heretics attracted men by persuasive means, by preaching and a great outward show of sanctity, whilst the legates were surrounded by a numerous suite of followers, with horses and rich apparel. Then he said, 'It is not thus, my brothers, that you must act. They seduce simple souls with the appearances of poverty and austerity: by presenting to them the contrary spectacle, you will scarcely edify them; you may destroy them, but you will never touch their hearts.' "

The words of Diego, if they convinced his hearers, were yet a little unwelcome. None had the courage to be the first to follow the hard counsel, and they felt the want of one possessed of the chief authority among them to set the example of an austere reform, and enforce its adoption by the others. "Excellent father," they said to Diego, "what would you have us do?" Then the spirit of God came upon him, and he said, "Do as I am about to do"; and, calling his attendants, he gave orders that they should return to Osma with all the equipages and followers who accompanied him. A little company of ecclesiastics alone remained, of whom Dominic was one; but they retained nothing of external pomp, and affected only the bearing and manners of the humblest missioners.

The example was instantly followed by the other legates,

and each one sent away all his followers and baggage, retaining only the books necessary for the recital of the Divine Office and for the confutation of the heretics. More than this, feeling the power of Diego's character and influence, they unanimously elected him as head and chief of the Catholic body, and Innocent III, to whom the whole of the circumstances were made known, hesitated not to grant him the permission which he had before refused in the case of the Cumans: he was authorized to remain in the French provinces for the service of the Faith.

CHAPTER 4

Dominic in Languedoc. The miracles of Fanjeaux and Montreal. The foundation of the Convent of Prouille.

A new impulse had been given to the enterprise on which the Catholics of Languedoc had embarked: with the apostolic life came a daily increase of the apostolic spirit. It was a very difficult thing to set about evangelizing a country encumbered with the pomp of a feudal retinue, and to traverse the same country on foot with "neither purse nor scrip," as Diego was wont to send out his companions daily into the neighboring towns and villages to preach the Faith. For after the conference at Montpellier they all set out together towards Toulouse, stopping at different places on the road to preach and hold disputations with the heretics, as they were moved by the Spirit of God. We are assured that they made this journey barefooted, and trusting to God's providence alone for their daily wants; and the effect of this new way of proceeding was soon evident in the success which attended their labors.

At Carmain, a town near Toulouse, the residence of two of the principal Albigensian leaders, Baldwin and Thierry, the people received the missionaries so warmly that they were only prevented from expelling the Albigenses from their territory by the authority of the lord of the place, and accompanied the legates out of the town on their departure with every sign of respect. They proceeded in this way to Beziers, Carcassona, and other places in the surrounding country, confirming the faith of the Catholics and in many instances reconciling great numbers of the heretics to the Church.

Hitherto Dominic's part in these transactions has seemed to be a secondary one: he has appeared before us rather

16

as the follower and companion of the bishop of Osma, than as the man whose name was to be forever remembered in future histories as the chief leader in this struggle of the Faith. Few probably of those who witnessed these first openings of the campaign against the Albigenses would have believed that the award of a deathless fame was to fall, not to the bishop whose prompt and commanding spirit had been so readily recognized by those who had unanimously chosen him to be their chief, but to one who followed in his train, known only as Brother Dominic; for he had laid aside even the title of sub-prior, and took on him nothing but the inferior part of the subject and attendant of another.

As soon, however, as the disputes with the heretics began to be held of which we have spoken, his power and value were felt. Perhaps they were best evidenced by the bitter hatred which the heretics conceived against him. The same sentiments had been so unequivocally evinced towards the legate Peter de Castelnau, that the others had persuaded him to withdraw for a while from the enterprise, in order not to exasperate those whom it was their object to conciliate.

The masterly arguments and captivating eloquence of Dominic, which time after time silenced his adversaries and conquered the obstinacy of vast numbers who returned to the obedience of the Church after many of these conferences, excited a no less vindictive feeling against him in the minds of those who might be confounded, but would never yield. They spoke of him as their most dangerous enemy, and did not even conceal their resolve to take his life, whenever chance should give them the opportunity. He behaved on this occasion with a surprising indifference: the service of God was the only thing that he saw before him; and as his days were spent in public disputations, his nights were consumed in interviews with those who secretly sought his counsel, or more frequently in those prayers, and tears, and strong intercessions with God for the souls of His people, which were more powerful arms in fighting the battle of the Faith than were the wisdom and eloquence of his words.

Among the conferences held at this time, that of Fanjeaux was the most important, both from the preparations made by both sides and the extraordinary nature of its termination. It would seem that the heretics had appealed to some final arbitration of their differences, and that the Catholic leaders had not only responded to the challenge but even accepted as judges in the controversy three persons whose sentiments were commonly known as favorable to the Albigenses themselves.

Each side had put together in writing the strongest defense of their cause; that of the Catholics was the work of Dominic. The three arbitrators having heard both parties and read the written apologies, absolutely refused to pronounce any decision on the case; and in this perplexity the heretics loudly demanded a different mode of trial and proposed that both books should be committed to the flames, that God might declare by His own interposition which cause He favored. "Accordingly a great fire was lighted" (says Blessed Jordan), "and the two volumes were cast therein; that of the heretics was immediately consumed to ashes; the other, which had been written by the blessed man of God, Dominic, not only remained unhurt, but was borne far away by the flames in presence of the whole assembly. Again a second and a third time they threw it into the fire, and each time the same result clearly manifested which was the true Faith, and the holiness of him who had written the book."

This miracle is given by every contemporaneous writer. It is mentioned in the lessons for the Divine Office composed by Constantine Medici, bishop of Orvieto, in 1254; and in the following century Charles le Bel, king of France, purchased the house where the event took place and erected it into a chapel under the invocation of the Saint. A large beam of wood on which the paper fell when tossed away by the flames was still preserved when Castiglio wrote his history; and there does not even seem to have been any attempt on the part of the heretics themselves to deny the fact.

Yet in spite of this, there is a melancholy significance in the expression of the historian. "A *few* of the heretics were converted to the truth of our holy faith, but as to the rest, it produced no effect; this being the just reward of their great sins."* It would seem as if every age and every heresy were to act over again the scenes of Christ's ministry in Judea: signs and miracles were thrown away on those who had Moses and the prophets, and would not believe.

This was not the only occasion when a miracle of this kind was wrought. A similar prodigy took place at Montréal, in the diocese of Carcassona, under different circumstances. Dominic had, in the course of one of his public disputations, written down on a sheet of paper various quotations from the Holy Scriptures which he had cited in the course of his argument, and these he gave to one of the heretics, praying him to consider them well, and not to resist the conclusion to which they might bring him. The same evening, as this man sat over the fire with some of his companions discussing the subjects of dispute, he drew out the paper and proposed submitting it to the flames, as a test of the truth of its contents. They consented; and thrusting it into the fire, kept it there for some time, and then drew it out unscorched. Again and again they repeated the experiment, and always with the same result.

And a second time what do we find to be the effect on the witnesses of this new miracle? "Then the heretics were filled with great wonder, and, instead of keeping the promise they had made of believing the truths preached by the Catholics, agreed to keep the prodigy a close secret, lest it should reach the ears of the Catholics, who would be certain to claim it as a sign of victory."† One, however, more noble-minded than the rest, was converted by what he saw and published it to the world; and from his testimony it was inserted by Peter de Vaulx Cernay in his history of the Albigenses.

---

*Castiglio, part 1. cap. 8.   †Polidori, cap. 6.

It is to be regretted that more particulars have not been preserved of these memorable conferences, but we are only told in general that great success everywhere followed the footsteps of the missionaries, and that the numbers of the Catholics daily increased, which reduced the heretics to the necessity of using frauds and the most incredible ingenuity to preserve their ground against the power of their adversaries.

It will be observed that we have made no attempt in these pages to give any account of the nature of that celebrated heresy, the name of which will be forever inseparably united with that of St. Dominic; neither is it our intention to do so. An ample account of its doctrines may be gathered from so many works within the reach of the Catholic reader, that we feel it is wholly unnecessary to devote any space here to the task of unveiling its true character.

Indeed, whilst alluding to its connection with this period of St. Dominic's life, we cannot but feel that this connection has been greatly overrated by many, who have made his biography little more than a history of political and ecclesiastical affairs with which he had personally but little to do. In this way his own personal life and character have often been lost sight of and confused with the troubles of the times, and the portrait of the Saint has been hidden by the shadow which rests, in some degree, on the Count de Montfort's crusade. With all this we have nothing to do; nor shall we allude to the political history of the time, except insofar as is necessary to explain and illustrate the details preserved to us of the life of Dominic.

There is little doubt that the Albigensian heresy, besides its corruptions of the Faith and its frightful immorality, had a directly political character, and was mixed up with a spirit of revolution and sedition, which goes far to explain the bitterness of those civil wars of which it was the immediate cause; and like all revolutionary movements, it had a disorganizing effect on all social ties, so that the south of France was plunged by it into a state of civil anarchy, which was doubtless the chief reason which moved the civil arm against its followers with such peculiar severity.

One of the consequences of these political commotions was the impoverishing of many noble families engaged in them, and this often led to their concealing their faith through the pressure of necessity and suffering their children to be educated by the heretics, who eagerly made use of the worldly temptations which were in their power to offer in order to get the children of Catholics into their hands.

This evil was very soon perceived by the quick eye of Dominic, and so deplorably did he feel the cruelty which exposed these souls to the certain ruin of their religious principles that he determined on a very strenuous effort to oppose it and to provide some means for the education of the daughters of Catholics in the true Faith.

For this purpose he resolved to found a monastery where, within the protection of strict enclosure and under the charge of a few holy women whom he gathered together out of the suffering provinces, these children might be nurtured under the Church's shadow. The spot chosen for the purpose was Prouille, a name illustrious in the Dominican annals, for there, unconsciously probably to its founder, rose the mother house of an institute which was to cover the world. It was a small village near Montréal, at the foot of the Pyrenees; and a church dedicated to Our Lady, under the familiar title of Notre Dame de Prouille, was the object of considerable veneration among the people.

There, with the warm sanction and cooperation of Fulk, bishop of Toulouse, Dominic founded his monastery. The church we have spoken of was granted to the new foundation, and it seemed as if the plan had no sooner been proposed than everyone saw its fitness for the necessities of the times, and vied one with another in forwarding and contributing to it. Peter of Castelnau, stretched on a bed of sickness, gave thanks to God with clasped hands for what he deemed so signal a mercy. Berenger, archbishop of Narbonne, immediately granted it considerable lands and revenues; and all the Catholic nobles, with the Count de

Montfort at their head, gave their prompt and liberal aid to a scheme from which they themselves were sure to derive such lasting advantage.

The little community consisted at first of nine members, all of them converted from the Albigensian heresy by the preaching and miracles of Dominic. They were joined by two noble ladies of Catholic families, one of whom, Guillemette de Fanjeaux, though the last to receive the habit, was chosen by Dominic as their Superior. She continued in that office until the year 1225; but he himself governed in the monastery, and thenceforth received the title of Prior of Prouille, residing in a house outside the enclosure when his apostolic labors did not call him elsewhere. The community took possession of their new retreat on the 27th of December, 1206. Their habit was white with a tawny mantle; of the rule given them by their founder we know nothing, save that it bound them, besides attending to the education of children, to devote certain hours to manual labor such as spinning. Prouille, afterwards associated to the Order of Preachers, became in time a flourishing monastery, never numbering less than a hundred religious; it was the mother house of no less than twelve other foundations, and reckoned among its prioresses several of the royal house of Bourbon.

CHAPTER 5

Diego returns to Spain. His death. Dominic remains in Languedoc. The murder of Peter de Castelnau, and the commencement of the Albigensian war.

Diego of Azevedo saw the foundation of Prouille before returning to his diocese of Osma. He had now been two years in the French provinces, and he felt it was time to revisit his own church and people. He left the country in which he had labored so truly and nobly, with the promise soon to return with fresh laborers in the cause; but this promise was destined never to be fulfilled. His companions attended him to the confines of the province of Toulouse, all journeying on foot and preaching as they went. These last missionary labors of Diego were crowned with new successes. At Montreal 500 heretics abjured their errors. A meeting of the legates and chief Catholics also took place at the same town, and another at Pamiers, when the increased courage and strength of the Catholic party were plainly visible, and some of the principal of the Albigenses made their submission with the most unequivocal marks of sincerity.

After this last conference Diego turned his steps toward Spain, and still travelling on foot reached Osma, having been absent from his diocese exactly three years. He died before he could carry his intention of returning to France into execution; and thus he and Dominic never met again. He was the first of a long line of great men with whom the founder of the Friars Preachers was united in bonds of no common friendship, nor was he the least worthy of the number. So holy and stainless was the life he led that even the heretics were wont to say of him in the words of Blessed Jordan that it was "impossible not to believe such

23

a man predestined to eternal life, and that doubtless he was sent among them to be taught the true doctrine."

It was Diego's influence that had consolidated the weak and scattered elements of the Catholic party into a firm and united body, and his loss was felt by all to be that of a father and chief. Nay, it seemed as if his death dissolved in a moment the tie which had bound them together. They were again scattered, each in different directions, and a few weeks after the news of his friend's death reached the ears of Dominic, he found himself alone.

We cannot guess, or rather we can but guess, what kind of solitude that was when the work remained to do, but the fellow laborers, and he among them whose company had been a brotherhood of fourteen years, were gone. Yet Dominic was equal to the shock of that great loneliness: he saw one after another of the missioners depart—the Spanish ecclesiastics to Spain, the Cistercians back to their abbey, but he remained firm and tranquil at the post where God had placed him. The sweetness of human consolation had left it, but the will of God was clear as ever, and that was the law of his life; and if hitherto he had been displayed to the world as following rather in another's track than as himself the originator of the enterprise in which he was engaged, it was for the test of a crisis like this to show him to the world in his true light. We have mentioned Fulk, bishop of Toulouse, as cooperating in the foundation of the convent of Prouille. His presence and influence in some degree supplied the loss which the Catholics had sustained by the death of Diego. Until his elevation to the episcopate, one of the greatest drawbacks to the Catholic cause had been the coldness and indifference of their own bishops; but the vigorous example of the new prelate roused many of his colleagues from their negligence and infused new life into the ecclesiastical administration of the diocese.

He was indeed in every way a remarkable man, one in whom the energy of human passion had been, not laid aside, but transformed and sanctified by the influence of grace.

Not many years before he had been known to the world only as a brilliant courtier, a successful cultivator of the "gaie science," the very embodiment of the Provencal character. The world spoiled him for a time, and then deserted him; or we might rather say that God had determined to draw to Himself a soul too noble for the world's spoiling. Deaths came one after another to strip his life of everything that made it desirable; then there followed that period of bitter conflict and agony which precedes the putting off of the old nature; and when it was over, Provence had lost her gayest troubadour, and Fulk was a monk in the abbey of Citeaux. In 1206 he was raised to the bishopric of Toulouse, and in that capacity his energy and enthusiasm of character was of special service in animating the chilled and timorous spirit of his colleagues. Towards Dominic and his companions he was ever a liberal benefactor.

And indeed there was need of some support in the position in which the departure and death of Diego had left his friend. He was not only alone, but alone just as the difficulties of the cause to which he was bound were about to be increased tenfold by the horrors of civil war. This conflict, associated as it was with the religious contest in which he was engaged, could scarcely fail to entangle him in something of its confusion: so at least it would seem, if we remember that the war was that crusade against the Albigenses which history has persisted in linking with the name of Dominic.

The reader of his life who comes full of this prepossession will turn to the chapter of the Albigensian crusade with the natural expectation of finding there the most striking details of the man he has been accustomed to think of as its hero. Whereas it is literally true that it is just during the ten years of the Albigensian war that we find least record of Dominic's life, so far as the world knew it. He had a life, and a work, but one so wholly distinct from the conflict that was raging around him that it has hidden him from sight. Here and there we find a trace of him, but in no case are those scattered notices connected with any of the warlike or political movements of the times. They are the anecdotes of an apostolic life whose course has been thus briefly sketched by Blessed Humbert in a few lines: "After the return of the bishop Diego to his diocese," he says, "St. Dominic, left almost alone with a few companions who were bound to him by no vow, during *ten years* upheld the Catholic Faith in different parts of the province of Narbonne, particularly at Carcassona and at Fanjeaux. He devoted himself entirely to the salvation of souls by the ministry of preaching, and he bore with a great heart a multitude of affronts, ignominies, and sufferings for the name of Jesus Christ."

And this is all. The few details preserved of these ten years of suffering and silent work will disappoint any who look for stirring pictures of the crusade. Some trait of humility and patience exhibited amid the insults of his enemies—or, it may be, a few words redolent with the spirit of prayer and trust in God, which have come down in the tradition of ages—or the record of miracles worked, like those of the Master whose steps he followed, as he went up and down the hills of Narbonne and among the towns and villages, preaching the Faith, and seeking for the sheep that were lost—this is all we find.

There is an evangelical sweetness of simplicity about these broken notices of his life which, coming in the midst of the troubled and bloody history of the period, sounds like the rich notes of a thrush's song falling on the ear between the intervals of a thunderstorm—lost every now and then, and hushed by the angry roll of the elements, then sounding sweetly again in the stillness when the storm is over. We shall give them as we find them, in their proper place, but it is necessary first of all to notice very briefly some of those events which followed on the departure of Diego of Azevedo, and which plunged the southern provinces of France into the bloody contest of which we have spoken.

It will be remembered that among the legates and missioners whom Dominic and Diego met at Montpellier on their first entrance on the mission, mention was made of Peter de Castelnau, against whom the hatred of the heretics had been so strongly evinced that he had been persuaded for some time to withdraw from the enterprise. Something of severity and harshness in his character may probably account for the peculiar vindictiveness of which he was the object. He had often been used to say that religion would never raise its head in Languedoc till the soil had been watered with the blood of a martyr; and his constant prayer was that he himself might be the victim. It was even as he desired. Count Raymond of Toulouse, the sovereign of the distracted provinces, had been the constant but not always the avowed protector of the Albigenses during the whole period of his government. Again and again, in reply to the pressing entreaties of the Holy See, he had promised to use his authority to suppress their disorders and to defend the property and liberty of the Catholics; and again and again, when the dread of excommunication was withdrawn, he had failed to fulfill his engagements.

It is no part of history to asperse its characters with epithets of reproach. Count Raymond has been the hero of one party, and the object of unlimited abuse from the other; but we may well content ourselves with such conclusions as may be drawn from facts which none have attempted to dispute. He had bound himself by solemn oaths to suppress those violent disorders, the frightful increase of which had opened the eyes of his predecessor and forced from him the unwilling acknowledgment that "The spiritual sword was no longer enough; the material sword was needed also."

These oaths were made, and as often violated; after incessant remonstrances, Peter de Castelnau, in his office of papal legate, pronounced the final sentence of excommunication against him. The result was an earnest entreaty from the count to meet him at Saint Gilles, in order that by fresh submissions he might be once more reconciled to the Church. His request was agreed to, but it seemed impossible for Raymond to act with good faith. No sooner were the legates in his power than he changed his tone of submission and haughtily threatened them with imprisonment if they did not grant him the unconditional repeal of his sentence. Such threats were lightly felt by men who counted their lives as nothing in the cause in which they were engaged, and they answered him only with a stern reproof.

The next day, as they stood by the rapid waters of the Rhone, on the banks of which they had passed the night and which they were preparing to cross, two members of the count's household came up in pursuit of them, and one plunged his lance into the body of Peter de Castelnau. It was the death for which he had so often longed; he fell without a struggle, and summoned his departing strength to utter words worthy of a martyr. "May God pardon you," he said to his murderer; "as for me, I forgive you—I forgive you"; then turning to his companion, "Keep the Faith," he said, "and serve God's Church without fear, and without negligence," and, with these words upon his lips, he died.

When the news of this murder reached the ears of the Pope and the Catholic potentates of Europe, there seemed a unanimous feeling that all time for further treating with the heretics was at an end. Let us remember that the south of France had now been at their mercy for more than a century; that during that time these atrocious wretches, whom Protestants are not ashamed to boast of as their ancestors in the faith, had ravaged the country like bandits, setting fire to churches, torturing priests and nuns, trampling underfoot the Holy Eucharist and committing every violence most shocking to human feeling; and that during this century of crime the Church had opposed only her censures and her entreaties, sending among them missionaries and preachers, but never unloosing the temporal sword.

Nay, she had even interposed with peaceful measures when the civil arm was at length raised against them. Raymond of Toulouse, the predecessor of the present count and himself a favorer of the heretics, had at length become aware of the danger threatened to his own government, and to the very existence of all law, by their continued excesses.

Too late he strove to check the evil he had fostered, but he found the task was far beyond his strength. In his terror he wrote to the French king a memorable letter which, as coming from his pen, may fairly be received as impartial testimony. "Our churches," he says, "are in ruins, penance is despised, the Holy Eucharist is held in abomination, all the Sacraments are rejected—*yet no one thinks of offering any resistance to these wretches.*" He then makes an earnest appeal to the king for assistance, and would have obtained it had not the reigning Pontiff, Alexander III, interfered and proposed once more to try the effect of an ecclesiastical mission before harsher measures were adopted.

But however well fitted a legation of monks and preachers might be for the suppression of theological errors, it scarcely had the strength necessary for delivering Languedoc from its swarms of bandits. The sufferings of the country were not simply doctrinal: Stephen, abbot of St. Geneviève, sent to Toulouse by the king and an eyewitness of what he describes, gives us a picture of the state of things in his time in a few words which occur in one of his letters: "I have seen," he says, "churches burnt and ruined to their foundations; I have seen the dwellings of men changed into the dens of beasts." Is it any wonder, therefore, that after these terrible disorders had been endured for more than a century and opposed only by the weapons of ecclesiastical censures, the murder in cold blood of the Papal legate by the avowed leader of the Albigenses seemed to fill up the measure of their iniquity? War at once burst out; and surely if ever war is just, it must be deemed so when waged to defend society from outrage, and the Faith from ruin. This at least we may affirm without in any way binding ourselves to vindicate the manner in which it was carried on, when man's passions and personal interests were once irretrievably engaged; but we cannot think that the act which proclaimed the crusade against the Albigenses, after a century of forbearance, can be condemned by any who will patiently go over that century's most melancholy history.

CHAPTER 6

Proclamation of the Crusade. Simon de Montfort. Dominic among the heretics. His apostolic labors.

The death of de Castelnau took place in the February of the year 1208. Early in the following month Pope Innocent addressed letters to the kings of France and England, and to the sovereign nobles of France, calling on them to lay aside their private quarrels and join in an unanimous effort against "the rage of heresy." The crime of the Count of Toulouse was declared to be one which freed his subjects from their allegiance until such time as he should return to his own allegiance to the Church; and a new commission of bishops and abbots was appointed to preach the crusade, and undertake the ecclesiastical government of the country. In this commission Dominic's name does not occur; Arnold of Citeaux is the man charged with the chief burden of the whole undertaking, and his fiery and inflexible temper caused him to fulfill his charge with an unrelenting severity which can never be excused. If indeed we had to make any religious body responsible for the severities of the Crusade, it certainly seems as though the Cistercians had done more to merit such a reproach than any other. We find their leader, Arnold, eagerly and zealously engaged in all the movements of the Catholic chiefs, often accompanying them to the field and rousing the country to arms with the energy of his preaching. Every representation of the progress of the war which reached the Pope came through him and his followers; and these representations seem, in more instances than one, to have been colored by partiality, and to have misled the Pontiff whom they were intended to direct. For more than a year after the war first broke out, Arnold was the only acknowledged leader and director of the Catholic forces; and the unfortunate plan of setting the two houses of Montfort and Toulouse in rivalry one against the other, as the means of destroying the latter by the vindictiveness of a personal quarrel, was the invention of his own scheming brain.

Yet this man, who really played so conspicuous a part in the history of his time and who stands bound to every detail in those proceedings of which he was the animating spirit, is almost forgotten by Protestant historians and their readers, so eager are they to heap terms of reproach on one who had little or no share in them. Doubtless in their own day, Dominic Guzman was a very insignificant person compared to the legate, Arnold of Citeaux; but the Church, in her unerring justice, has raised one to her altars, and left the other to the mercy or indifference of future ages; and this explains what would otherwise be an unaccountable phenomenon. Arnold of Citeaux, though a busy man in his time, is in no way a representative of the Catholic Church; she has not identified herself with him, and so there is no good reason for attacking him and his order, and holding up their names for popular abuse, however deeply they were responsible for the excesses of the Crusade.

But it is quite another thing to vilify a Catholic saint. Dominic bears on his brow the indelible seal of the Church's canonization, and therefore no Protestant can touch on the history of the Albigensian war without assuring us that it was "preached by the infamous Dominic," with a thousand other like expressions which would give us to understand that he was the foremost character in the whole affair, but which are simply inexplicable to anyone who, in studying his life, finds it his chief difficulty to come on any trace of him during this period.

It must be acknowledged that the perpetual insincerities of the Count of Toulouse render it difficult to follow, with anything like clearness, a history which shows him to us submitting to public penance in the church of St. Gilles in 1209, and swearing at the same time, on holy relics and

the very Body of Our Lord, to drive away the heretic insur-
gents, to repair the churches, and replace the lawful bishops
in their sees; then, a year afterwards, evading the demands
of the council, held at the same place, which called on him
to fulfill his engagements and persisting in his refusal, even
whilst he supplicates to be heard in justification of the ac-
cusations brought against him. A little while after we find
him at Toulouse, preparing to take up arms against the Catholic forces whom he had sworn to assist; and in return for
this breach of faith, we have a touching and affectionate
letter from Pope Innocent, calling on him once more to stand
to his plighted word. Then more conferences and more evasions. In 1211, at a meeting held at Montpellier, he seems
about to yield, but suddenly leaves the city without a word
of explanation. Then at length the thunder of excommunication falls on his head a second time; and the war begins
in earnest.

Raymond had the powerful protection of his brother-in-
law, the king of Arragon, together with many of the ter-
ritorial lords of the south. The power of the crusaders under
the leadership of Count Simon de Montfort was certainly
in no overwhelming disproportion, and we are told that
more than a thousand cities and towns were in the hands
of the heretics. Two of these towns, Beziers and Carcassona,
had yielded to the Catholic confederates after a bloody contest at the very commencement of the war and before the
final rupture with Raymond. The cruelties practiced on the
inhabitants of the former, and the pillage of the latter, gave
a vindictive character to the very opening of the campaign.
For the enormities perpetrated by the heretics had lashed
the Catholics of Languedoc to fury; and when the day of
retribution came and vengeance was in the power of men
who had so long suffered the worst injuries without redress,
it broke out into the usual excesses. There is no temptation
to justify such excesses, yet surely there is an astonishing
unfairness, may we not say an astonishing hypocrisy, in those
who can find no words to express their horror at the slaughter

of Beziers, yet forget the tortures of helpless women, profanation of holy things, the murders and oppressions of the century which had passed, the recollection of which was doubtless too terribly alive in the minds of the crusaders for them to find much mercy in their hearts for those who were in turn their victims.

Where was Dominic all this time? Some of his historians give the year 1207 as the date of the foundation of his order; inasmuch as it was then that he took the command of that little company of missionaries who remained with him after the departure of Diego. But they were bound to him by no other tie than a common interest; and the only ground for the supposition seems to be that they lived together in a kind of community life, and were known by the name of the Preaching Brothers. It does not, however, seem that they had anything of the formation of a regular religious body, and probably no plan for such a formation had yet been clearly developed in Dominic's own mind.

Of their manner of life we can form some notion from those scattered anecdotes which are all that are left us. Even amid the hottest period of the war, it was the same as it had ever been; they went about barefoot from village to village preaching the Faith. The only commission which Dominic held was the original one he possessed in virtue of that first legation to which he and Diego had been associated before the Crusade began. It gave him the power of reconciling heretics and receiving them to penance, an office which has acquired him the title of the first Inquisitor. If by this is meant that the office of the Inquisition, as afterwards constituted, was established at this time, such title is certainly an error; no such office existed before the Lateran Council of 1215, and it was not until 1230, nine years after the death of Dominic, that the Council of Toulouse gave it a new form, and entrusted a large share of its government to the recently instituted order of Friars Preachers.

It is singular also that the first commission for denouncing heretics to the civil magistrate was granted to the Cistercians.

But, on the other hand, there is no doubt that the commission of reconciling heretics, held by St. Dominic, was the germ from which the Inquisition afterwards sprang; and so Dominic may be called the first Inquisitor, in the same sense as the Marquis of Worcestor is called the inventor of the steam engine, or Roger Bacon the discoverer of gunpowder— without supposing that the marvels of a cotton mill, or the broad side of a three-decker, ever crossed the imagination of either.*

His chief residence was at Fanjeaux and Carcassona. Fanjeaux he chose for its proximity to Notre Dame de Prouille, and Carcassona for another reason. "Why do you not live in Toulouse, or the diocese?" was a question one day asked him. "I know many people in Toulouse," he replied, "and they show me respect; but at Carcassona, everyone is against me." They certainly were: it was their diversion to treat the humble, barefooted friar who was to be seen about their streets as a fool; rather let us say, they gave the truest testimony to his likeness to his Lord by the likeness of their treatment of him.

They were wont to follow him, throwing dirt at him and spitting in his face; tying straws to his cloak and hat, and pursuing him with shouts of derisive laughter. He never seemed to heed them, or to let the singular quietude of his

---

*It is no part of the plan which we have laid down for ourselves to enter at any length into the vexed question of the character of the Inquisition. But we cannot resist referring to one authority, quoted by Père Lacordaire, in his well-known "Memorial to the French People," whose partiality can scarcely be questioned. It is from the Report presented to the Cortes on the character of that tribunal, which was followed by its suppression and bears the date of 1218. Considering that it proceeded from the party most violently opposed to the Inquisition, and whose political successors, the Progressistas of Spain, have succeeded in abolishing all religious orders in that country, its testimony is of peculiar value. "The early Inquisitors," they say, "encountered heresy with no other arms than those of prayer, patience, and instruction; and this remark applies more particularly to St. Dominic, as we are assured by the Bollandists, with Echard and Touron. Philip II was the real founder of the Inquisition." For a minute and careful account of the change introduced into the character of the tribunal by the royal influence, we must refer the reader to the celebrated work of Balmez, on "Protestantism and Catholicity compared in their Effects on the Civilization of Europe."

soul be once disturbed by these affronts. Sometimes their insults were accompanied with blasphemous oaths and threats of death. "I am not worthy of martyrdom," was the only answer they were able to draw from him. He was warned once of a party of heretics who lay in ambush in a certain place to assassinate him. He treated the information with his usual indifference, and passed by the place singing hymns with a joyful aspect. The heretics, who were probably not prepared for the actual execution of their threat, accosted him on their next meeting in their usual style. "And so thou dost not fear death? tell us, what wouldst thou have done if thou hadst fallen into our hands?" Then the great and courageous spirit of Dominic spoke in a memorable reply: "I would have prayed you," he said, "not to have taken my life at a single blow, but little by little, cutting off each member of my body, one by one; and when you had done that, you should have plucked out my eyes, and then have left me so to prolong my torments, and gain me a richer crown." It is said that the reply so confounded his enemies that for some time afterwards they left him unmolested, being convinced that to persecute such a man was to give him the only consolation he desired. The place of the intended attempt on his life is still shown, halfway between Prouille and Fanjeaux, and its name "Al Sicari," in the dialect of the country, commemorates the event.

On another occasion a great conference was appointed to be held with the heretics, at which one of the neighboring bishops (who, some writers tell us, was Fulk of Toulouse) was to attend. He came in great pomp, to the great displeasure of Dominic. "Then the humble herald of God spoke to him, and said, 'My father, it is not thus that we must act against this generation of pride. The enemies of the truth must rather be convinced by the example of humility and patience, than by the pomp and grandeur of worldly show. Let us arm ourselves with prayer and humility, and so let us go barefooted against these Goliaths.'" The bishop complied with his wishes, and they all took off their shoes and went to meet the heretics, singing Psalms upon the way.

Now, as they were not sure of their road, they applied to a man whom they met and believed to be a Catholic, but who was in truth a concealed and bitter heretic and who offered to be their guide to the place of meeting, with no other design than that of embarrassing and annoying them. He led them, therefore, through a thorny wood, where the rough stones and briars tore their naked feet and caused them to dye the ground with their blood. The bishop and his suite were a little disconcerted at this, but Dominic encouraged them to persevere. Joyous and patient as ever, he exhorted his comrades to give thanks for their sufferings, saying, "Trust in God, my beloved; the victory is surely ours, since our sins are expiated in blood; is it not written, 'How beautiful are the feet of them who bring the gospel of peace?'" Then he intoned a joyful hymn, and the hearts of his companions took courage, and they also sang with him; and the heretic, when he witnessed the patience and courage of the saint, was touched to the heart, and falling at his feet confessed his malice and abjured his heresy.

As we have said, these anecdotes of Dominic's apostolic life in Languedoc can hardly be given in successive order as they occurred; the most ancient writers tell us only in general terms that during this time he suffered many affronts from his enemies and overcame their wiles by his patience, giving these disconnected stories without anything to guide us as to the particular times when they happened.

One anecdote, however, in which the miraculous powers of the Saint are first exhibited to us, is given with greater exactness. It was in 1211, whilst the crusaders were under the walls of Toulouse, and just after open hostilities had for the first time broken out with Count Raymond, that the course of Dominic's apostolic wanderings led him to the bank of the river Garrone. Whilst he was there, a band of English pilgrims also arrived in the neighborhood. They were about forty in number, bound to the shrine of St. James of Compostela. In order to avoid the town, which lay under the Papal interdict, they took a boat to cross the river; but the boat being small and overladen was upset, and all those who were in it sank to the bottom. Dominic was praying in a small church which stood near the scene of the accident, but the cries of the sufferers and some of the soldiers who saw their danger roused him from his devotions. He came to the river's bank, but not one of the pilgrims was to be seen. Then he prostrated himself on the earth in silent prayer, and, rising full of a lively faith, "I command you," he cried, "in the name of Jesus Christ, to come to the shore alive and unhurt." Instantly the bodies rose to the surface, and with the help of the soldiers, who flung them their shields and lances, they all safely reached the bank, praising God and His servant Dominic.

Several other miracles are related as having happened at this period. They are the only footprints left us of his apostolic journeys over Languedoc. At one time we hear of him dropping his books into the river Ariege as he forded it on foot, and after three days they are recovered by a fisherman, and found perfectly dry and uninjured. At another time he is crossing the same river in a little boat, and being landed on the opposite shore finds he has no money to pay the boatman. The boatman insisted on his fare: "I am," said Dominic, "a follower of Jesus Christ; I carry neither gold nor silver; God will pay you the price of my passage." But the boatman, being angry, laid hold of his cloak, saying, "You will either leave your cloak with me, or pay me my money." Dominic, raising his eyes to heaven, entered for a moment into prayer; then, looking on the ground, he showed the man a piece of silver which lay there, which Providence had sent, and said to him, "My brother, there is what you ask; take it, and suffer me to go my way."

Cardinal Ranieri Capocci, who lived during the time of St. Dominic, in a sermon preached shortly after his canonization relates the following fact which had come to his own knowledge. A certain religious chanced to be the companion of the saint on a journey of some days, but being of another country, and neither of them understanding the language of the other, they were unable to hold any conversation together. Desiring very much, however, to profit by the time he should spend in his society, this religious secretly prayed to God that, for the three days they should be together, they might be intelligible to one another, each speaking in his own tongue; and this favor was granted until they reached their journey's end.

We read also that, after a night spent in long disputes with the heretics, Dominic left the place of conference in company with a Cistercian monk, and desired to retire into a neighboring church in order, according to his custom, to spend the remainder of the night in prayer. They found the doors locked, and were therefore obliged to kneel outside. But scarcely had they done so, than without being able to say how, they found themselves before the high altar inside the church, and remained there until break of day. In the morning the people found them there, and crowding together, brought them the sick and infirm in great numbers to be healed. Among these were several possessed persons, whom the Holy Father was entreated to restore by his touch. He took a stole and fastened it on his shoulders as if about to vest for Mass; then, throwing it round the necks of the possessed, they were immediately delivered.

These miracles, some of which are mentioned in the process of his canonization, were commonly known and talked of both by the crusaders and by the people of Toulouse. Among the latter their effect was sensibly felt, and in no small degree aided the success of his preaching. Yet the marvels produced by his simple eloquence were perhaps as great in their way as those directly supernatural gifts communicated to him by God.

One day as he prayed in the church of Fanjeaux, nine women who until then had been of the heretical sect came to him, and threw themselves at his feet in great anguish. "Servant of God," they cried, "if what you preached to us this morning is true, we have till now been living in horrible darkness; therefore have compassion on us, and teach us how we may be saved." The holy man looked on them with a bright and cheerful countenance, and comforted them with words of hope. Then he prayed awhile, and turning to them bade them be of good heart, and not be afraid at what they should see. Scarcely had he spoken, when they saw in the midst of them a hideous animal of a ferocious and horrible aspect. It fled from among them and seemed to escape from the church through the bell tower. The women were greatly terrified, but Dominic spoke and reassured them. "God has shown you, my daughters," he said, "how terrible is the devil whom till now you have served; thank Him, therefore, for the evil one has from this moment no more power over you." These women, who were all of noble birth, he afterwards caused to be instructed in the Faith and received into the monastery of Prouille.

Miracles and preaching, however, are not the only means, scarcely the most powerful, by which the saints of God extend the kingdom of their Master. The silent eloquence of a holy life has a larger apostolate than the gifts of tongue or of healing; and we find some records of the harvest of souls which were gathered to the faith solely by the example of the servant of God. There were living, near Toulouse, some noble ladies who had been led to join the heretics, being seduced into this error by the show of pretended austerity which their preachers affected. Dominic, who had their conversion greatly at heart, determined to preach there that Lent; and, going thither with one companion, it chanced, by the providence of God, that they were received to lodge in the house occupied by these ladies. He remained there during the whole time of his stay, and they saw with wonder the reality of that life of penance which differed so widely from the empty professions of the heretics. The soft beds which had been prepared for them were never used, for Dominic and his companions slept upon the ground. Their food was scarcely touched; until Easter time they took only bread and water, and that in scanty measure. Their

nights were spent in prayer and austerities, their days in
labors for God; and so new and wonderful did this life seem
to those who beheld it, that it opened their eyes to the truth
of the Faith which inspired it; and the whole household
made their recantation in his hands before the time of his
stay was ended. In after days he was often accustomed to
exhort his brethren to this as the best method of preaching,
reminding them that it was by good works and by the outward habit, even more than by holy words, that we must
let our light shine before men to the glory of God.

It was this singular holiness of life which endeared him
so wonderfully to all those among whom he was thrown.
Three times the episcopal dignity was offered to him, but
he refused it with a kind of horror. He was used to say
he would rather go away by night with nothing but his
staff than accept any office or dignity. He could not, however, succeed in avoiding a temporary appointment as vicar
to Guy, bishop of Carcassona, during the time that the latter was absent from his diocese preaching the Crusade, and
gathering together fresh forces to join the army of the Count
de Montfort.

He held this charge during the Lent of the year 1213,
during which time he resided in the episcopal palace, and
discharged all the duties of the office without, however,
suffering them to interfere with his customary occupation
of preaching and instructing in the Faith. During the Lent
we again find him spoken of as fasting on bread and water
and sleeping on the ground. "When Easter came," says his
historian, "he seemed stronger and more vigorous than before, and of a better aspect." We may remark in this appointment how entirely distinct Dominic's mission was from
the military or political affairs in which many other of the
Catholic clergy and prelates took their share. So far from
being himself the preacher of the Crusade, we see him taking the place and duties of another who is engaged in that
undertaking, as if the purely spiritual character of his ministry were generally recognized. Once, and once only, do we

find his name in any way associated with any of the judicial severities of the time; it is in an anecdote given by Theodoric of Apoldia, but it will be hard to draw from it the conclusion that Dominic was the bloody persecutor represented in popular fiction; for as we shall see, his part was to *release*, and not to *condemn* the prisoner in question.

"Some heretics," says the historian, "having been taken and convicted in the country of Toulouse, were given over to secular judgment, because they refused to return to the Faith, and were condemned to the flames. Dominic looked at one of them with a heart to which were revealed the secrets of God, and said to the officers of the court, 'Put that man aside, and see well that no harm befall him.' Then, turning to the heretic, he said with great sweetness, 'My son, I know that you must have time, but you will at length become a saint.' Wonderful to relate, this man remained for twenty years longer in the blindness of heresy, till at length, touched by the grace of God, he renounced his errors, and died in the habit of the Friars Preachers, with the reputation of sanctity."

The presence of Dominic at this execution will be understood, if we remember that before the deliverance of any heretic to the secular arm for punishment, every effort was made, by the exhortations of persons appointed for that purpose, to convince them of their errors and reconcile them to the Church; in which case their sentence was rescinded, and they were admitted to canonical penance. This course was always followed in the later proceedings of the Inquisition; the part of the Church was to reconcile and convince, and not to condemn; in the instance just quoted, we might call it to pardon.

This office was exercised by Dominic in virtue of the powers he held from the papal legates; two letters proving this fact are given us by Echard, but have no date attached, although there is little doubt they belong to this period of his life. They are as follows: "To all the faithful in Christ to whom these presents may come, Brother Dominic, canon of Osma, the humble minister of preaching, wishes health and charity in the Lord. We make known to your discretion, that we have permitted Raymund William de Hauterive Pelaganira to receive into his house of Toulouse, to live there after the ordinary life, William Huguecion, whom he has declared to us to have hitherto worn the habit of the heretics. We permit this until such time as it shall be otherwise ordered either to him or to me by the Lord Cardinal; and this shall not in any way turn to his dishonor or prejudice." If it seems singular to us in these days that a written permission was necessary in order to allow any man to receive into his house a reconciled heretic, we must remember the double character attaching to these people. They were not merely heretics, but the disturbers of the public peace; and, as the authors of every kind of outrage against society, it is not singular that some kind of pledge for their future good conduct was reasonably demanded.

The other letter is of a severer character; it is as follows: "To all the faithful in Christ to whom these presents may come, Brother Dominic, canon of Osma, wishes health in the Lord. By the authority of the Lord Abbot of Citeaux, who has committed to us this office, we have reconciled to the Church the bearer of these presents, Ponce Royer, converted by the grace of God from heresy to the Faith; and we order, in virtue of the oath which he has taken to us, that during three Sundays or feastdays he shall go to the entrance of the village, bare to the waist, and be struck with rods by the priest. We also order him to abstain forever from flesh, eggs, cheese, and all which comes from flesh, except at Easter, Pentecost, and Christmas, when he shall eat some to protest against his former errors. He shall keep three Lents each year, fasting and abstaining from fish, unless from bodily infirmity or the heat of the weather he shall be dispensed. He shall dress in a religious habit, as well in the form as in the color, to the ends of which shall be hung two little crosses. Every day, if possible, he shall hear Mass, and he shall go to vespers on festival days. Seven times a day he shall recite ten 'Pater Nosters,' and he shall say twenty in the middle of the night. He shall observe chastity, and once a month he shall, in the morning, present this paper to the chaplain of the village of Céré. We desire this chaplain to have great care that his penitent lead a holy life, and observe all we have said until the lord legate shall otherwise ordain. If he neglect to do so through contempt, we will that he be excommunicated as perjured and heretic, and be separated from the society of the faithful."

Such was still the Church's discipline in the thirteenth century. We who live in days when that discipline has been gradually, though reluctantly, relaxed, because of the relaxing love and faith of penitents, are amazed at its severity: we are even disposed to lay the responsibility of its seeming harshness on the head of him who pronounced the sentence. But Dominic was in no way the legislator in such a case as this: he was simply the executor and dispenser of the Church's law. The above diploma is one of those monumental records of canonical penances which we occasionally find preserved in the course of history, and which, when so stumbled on, are almost invariably rocks of offense to those who are accustomed to look on a litany, or a *"Salve Regina,"* as a reasonable penance for the sins of a life.

The accumulation of indulgences in modern times ought surely to have its significance to such minds. In those days, men really *performed* the penances which are now dispensed. The rod which descends so gently on the head of the wondering stranger in the Roman basilicas—that ghost of the ancient penitential discipline—fell with a hearty earnestness on the shoulders of our fathers; and we cannot too often remind ourselves, by means of such documents as that we have just read, of a difference which should cover us with humiliation for the feebleness of modern penitence, rather than send us to criticize the severity with which the Church has ever looked on sin.

CHAPTER 7

The institution of the Rosary. The Council of Lavaur. The battle of Muret.

We have given a few anecdotes of the life led by Dominic during a time when war and bloodshed were raging around him. They are all that are left us to mark his course for many years. But it was during this time, though it would be difficult to affix the precise date, that he propagated that celebrated devotion which would alone entitle its author to our veneration, did we know him in no other way than as the first institutor of the Rosary.

The universal voice of tradition affirms this devotion to have been revealed to him by the Blessed Virgin herself; and if we consider its almost supernatural character, combining as it does the simplest prayers with the profoundest meditations, or again if we remember the extraordinary power with which it has been blessed, and its adoption through the universal Church as the very alphabet of prayer, it is difficult for us not to believe it something more than a human invention, but rather as a gift which came to us as the most precious token of the love of our dear Mother. Although, however, there is ample ground for this belief, the details of any such revelation have not been preserved to us, for the circumstantial accounts of the giving of the Rosary, which are so popular with later writers, are not to be found in any of the more ancient authors, who leave the date and the manner of its first institution in obscurity.*

---

*Local tradition declares the sanctuary of Notre Dame de Dreche, near Albi, to have been the scene of the vision of Our Lady; it is certain that this sanctuary first attained celebrity during the Albigensian troubles, and was one of the favorite resorts of St. Dominic in the course of his apostolic labors.

St. Dominic's life during these years was, for the most part, a lonely and hidden one: his communications with Heaven remained locked within his own breast; for it was not with him as with so many other saints, on whom a hundred busy eyes were always fixed to mark every indication of supernatural grace, every phenomenon, if we may so say, of their ecstasy and prayer: his own lips were the only source from whence the secret favors of God could ever have been made known, and they certainly were the last which were ever likely to speak of them to another.

We again remark in the institution of the Rosary something of that character feature of St. Dominic to which we have before alluded. It was not altogether a new devotion. There was nothing novel in the frequent repetition of the "Angelical Salutation" or the *"Pater Noster"*: such devotion had been common in the Church from time immemorial, and we read of the hermits of the deserts counting such prayers with little stones, in the same way as we use the beads. The novelty was the association of mental and vocal prayer in those mysteries which gather together, under fifteen heads, all the history of the life of Christ. This working out of the materials which lay before him, and which others had used before him, is the peculiarity of which we have spoken. It is the distinctive humility of our Saint. If we reflect on the way in which all his greatest actions were performed, we may safely say that they came from a soul in which the petty desire of personal reputation, of making a noise in the world, of being known as the founder of an institution or the originator of a noble thought, was never felt.

Nay, if we may so say, there is something which perpetually reminds us of Our Lord's own way of working; when He took His parables and similitudes from the common things before His eyes, and was content to let His Church grow out of the relics of Judaism, as its visible temples may sometimes be seen standing among the ruins of heathen fanes, converting all their beauty to a sacred use. In

all St. Dominic's institutions we see this unconsciousness
of self, which is an evidence of the highest class of mind,
and it is probably from this cause that, in the commencement of all of them, there is an obscurity and uncertainty
of date which is rarely found to attach to the inventions
of human genius.

We may, however, consider it as certain that the Rosary
had begun to be propagated before the year 1213, as we
are assured that it was used by the soldiers of the Count
de Montfort's army before the battle of Muret, which took
place in that year. Many stories are told of the wonders
which followed on its first adoption. Some despised it, and
ridiculed its use; among whom was one of the bishops of
the country of Toulouse, who, hearing the Rosary preached
by St. Dominic, spoke of it afterwards with contempt, saying it was only fit for women and children. He was soon
convinced of his error; for shortly afterwards, falling into
great persecution and calumnies, he seemed in a vision to
see himself plunged into thick mire from which there was
no way of escape. Raising his eyes, he saw above him the
forms of Our Lady and St. Dominic, who let down to him
a chain made of a hundred and fifty rings, fifteen of which
were of gold; and laying hold of this he found himself safely
drawn to dry land. By this he understood that it was by
means of the devotion of the Rosary he should be delivered
from his enemies, which shortly took place after he had
devoutly commenced its use.

Another similar story relates how a noble lady opposed
the new confraternities of this devotion with all her power,
but was converted by the following vision, which was
granted to her one night in prayer. Being rapt in ecstasy,
she saw an innumerable company of men and women, surrounded by a great splendor, who devoutly recited the Rosary together; and for every *"Ave Maria"* which they
repeated a beautiful star came forth from their mouths,
and the prayers were written in a book in letters of gold.
Then the Blessed Virgin spoke to her and said, "In this

book are written the names of the brethren and sisters of my Rosary, but thy name is not written; and because thou hast persuaded many not to enter it, there shall befall thee a sickness for a time, which yet shall turn to thy salvation." The lady was soon after seized with sickness, and recognizing the truth of the prediction, she caused herself on her recovery to be inscribed among the members of the confraternity. The spread of this devotion was the most successful weapon in the eradication of the <u>Albigensian heresy</u>. The child of ignorance, it fled before the light of truth; and as the mysteries of the Faith were gradually brought back to the minds and hearts of the people, the mysteries of falsehood disappeared. <u>The doctrine of the Incarnation,</u> so specially commemorated in the Rosary, became then, as ever, the bulwark of the truth; and wherever the society was established and the name of Mary was invoked, that name, as the Church sings, "alone destroyed all heresies."

During the time that Dominic exercised the office of vicar to the Bishop of Carcassona, the position of the contending parties in Languedoc was considerably altered by the arrival of Peter, king of Arragon, who joined the forces of the Count of Toulouse with a powerful army. He was allied to the count by marriage, but had hitherto contented himself by negotiating in his favor with the court of Rome.

In the beginning of the year 1213, however, a council was summoned at Lavaur, at which the king formally demanded from the legates and Catholic chiefs the restitution of the towns and lands which they had taken in the course of the war from the Count of Toulouse and the other nobles who had espoused his cause, and their restoration to the communion of the Church. The council consented to admit the others on the terms proposed, but refused to include the Count of Toulouse, whose repeated perjuries and evasions had rendered him unworthy of trust. This answer was considered by the king as an evidence that there was a resolve to destroy the house of Toulouse, from motives of personal ambition on the part of the Count de Montfort; and he, therefore, declared the family of Raymond under his protection, and appealed to the Holy See against the decision of the council. The legates, on their part, represented to the Pope that the only chance of restoring peace to the distracted country was by the entire removal of the house of Toulouse, and the destruction of its hereditary power. The contradictory appeals and reports which were sent him rendered it difficult for Innocent to judge in a cause involved every way in embarrassment. That he was very far from advocating unnecessary or undue severity toward Raymond and his family, we may gather from his own letters to the Count de Montfort, in which he urges him not to let the world think that he fought more for his own interest than for the cause of the Faith. On the other hand, he complains in a later letter that the king of Arragon had misled him as to the state of affairs, and enjoins him to proceed no further against the Count de Montfort, until the arrival of a cardinal whom he is about to despatch to the spot to examine the whole question as his delegate.

It was too late. Before the order arrived, the king had passed the Pyrenees, and joining the troops of the Counts of Toulouse, Foix, and Comminges, prepared to advance against the army of the crusaders. Their position seemed indeed but gloomy, for the forces of the heretic leaders far outnumbered those of the Catholics. A lay brother of the Cistercians, who watched the progress of the war with painful interest, went in company with Stephen de Metz, another religious of the same order, to consult Dominic at this juncture, well knowing that God often revealed to him the secrets of coming events. "Will these evils never have an end, Master Dominic?" asked the afflicted brother. He repeated his question many times, but Dominic remained silent. At length he replied, "There will be a time when the malice of the men of Toulouse will have its end; but it is far away; and there will be much blood shed first, and a king will die in battle." Brother Stephen and the Cistercian interpreted this prediction to allude to Prince Louis of France, the son of Philip Augustus, who had joined the army of the crusaders in the previous February.

"No," replied Dominic, "it will not touch the king of France: it is another king whose thread of life will be cut in the course of this war." This prophecy was very shortly to be accomplished, and Dominic himself was destined to be present on the spot where the decisive struggle took place which witnessed its fulfillment.

Very shortly after uttering the prediction, he left Carcassona on the return of the bishop, intending to join a congress of the Catholic prelates and legates which was to be held at Muret. On the road thither he passed through the city of Castres, where the body of the martyr St. Vincent was preserved for the veneration of the faithful. Entering the church to pay his devotion at the shrine of the saint, he remained so late that the prior of the collegiate canons of Castres, who was his host for the time, despatched one of the brethren to call him to dinner. The brother obeyed, but on going into the church, he saw Dominic raised in the air in ectasy before the altar; and not daring to disturb him, he returned to the prior, who himself hastened to the spot, and beheld the spectacle with his own eyes. So forcible was the impression it left on his mind of the sanctity of the man of God that shortly after he joined himself to him, and was one of those who formed the first foundation of the order. This was the celebrated Matthew of France, afterwards the prior of the convent of St. James in Paris, and the first and last who ever bore the title of abbot among the Friars Preachers. After this incident, Dominic proceeded on his road to Muret.

It was on the 10th of September of the same year that the king of Arragon suddenly appeared before the walls of this place, with an army, according to some writers, of 100,000 men, or as others more probably state, of 40,000. The intelligence of his approach reached de Montfort at Fanjeaux. It seems probable that this hostile movement took the Catholic chieftain by surprise; for only a few weeks previously he had been invited to a friendly conference by the king, and so little was he prepared for any active measures at that time (owing to the pending negotiations with the Roman court), that he had no more than 800 horses and a small number of men-at-arms with him with which to come to the relief of the besieged. To oppose so contemptible a force to the army of the king seemed little less than madness, yet he never hesitated. On the day following that on which the news reached him he set out from Fanjeaux, taking with him the bishops and legates, amongst whom was Fulk, bishop of Toulouse, with the intention of at least attempting a pacific settlement before the last appeal to arms.

He stopped on his way at the Cistercian monastery of Bolbonne, and going into the church laid his sword on the altar, as though to commend his cause to God, and remained for some time in prayer; then taking back his sword, as now no longer his, but God's, he proceeded to Saverdun, where he spent the night in confession and preparation for death. His little company of followers did the same, and on the morning of the following day they all communicated, as men who were about to offer their lives as a sacrifice. Some authors tell us that Dominic was present with the other legates and ecclesiastics in the army; others name him as being in their company only at Muret; but it seems probable that he had joined them previously, and if the current tradition is the correct one—that the crusaders ascribed their subsequent victory to the particular assistance of Mary, whom they had united to invoke in the prayers of the Rosary—we may well believe that this appeal to Our Lady of Victories came from his counsel and exhortation.

The army reached Muret on the side of the town opposite to that where the forces of the king of Arragon were drawn up; but, before entering the gates, the bishops were despatched with propositions of peace to the enemy's camp. A contemptuous sarcasm was the only reply they received, and returning to the army, they all entered Muret together. But they determined on one more effort, and very early in the morning despatched another message to the king, to the effect that they would wait upon him barefoot to bring about the terms of reconciliation. They were preparing to execute this design when a body of cavalry attacked the gates; for the king had ordered the advance, without even deigning a reply to this second embassy.

The scene that morning within the walls of Muret was surely a religious one. Eight hundred devoted men, fortified by prayer and the Sacraments of reconciliation, were about, as it seemed to human judgment, to lay down their lives as a sacrifice for the Faith. There might be seen how the Holy Sacrifice was celebrated in the presence of them all; and how, when the Bishop of Uzès turned to say the last *"Dominus vobiscum,"* de Montfort knelt before him, clad in armor, and said, "And I consecrate my blood and life for God and His Faith"; and how the swords and shields of the combatants were once more offered on the altar; and when it was over, and the horsemen were gathering together, and the very sound of the attack was at the gates, these men all once more dismounted and bent their knee to venerate and kiss the crucifix, extended to them by the Bishop of Toulouse. He had come to give them his parting words and blessing.

Did his voice falter, or his eye grow dim at the spectacle before him? Something there certainly was of human emotion at that moment which history does not notice; for we are told it was not he, but the Bishop of Comminges who stood by his side, that spoke the last charge to the army, and taking the crucifix from the hands of Fulk, solemnly blessed them as they knelt. Then they rode out to battle, and the ecclesiastics turned back into the church to pray.

Nothing more heroic is to be found in the whole history of chivalry than this battle of Muret.* It was a single charge. They rode through the open gates, and after a feigned movement of retreat, they suddenly turned rein and dashed right

---

*See No. II of "Tales and Legends from History," in this series.

on the ranks of their opponents, with the impetuosity of a mountain torrent. Swift as lightning they broke through the troops that opposed their onward course, scattering them before the horses' hoofs with something of supernatural energy, nor did they draw bridle till they reached the center of the army, where the king himself was stationed, surrounded by the flower of his nobles and followers. A moment's fierce struggle ensued; but the fall of the king decided the fortune of the day. Terrified by the shock of that tremendous charge, as it hurled itself upon them, the whole army fled in panic. The voice and example of their chief might again have rallied them, but that was wanting: Peter of Arragon lay dead on the field, and Dominic's prophecy was fulfilled.

And where was he meanwhile—and what place has this page of chivalry in the annals of his apostolic life? The flash of swords and the tramp of those galloping steeds startle us strangely from the story of his quiet, lonely wanderings over the mountains, filling their echoes with the sound of his hymns and litanies, as he goes about to preach. Where are we to look for him in such a scene? Protestant writers are ready enough to tell us he was *at the head of the crusaders*, carrying a crucifix, and urging them on to slaughter. We must be suffered to think, however, that neither in the schools of Palencia nor in the canonry of Osma could he have fitted himself for such a post as the leader of a cavalry charge whose equal is scarce to be found in history.

Yet the battle of Muret forms part of the story of Dominic's life; he had his place there: for that one moment, and so far as history gives us any token, for that one alone, he was brought in contact with the stormy scenes of the Crusade. He had his place; but, to find it, we must leave the battlefield and go back to the church of Muret, where a different sight will greet us.

When the Christian knights were ridden forth to the battle, the churchmen had gone before the altar to pray. They had sent their comrades, as it seemed, to certain death; and their prayer had in it the anguish of supplication. Prostrate on the pavement, which they bathed with their tears, they poured out their souls to God. F. Bernard, of the Order of Preachers, who lived in Toulouse at the beginning of the following century and who wrote whilst the memory of these events was still fresh in the minds of the people, thus describes them: "Then going into the church, they prayed, raising their hands to heaven, and beseeching God for His servants who were exposed to death for His sake, with such great groans and cries that it seemed not that they prayed, but rather howled."*

But from this agonizing suspense they were roused by the shouts of the populace. The cry of victory sounded in their ears; they hastened to the walls and beheld the plain covered with the flying companies of the heretics. Some plunged into the waters of the Garonne and perished in their armor; others trampled their own comrades to death in the confusion of their flight; many died under the swords of the crusaders. It is computed that no fewer than 20,000 of the heretic forces were slain, whilst we are assured by all authorities that *eight* only of the Catholics fell during the combat of that day. As the Count de Montfort rode over

---

*A very popular tradition has represented St. Dominic as ascending one of the towers on the wall and displaying the crucifix for the encouragement of the Christian troops. This assertion has been supported by the exhibition, in later ages, at Toulouse, of a crucifix pierced all over with arrows, which is supposed to have been the identical one used by him on the occasion. Polidori, who in all things strictly adheres to the ancient authors and is careful to repudiate every modern addition of less authority, rejects this tale as utterly unfounded, chiefly from the entire silence of F. Bernard concerning the whole matter; and as he was Inquisitor of Toulouse during fourteen years, if any such crucifix had been preserved by the Institute in his day, he could hardly have failed noticing it. Père Lacordaire, in his eloquent Life of St. Dominic, has followed the same argument. On the other hand, in the chapel of Our Lady in the church of St. James at Muret, which was built as a memorial of the victory in the course of the same year, we see a picture representing the Blessed Virgin giving the Rosary to St. Dominic, who holds in his right hand a crucifix pierced with *three arrows:* on the other side of Our Lady kneel Simon de Montfort and Fulk of Toulouse. A facsimile of this picture, and of the same date, was long kept in the Dominican church at Toulouse. Whether this picture alluded to any circumstance which really took place, or was itself the origin of the tradition, we do not pretend to determine.

that victorious field, he checked his horse by the bleeding
and trampled body of the king of Arragon. De Montfort
had some of the failings, but all the virtues, of his order:
he was cast in the heroic type of Christian chivalry. Descending from his horse, he kissed the body with tears and gave
orders for its honorable interment, as became a gallant
enemy; then, returning barefoot to Muret, he went first to
the church to return thanks to God, and gave the horse
and armor with which he had fought to the poor. It was
a true picture of the ages of faith.

We need scarcely be surprised that so wonderful a victory was looked on as miraculous, and counted as the fruit
of prayer. De Montfort himself ever so regarded it; and at-
tributing his success, under God, to the intercession of
Dominic, his love and gratitude to the Saint knew no bounds.
It has always been so associated in the traditions and chronicles of the time with the institution of the Rosary, as to
make many affirm that the first propagation of that devotion must be dated from this time.

The battle of Muret was a fatal blow to the cause of the
Count of Toulouse. Very shortly after, Toulouse itself opened
its gates to the victorious arms of de Montfort; and a council,* which assembled at Montpellier in the following year,
decided that the sovereignty of the country should be entrusted to him, until the general council about to assemble
at Rome should declare further. Cardinal Benvenuto, who
reached Toulouse just as the decisive blow had been struck,
was commissioned to receive the elder Raymond to absolution, and to put a stop to further hostilities; but the question as to his future enjoyment of the temporal rights he
had forfeited by breach of engagement was still deferred.

Twice again Dominic's name occurs among the busy scenes
of de Montfort's career. He was called on to baptize his

---

*In the Life of St. Francis we are informed that the holy founder of the Friars
Minor was present at this council, being then on his return to Spain. He had,
however, no opportunity of meeting St. Dominic, as the latter was then absent
at Carcassona, and took no part in the proceedings.

daughter, and to celebrate the marriage of his eldest son with the daughter of the dauphin of France.

But the favor of the victorious chieftain, and the distractions of the camp and court, were scarcely felt by him at this moment. The shifting chances of the war, guided by the hands of Providence, were opening to him, after long waiting, the way to that design which had ever floated before his mind's eye. The clouds which had so long hung over that distant horizon rose at last; and when Toulouse opened her gates and the storm of the combat was lulled, and the favor of man was at hand to help on the will of God, Dominic, in his forty-sixth year, prepared to lay the foundation of that order which was to bear his name to future ages so long as the world and the Church should last.

CHAPTER 8

Dominic commences the foundation of his order at Toulouse. The grant
of Fulk of Toulouse. Dominic's second visit to Rome. The Council
of Lateran. Innocent III approves the plan of the Order. Meeting of
Dominic and Francis.

Dominic came to Toulouse soon after the Crusaders had
entered it, and was joyfully received both by Fulk and by
the Count de Montfort. Neither of these distinguished persons was, however, destined to be the immediate cooperator
with him in the foundation of the order.

Peter Cellani, an opulent citizen of Toulouse, and another
of the same rank known to us only under the name of
Thomas, presented themselves to him shortly after his arrival at Toulouse and placed themselves and all they had
at his disposal. Peter Cellani offered his own house for the
use of the few companions whom Dominic had gathered
together to commence his work. They were but six in all,
and in after years Peter was accustomed to boast that he
had not been received into the order, but that it might rather
be said he had received the order into his own house. With
these six followers, whom he clothed in the habit of the
Canons Regular, which he himself always wore, Dominic
accordingly commenced a life of poverty and prayer under
rules of religious discipline.

But this alone did not satisfy him; the first design which
he had conceived, and which had never left his mind, had
preeminently as its object the salvation of souls, by means
of such a ministration of the Divine Word as should proceed from a knowledge of sacred science, large enough for
the defense of the Christian dogmas against all the assaults
of heresy and infidelity. The whole future scope of the Friars

Preachers was in the mind of Dominic at the moment of their first foundation. That it was so is evinced by his first step after assembling these six brethren in the house of Peter Cellani. He explained to them the extent and nature of his design and showed them that, in order to carry it out and fit themselves for the task of teaching truth, they must first learn it. Now it so happened that there was then in Toulouse a celebrated doctor of theology named Alexander, whose lectures were greatly admired and frequented. It was to him that Dominic resolved to entrust his little company.

On the same morning Alexander had risen very early and was in his room engaged in study, when he was overcome by an unusual and irresistible inclination to sleep. His book dropped from his hand, and he sank into a profound slumber. As he slept he seemed to see before him seven stars, at first small and scarcely visible, but which increased in size and brightness till they enlightened the whole world.

As day broke he started from his dream, and hastened to the school where he was to deliver his usual lecture. Scarcely had he entered the room when Dominic and his six companions presented themselves before him. They were all clad alike, in the white habit and surplice of the Augustinian canons, and they announced themselves as poor brothers, who were about to preach the Gospel of Christ to the faithful and heretics of Toulouse, and who desired first of all to profit by his instructions. Alexander understood that he saw before him the seven stars of his morning dream; and many years after, when the order had indeed fulfilled the destiny predicted and had covered Europe with the fame of its learning, he himself being then at the English court related the whole circumstances with an almost fatherly pride, as having been the first master of the Friars Preachers.

These first steps of the brethren were marked by the bishop, Fulk of Toulouse, with unmixed satisfaction. The piety and fervor displayed by them and their exact following in the footsteps of Dominic, for whom he had ever entertained

a peculiar reverence, determined him to give the infant order
the support of his powerful protection. With the consent
of his chapter he assigned the sixth part of the tithes of
the diocese for their support, and the purchase of the books
necessary for their studies.

The document in which he makes this grant will not be
without its interest:

> "In the name of our Lord Jesus Christ. We make
> known to all present and to come, that we Fulk,
> by the grace of God the humble minister of the
> see of Toulouse, desiring to extirpate heresy, to expel
> vice, to teach the rule of faith, and recall men
> to a holy life, appoint Brother Dominic and his
> companions to be preachers throughout our dio-
> cese; who propose to go on foot, as becomes reli-
> gious, according to evangelical poverty, and to
> preach the word of evangelical truth. And because
> the workman is worthy of his hire, and we are
> bound not to muzzle the mouth of the ox who
> treadeth out the corn, and because those who
> preach the Gospel shall live by the Gospel, we
> desire that, whilst preaching through the diocese,
> the necessary means of support be administered
> to them from the revenues of the diocese. Where-
> fore, with the consent of the chapter of the church
> of St. Stephen, and of all the clergy of our dio-
> cese, we assign in perpetuity to the aforesaid
> preachers, and to others who, being moved by zeal
> for God and love for the salvation of souls, shall
> employ themselves in the like work of preaching,
> the sixth part of the tenths destined for the build-
> ing and ornamenting all the parochial churches
> subject to our government, in order that they may
> provide themselves with habits, and whatsoever
> may be necessary to them when they shall be sick,
> or be in need of rest. If anything remain over at

the year's end, let them give it back, that it may
be applied to the adorning of the said parish
churches, or the relief of the poor, according as
the bishop shall see fit. For inasmuch as it is established by law that a certain part of the tithes
shall always be assigned to the poor, it cannot be
doubted that we are entitled to assign a certain
portion thereof to those who voluntarily follow
evangelical poverty for the love of Christ, labor-
ing to enrich the world by their example and
heavenly doctrine; and thus we shall satisfy our
duty of freely scattering and dividing, both by ourselves and by means of others, spiritual things to
those from whom we receive temporal things.
Given in the year of the Word Incarnate 1215,
in the reign of Philip king of France, the princi-
pality of Toulouse being held by the Count de
Montfort."

Neither was de Montfort wanting in a like liberality towards the young order. He had already made many grants
to the house of La Prouille, and in this year we find him
making over the castle and lands of Cassanel to the use of
Dominic and his companions.

In the autumn of the same year Fulk of Toulouse set out
for Rome to attend the approaching Council of the Lateran, and Dominic was his companion. Eleven years had
passed since his first visit in company with Diego: they had
been years of hard and solitary labor, and the work, the
plan of which had even then been formed within his mind
was now but just developing into actual existence. Most surely
he had within his soul the principle of a far higher strength
than mere human enthusiasm, or he might well have been
daunted as, coming for the second time within sight of the
eternal city, the forty-six years of his life lay before him,
so full of patient work and, as it seemed, blessed with so
little fruit. And something more than human enthusiasm

was needed to look forward to the task of the future—the task of teaching and reforming a world; whilst all the materials which he had as yet gathered for the struggle were to be found in the six unknown and unlettered companions whom he had left behind him at Toulouse.

Innocent III still filled the Papal chair, and the Council of Lateran formed almost the closing scene of a Pontificate which must be held as one of the greatest ever given to the Church. On the 11th of November, 1215, nearly 500 bishops and primates, above 800 abbots and priors and the representatives of all the royal houses of Europe, met in that ancient and magnificent church, the mother church of Rome and of the world. Few councils, save that of Trent, have higher claims on our veneration; for in it were defined some of the highest articles of Catholic Faith.

The Albigenses, like so many other heretical sects, were the involuntary means of drawing forth an explicit declaration of the Church's doctrine and discipline, and eliciting regulations of reform and Christian observance which have probably contributed more than any other to the well-being of the whole ecclesiastical body, as well as to each individual member thereof.

We allude to the decrees concerning the nature of the Sacraments, and in particular of the Holy Eucharist, and to the establishment of those two binding obligations of yearly confession and Communion, which, whilst they do indeed attest the lamentable decay from primitive fervor which could have rendered such regulations necessary, yet placed a barrier against further relaxation which no future age has been able to overstep. This council has always called forth the bitterest rancor from the supporters of heresy; a result which was but natural, considering the vigor and success with which it not only opposed itself to the evils which existed at the time, but with an astonishing spirit of discernment provided defenses for the future which have lost nothing of their power and stability even at the present day.

In fact, the singular energy displayed by this celebrated

council and the very nature of its decrees are a sufficient proof of the state in which the world and the Church were then found. There was everywhere a decay and a falling off. Old institutions were waxing effete, and had lost their power; whilst indications were everywhere visible of an extraordinary activity and restlessness of mind which was constantly breaking out into disorder for want of channels into which it might be safely guided.

Europe had taken some centuries to struggle through the barbarism which had fallen on her after the breaking up of the Roman Empire. As the waters of that great deluge subsided, life came back by degrees to the submerged world, and just at this period was quickening into a vitality which, in the succeeding century, was manifested in what we might call a luxuriance of growth. It was just one of those junctures in the world's history when God is wont to raise up great men who lay their hands on the human elements of confusion, and fashion them into shape. And it is not too much to reckon among these the founder of the Friars Preachers.

As yet the Church possessed only the more ancient forms of monasticism, with some institutes of later creation, which had, however, but a limited object, or a merely local influence; for the Friars Minor, though they preceded the Preachers by several years, could not as yet be said to have been formally established as a religious order. Dominic's idea included a much wider field than any of the more modern founders had attempted. He had designed an order for preaching and teaching; which for that purpose should apply itself to the study of sacred letters, with the express object of the salvation of souls.

But preaching and teaching had hitherto been considered the peculiar functions of the episcopate, and one of the decrees of this very Council of Lateran, after enumerating the evils flowing from the neglect or inability of the bishops in respect to these offices, empowers them to choose fit and proper persons in each diocese to discharge the "holy exercise of preaching" in their stead. This decree, however, in nowise contemplated the establishment of any body of persons exercising the office as an independent right, or in any other way than as deputies to the bishop, and the plan was, therefore, one full of novelty—and, as it seemed, of difficulty and even danger. But, apart from every other consideration, we may observe in it its admirable adaptation to the peculiar wants and feelings of the time.

The world was like an untrained, untaught child, just rising into manhood, and ready to learn anything. It wanted teachers, and whilst the want was unsatisfied, it made them for itself. During the eleventh and twelfth centuries, one wild sect after another had risen, and counted its followers by thousands, with scarcely any other reason for its success than the favor which was ready to attach to a popular leader. Dominic determined on nothing less than to give them truth in a popular form, and from the mouths of popular teachers; he felt that it had too long been buried in the cloister or the hermit's cell, and that the time was come for the world also to have evangelists. In short, whilst his idea was directly aimed at the guidance and taming of the wild spirit of the day, it had in it not a little of the prevailing tone of enterprise and enthusiasm. It was the very chivalry of religion.

His reception by the fathers of the council, and by the Pope himself, was cordial and flattering. Met as they were, in a great measure, to discuss the questions which had arisen out of the state of the French provinces, Dominic's name and the part he had taken during the last ten years were not unknown and unappreciated by them. Before the formal opening of the council, Pope Innocent granted him an apostolic brief by which he received the convent of Prouille under the protection of the pontifical see and confirmed the grants made to it. But when the plan for the foundation of the order was laid before him, its novelty and the vastness of its design startled him. It seemed to encroach on the privileges of the episcopate, and its boldness seemed dangerous at a moment when men's minds were so powerfully agitated. The troubles of the Waldenses were fresh in his mind, a sect which had grown out of the simple abuse of this same office of preaching, when usurped by men without learning or authority.

The Church, in short, was jealous of innovation, and had just ruled in the council then sitting that no more new orders should be introduced or allowed. In the face of this fresh regulation, it certainly required no small degree of boldness and confidence to present the scheme of a new foundation for approbation, and to persevere in the request; yet Dominic did so, and the result proved not only the strength of his confidence, but the source from whence it had been derived. Five years previously, when Francis of Assisi had visited Rome to solicit the approbation of his infant order from the same Pope, the like objections and difficulties had been raised; and we are assured that, on both occasions, they were removed by a similar interposition of Divine Providence.

Pope Innocent, doubtful as to the reply he should grant, saw, in a vision of the night, the Lateran Basilica about to fall—and Dominic supporting it on his shoulders. An exactly similar dream had before decided him to listen to the petition of St. Francis; and it is probable that the coincidence of the two visions had an additional weight in determining him on this occasion to favor that of Dominic.

Yet the language of the council was too strong to be entirely evaded; it was as follows: "In order that the too great diversity of religious orders be not a cause of confusion in the Church of God, we strictly prohibit that anyone do for the future form any new order; whoever desires to become a religious, let him do so in one of those already approved. In like manner, if anyone desire to found a new religious house, let him be careful that it observe the rule and constitutions of one of the approved orders." Not, therefore, to act in positive contradiction to a principle so recently and distinctly laid down, Innocent sent for the servant of God, and after commending his zeal and assuring him of his approval of the design, he desired him to return to France, that in concert with his companions he might choose one out of the ancient rules already approved, which should seem to them the best fitted for their purpose. When the selection was made he was to return to Rome, with the assurance of receiving from the apostolic see that confirmation which he desired.

Besides this encouragement and promise of future protection, Innocent was the first who bestowed on the order the name it has ever since borne. The circumstances under which he did so were a little singular, and have been preserved with unusual exactness. Shortly after granting the above favorable answer to the prayer of Dominic, he had occasion to write to him on some matters connected with the subject and desired one of his secretaries to dispatch the necessary orders. When the note was finished, the secretary asked to whom it should be addressed. "To Brother Dominic and his companions," he replied; then, after a moment's pause, he added, "No, do not write that; let it be, 'To Brother Dominic, and those who preach with him in the country of Toulouse'"; then, stopping him yet a third time, he said, "Write this, *'To Master Dominic and the Brothers Preachers.'*" This title, though not at first formally given by his successor Honorius in the bulls of confirmation, was, as we shall see, afterwards adopted, and has always continued to be used. It was one to which Dominic himself was attached, and which he had always assumed. So early as the June of 1211, when he was in the midst of his solitary missionary labors in Languedoc, we find a document bearing his seal, attached to which are these words, "The seal of Brother Dominic, *Preacher.*"

The object of his visit to Rome was now fully accomplished; yet he did not return to Languedoc until the spring of the following year. The council still sat, and it is probable that he was present at those deliberations concerning the future settlement of the French provinces, which terminated in the formal declaration that Raymond of Toulouse had forfeited his rights, and in the definitive transfer of

them to the Count de Montfort. But we do not feel that
these transactions require any further notice in a biography
of St. Dominic. His connection with the history of the
Albigensian struggle was now at an end; henceforth he was
to belong, not to Languedoc or to France alone, but to the
world.

During his stay in Rome his first acquaintance with St.
Francis was formed under the following circumstances. One
night, being in prayer, he saw the figure of Our Lord in
the air above his head, with the appearance of great anger,
and holding three arrows in His hand with which He was
about to strike the world in punishment of its enormous
wickedness. Then the Blessed Virgin prostrated herself before Him, and presented two men to Him whose zeal should
convert sinners and appease His irritated justice. One of
these men he recognized as himself; the other was wholly
unknown to him. The next day, entering a church to pray,
he saw the stranger of his vision, dressed in the rough habit
of a poor beggar, and recognizing him as his companion
and brother in the work to which both were destined by
God, he ran to him, and embracing him with tears, exclaimed, "You are my comrade, you will go with me; let
us keep together, and nothing shall prevail against us."

This was the beginning of a friendship which lasted during the remainder of their lives. From that time they had
but one heart and one soul in God; and though their orders
remained separate and distinct, each fulfilling the work assigned to it by Divine Providence, yet a link of fraternal
charity ever bound them together: "brought forth together,"
in the words of Blessed Humbert, "by our holy mother the
Church," they felt that "God had destined them from all
eternity to the same work, even the salvation of souls."

In the following century the storm of persecution bound
these two orders yet closer together; the blows aimed at
the one fell on the other, and when they eventually triumphed
over their enemies, the defense which so successfully silenced
all attacks came from the lips of the two greatest doctors

of either order, St. Thomas and St. Bonaventure; men who revived in their own day the friendship and the saintliness of their two great patriarchs.*

In the Life of St. Francis it is said that Angelus the Carmelite, afterwards a martyr of his order, was likewise in Rome at this time and preached in the church of St. John Lateran, in the presence of the two holy founders, predicting their future greatness and the extension of their orders. Some of the Franciscan writers place this meeting of Dominic and Francis in the following year, when both were again present in Rome for the confirmation of their institutes, but the Dominican authorities are generally agreed in giving it as occurring during this visit. The difference is of no great consequence, and might easily arise without throwing any discredit on the authenticity of the circumstance itself, which rests on the authority of one of St. Francis' constant companions, and has never been called in question.

---

*The friendship between the two orders was not a mere matter of sentiment. It was considered of sufficient importance to be noticed in their very rule. In the Chapter of Paris, held in 1236, the following was ordained, and still continues in the Constitutions of the Friars Preachers:—

"We declare that all our Priors and Brethren should have a diligent care that they always and everywhere bear, and heartily preserve, a great love to the Friars Minor; let them praise them with their lips, and by their words kindly receive and courteously treat with them; and be solicitous as far as they can to be at peace with them. And if any do contrary, let him be gravely punished. And let the Brethren beware, lest they ever speak otherwise than well of them, either among themselves or to any of their friends. And if anyone, under the show of friendship, shall report any evil of the aforesaid Friars, our brethren must not be easy in believing it; but shall rather endeavor as far as possible to excuse them. And if it chance that the Friars Minors shall have provoked us by speaking ill of us, nevertheless let us in nowise publicly contend with them."

It is in the same spirit that we find it ordered that there shall always be made a commemoration of "Our holy father St. Francis" in the little office of St. Dominic. (Such is the affectionate title given by the Friars Preachers to the founder of the order of Minors.) Whilst within the last twelvemonth (1855) the entire office of both holy Patriarchs has been ordered to be recited by the brethren of the two orders on their respective feasts.

CHAPTER 9

Dominic's return to France. The brethren assemble at Prouille to choose
a rule. The spirit of the Order. Some account of the first followers
of Dominic. The convent of St. Romain.

The Council of Lateran lasted but three weeks, and broke
up at the end of November, 1215. In the early spring of
the following year, Dominic found himself once more among
his brethren at Toulouse. In the short period of his absence
their numbers had increased from seven to sixteen, and we
may well imagine the mutual joy of their meeting. He explained to them the result of his expedition to the Holy See,
and the necessity which now lay on them to apply themselves to the choice of a rule. For this purpose he appointed
Notre Dame de Prouille as the place of meeting, where two
other of the brothers, Fr. William de Claret and Fr. Noel,
who had care of the religious of Prouille, were waiting for
them. It was April when they all gathered in this mother-
house of the order; and after earnest prayer and invocation
of the Holy Spirit, they agreed in choosing the rule of St.
Austin—a rule to which Dominic himself had long been
bound, ever since he had worn the habit of Canon Regular,
and which from its simplicity was the better fitted for their
purpose, as being susceptible of nearly any development
which the peculiar objects of their institute might require.
In choosing this rule, Dominic fulfilled the obligation imposed on him by the Pope and escaped the censure of the
late council, while at the same time he was left free to ex-
pand the general principles of religious life laid down by
St. Austin into particular constitutions of his own.

He had not been the first who had made a similar use
of this rule. If we compare the plan and work of St. Dominic

with that of St. Norbert, who had preceded him by nearly
a century, we shall find a very striking similarity. St. Norbert's rule was a reformation of that of the Regular Canons.
In its design he departed from the ordinary line of the more
ancient forms of monasticisim, and set before him as his
object active missionary labors for the salvation of souls.
His work was preaching. He himself preached over all the
provinces of France and Flanders, and obtained faculties
from Pope Gelasius II enabling him to preach wherever he
chose.

A mere cursory glance would induce us to judge the spirit
of these two orders identical; and there can be no doubt
that, in many points of interior discipline, Dominic took
the Premonstratensian rule as his guide. Yet we see clearly
that, whatever similarity existed between them, they were
not the same; they were called to different works, and were
to fill a different place in the Church of God. Religious
orders, we must never forget, are the result of Divine vocation, not the mere creations of human intelligence; and those
vocations they accomplish in an infinite variety of ways,
which human intelligence could never have planned or executed: they are like the varieties of plants and animals in
nature, whose mingled distinctions and similarities, multiplied in so many thousand forms, attest the authorship of
an infinite Creator. We cannot but be struck by this supernatural element in the formation of the order of Friars
Preachers. As a mere human work, critics might find so
much to say against it. If Dominic only wanted to join the
active and contemplative lives together, St. Norbert had done
it before him; why could he not be a Premonstratensian?
They followed the same rule, and wore the same habit. Or
if he and St. Francis really had the same thoughts, and were
raised up for the same purpose, why did they not amalga-
mate, and then their strength would have been concentrated,
instead of being divided?

These seem reasonable objections; they were doubtless
some of those which encountered the holy founder at his

first outset, for it is the way in which the world is wont to criticize the Church. It is certainly the way in which in our own day we do so, as though she were a vast piece of ingenious machinery, which we have a right to take to pieces and improve, as we like best. We often lose sight of the fact that great men and great institutions, popes and councils and religious orders, are but instruments in the hands of God, who works them like puppets without their will for the accomplishment of His own designs. The order of Friars Preachers had a place to fill in the Universal Church, never yet filled by any religious body, and in which it has since had no rival, even in the period of its decay. Only a hundred years from its first foundation, an Emperor* who was its avowed enemy, and who during his whole life had persecuted it to the last extremity, witnessing its remarkable contest against the alleged errors of a Pontiff† whom it had been foremost to defend when the aggressions of an antipope divided the allegiance of the faithful, pronounced this celebrated verdict, wrested from him, as it were, against his will: "The order of Preachers is the *order of truth.*"

This is the place which it has ever filled; which in God's Providence, we trust it ever will fill; and it was the place for which Dominic determined it should be fitted from the very first. His plan was threefold. The first and primary idea of the order was labor for the salvation of souls; but

---

*Louis of Bavaria.

†John XXII. This pontiff was reported to have given utterance, as a private individual, to some opinions of doubtful orthodoxy concerning the state of souls previous to the day of Judgment. He himself, in a brief which death alone prevented him from publishing in the consistory he had summoned for the purpose, made the most distinct and formal protest of his entire and hearty accordance with the doctrine of the Church. (Rohrbacher, *Histoire de l'Eglise Catholique,* tom. XX, 227.) Whether or not he ever did hold the opinions in question, the subject gave rise to a controversy in which the Friars Preachers took a distinguished part; particularly an Englishman, by name F. Thomas Walent, who is described as "a man of great zeal, great heart, and great learning": with daring courage he preached in the very presence of the Pope, denouncing the supposed error in no measured terms, and suffered for his boldness by a long imprisonment. The favorers of the disputed point had sufficient influence to cause considerable suffering and disgrace to the Order, which, however, never relaxed an inch in its obstinate defense of the teaching of the Catholic Church.

in setting this before him as his principal aim, he was not willing to abandon anything of the religious character which attached to the elder institutes of the Church. In short, the whole of the design is expressed in that passage of the constitutions where it is said that "the Order of Preachers was principally and essentially designed for preaching and teaching, in order thereby to communicate to others the fruits of contemplation, and to procure the salvation of souls."

Dominic well knew that to sanctify others, the teachers should first be sanctified themselves, and he was content to follow the guidance of antiquity in choosing the means of that sanctification whose fruits were to be imparted to the world. Those means had ever been considered as best found in the rigorous discipline of the cloister: in silence and poverty, prayer, fasting, and a life of penance, and the secret and magical influences of community life. He therefore included in his rule all the essential characteristics of monasticism, whilst at the same time a certain freedom and expansiveness was mingled with the strictness of its discipline, which enabled it ever to bend and mold itself so as to meet its great and primary intention, the salvation of souls. In the constitutions of the order, accordingly, we find, mixed with the usual enactments of regular discipline, certain powers of dispensation, to be used when a literal and unbending adherence to the letter of the rule would embarrass and impede the brethren in their more active duties. There are also express constitutions, both for the ordering of their own studies, and the regulation of such schools as they might open for the teaching of others; so that all their active and apostolic undertakings, instead of being departures from the rule, should be provided for in it, and partake of its own spirit and discipline. We may, therefore, consider contemplation, apostolic labor for souls, and the especial cultivation of theological science, as the three objects which Dominic sought to unite in the constitution of his order.

With what success he labored, and with what fidelity

his children have adhered to the character first imprinted on their institute by the hand of its founder, it is for history to show. The order of Friars Preachers has never lost anything of the monastic spirit, whilst at the same time it has never so exclusively adhered to it as to lose sight of the active duties imposed on it by its vocation to apostolic labor. The two characters have ever been preserved entire, and it has presented to the world, throughout six centuries, the spectacle of a body acting in the most perfect unity of government and design, producing at one and the same time the highest examples of contemplative saints, apostolic missionaries, and theological writers.

If we are dazzled by the fame of its doctors, we have but to turn over the page of the Dominican chronicles, and in exchange for the successes of a university contest, we shall find some tale of saintly life, redolent with the sweetness of evangelic simplicity. Its saints are not all great men in the world's reckoning; they are gathered from all ranks— from the shepherds of the Spanish mountains, the blind beggars of Italy, or the slaves of America, as well as from princes and Doctors of the Church. Or if, whilst dwelling on this side of the vast scene which it unfolds to us, absorbed, it may be, in the seraphic revelations of St. Catherine or the sweet mysticism of the German Suso, we are tempted to think that its genius grew to be contemplative only, and that in time it shrank from close contact with the world for which it was called to labor, other pages lie open before us rich with tales of the strife of martyrs.

Poland, Hungary, Ethiopia, America, and China—these, and many other countries have the children of Dominic evangelized by their preaching and watered with their blood. Nor is this all; it has constantly been true to its vocation as the organ of popularizing truth. It has borrowed from the spirit of the age to supply the wants of the age. When the world was accustomed to gather science from the lips of living orators, it gave out its companies of preachers and lectures. When books became more popular vehicles of teaching, there was no want of Dominican writers. Nay, it knew how to use other and lighter kinds of instruction, and laid a strong hand upon the magic of the arts. How many a sermon has Angelico left us in the colors which still charm us on the walls of his convent; and after him, painting still remained the heritage of the order which gave him birth, and in its hands has never ceased to be Christian. And if we cannot say of the greatest poet of the Middle Ages that he was himself a child of Dominic, it must at least be confessed that he found means to clothe his verse in the spirit of a theology whose master and teacher was St. Thomas.

Preeminently the order of the Church, it has shared her destinies, as it has clung to her teaching. Like her, it has never lost its unity; we do not indeed pretend to say of either that time has never seen their children waxing cold and unfaithful, but with both the power of reformation has ever been found to exist within their own bosoms. The only occasion when the Order of Preachers can ever be said to have endured a divided government was the unhappy period when it shared in a schism which rent the allegiance of the Church herself; when one regained unity of obedience, it was restored also to the other. After all its sufferings we constantly see it renewing its strength like the eagle; and even in our day, we can scarcely fail to observe that astonishing vitality and power of fresh development, which after six centuries bursts out as vigorous as ever, attesting its principle of eternal youth.

Before closing this chapter, we must give a brief account of those brethren who joined with St. Dominic in the deliberations of Prouille, and who with him may be considered the first founder and propagators of the order. They were, as we have said, sixteen in number. Matthew of France we have before mentioned in relating the circumstances of his first acquaintance with St. Dominic, when prior of St. Vincent's church at Castres; Bertrand of Garrigues, a little village in the province of Narbonne, was the constant companion of the Holy Father in all his journeys, and a most faithful imitator of his life and austerities. It is of him that it is related how, being constantly weeping for his sins, St. Dominic reproved him, and enjoined him rather to weep and pray for the sins of others. This circumstance throws light upon another story, very commonly repeated, but which we venture to think has not always been fully understood.

It is thus related by Surius: "This Brother Bertrand, a holy man, and, as we have said, the first prior provincial of Provence, was accustomed every day to celebrate Mass for sins; and being asked by one Brother Benedict, a prudent man, why he so rarely celebrated Mass for the dead, and so frequently for sins, he replied, 'We are certain of the salvation of the faithful departed, whereas *we* remain tossed about in many perils.' 'Then,' said Brother Benedict, 'if there were two beggars, the one with all his limbs sound, and the other wanting them, which would you compassionate the most?' And he replied, 'Him certainly who can do the least for himself.' 'Then,' said Benedict, 'such certainly are the dead, who have neither mouth to confess nor hands to work, but ask our help; whereas living sinners have mouths and hands, and with them can take care of themselves.'

"And when Bertrand was not persuaded in his mind, on the following night there appeared to him a terrible figure of a departed soul, who with a bundle of wood did in a wonderful manner press and weigh upon him, and waking him up more than ten times that same night, did vex and trouble him. Therefore on the following morning he called Benedict to him, and told him all the story of the night; and thence religiously, and with many tears, going to the altar, he offered the holy sacrifice for the departed, and from that time very frequently did the same. This is the same Brother Bertrand, a most holy and venerable man, to whom St. Dominic enjoined that he should not weep for his own, but for others' sins; for he well knew that he was wont to do excessive penance for his sins. And this charge of the Blessed Dominic had such an effect on the soul of

Brother Bertrand that from that time, even if he wished, he was not able to weep for his own sins; but when he mourned for those of others, his tears would flow in great abundance."

The next of St. Dominic's companions whom we find noticed are the two whom we have before mentioned as residing at Prouille, where they had care of the nuns; William de Claret of Pamiers, and Brother Noel, a native of Prouille. The former of these had been one of the first missioners among the Albigenses, in the time of Diego of Azevedo. After remaining in the habit of the Friars Preachers for twenty years, he left the order and joined the Cistercians. Not content with this, he even attempted to induce the nuns to follow his example, but it is unnecessary to say, without success. Then there was Brother Suero Gomez, a Portuguese of noble birth, who left the royal court to join the army of de Montfort against the Albigenses. He was one of those who witnessed the deliverance of the fourteen English pilgrims and who assisted in bringing them to shore, and shortly afterwards passed to the company of Dominic; he is said to have been distinguished for many virtues, and was the founder of the order in Portugal.

Michael de Fabra, a Spaniard of noble blood, was the first lecturer on theology in the order and held that office in the convent of St. James, at Paris. He was also a celebrated preacher, and accompanied King James of Arragon in his expedition against Majorca, where it is said, "So great was the esteem had of him, that during the fifteen months that the siege lasted nothing was done in the camp, either by soldiers or captains, save what was by him ordered."* Such was the reverence in which he was held, that after the conquest of the island he was looked on as the father and ruler of it; and his name was always invoked next after God and the Blessed Virgin. Diverse stories of his apparitions and supernatural assistance to the Christian soldiers are to be

---

*Michaele Pio—*Uomini illustri.*

found; and the Moors were themselves accustomed to say that it was Mary and Brother Michael, not the Spaniards, who conquered the island.

Another Michael, called De Uzero, was afterwards sent by Dominic to establish the order in Spain. Brother Dominic, called sometimes the little, on account of his stature, or by others Dominic the second (and confused by some writers with Dominic of Segovia,* or the third), had also been one of the holy patriarch's first companions in the missions of Toulouse. "He was," says his historian, "little of body, but powerful of soul, and of great sanctity." He too was a wonderful preacher, and cleared the court of king Ferdinand, "as it were in a moment," of all buffoons, flatterers, and other evil company.

Next comes Lawrence the Englishman. He is said to have been one of the pilgrims whom Dominic saved from death, as before related. By many he is called Blessed Lawrence, a title he seems to have deserved by his sanctity and his gifts of prophecy and miracles. Then there was Brother Stephen of Metz, a Belgian, "a man of rare abstinence, the frequent macerator of his own body, and of burning zeal for the eternal salvation of his neighbor"; and Brother John of Navarre, whom St. Dominic had brought with him to Toulouse from Rome, and there given the habit. He it was to whom St. Dominic gave the celebrated lesson on holy poverty, which we shall notice in its proper place. "He was then imperfect," says his biographer, "but he afterwards made many journeys with St. Dominic, and by familiar conversation with him learnt how to be a saint, which indeed he became." He was one of those who gave his evidence on the canonization of the holy father.

Peter of Madrid is the next name, but we find no particu-

---

*Many authors tell us that "Dominic the little" was the first Provincial of Lombardy, and afterwards of Spain; and that he was likewise called "Dominic of Segovia." It is clear, however, from the account of Michaele Pio, that the two Dominics were distinct persons, and that Dominic of Segovia, the Provincial of Lombardy, was *not* the same as the early companion of the holy patriarch of his order.

lars of his life. The two citizens of Toulouse, Peter Cellani
and Thomas, have already been mentioned. Oderic of Nor-
mandy was a lay brother, and accompanied Matthew of
France to Paris, where he was known and reverenced for his
"perfection of sanctity." Lastly, there was Manez Guzman,
St. Dominic's own brother, "a man of great contemplation,
zealous for souls, and illustrious for sanctity"; the only one
of the sixteen who has received the solemn beatification of
the Church. He had a great gift of preaching, although his
attraction was wholly to contemplation. Michaele Pio gives
us his character in a few expressive words: "Above all things
he loved quiet and solitude, taking most delight in a contemplative life, in the which he made marvelous profit; and in
living alone with God and himself, rather than with others.
He had the government of the nuns who were established
at Madrid. Sincerity and simplicity shone in him above all
things; and many miracles declared to the world how dear
he was to Heaven."

As soon as the little council of Prouille had concluded its
deliberations, Dominic returned to Toulouse. There fresh
demonstrations of the friendship of Fulk awaited him. With
the consent of his chapter he made him the grant of three
churches: Saint Romain at Toulouse, and two others; one at
Pamiers, and another, dedicated to Our Lady, near Puy-
Laurens. These in time had each a convent attached to them;
but that of St. Romain was commenced immediately, for Peter
Cellani's house was no longer adapted to their increased numbers. A very humble cloister was therefore built contiguous
to the church, and over it were placed the cells of the brethren. This was the first monastery of the order. The friars left
it in 1232, in order to remove to a larger and more magnificent building. The convent of St. Romain was poor enough,
and soon completed; the brethren went into it in the summer of the same year, 1216; and the house of Peter Cellani
became the future residence of the Inquisitors.

Previous to his last departure to Rome, Dominic had, with
the concurrence of his brethren, made over all the lands and

property granted to him and his brethren to the nuns of Prouille. Afterwards he had accepted, as it seems a little reluctantly, the revenues provided by the generosity of Fulk of Toulouse. But though he himself felt attracted towards the entire observance of poverty in its strictest form, the mendicity which was afterwards made a law of the Order was not among those constitutions drawn up at Prouille and immediately adopted. It was reserved for the test of experience, and for future deliberations. Nevertheless poverty was scarcely less dear to Dominic than it was to Francis; he honored it in his own person, and was vigorous in seeing it observed by those he governed; and we are assured that every detail of the convent of St. Romain was executed from his orders, and under his own eye, so as to ensure its conformity to the strictest requirements of his favorite virtue.

CHAPTER 10

Dominic's third visit to Rome. Confirmation of the Order by Honorius III. Dominic's vision in St. Peter's. He is appointed master of the Sacred Palace. Ugolino of Ostia.

As soon as the convent of St. Romain had been taken possession of by the brethren, Dominic prepared to return to Rome, to lay the result of his consultation with the other brethren before the Sovereign Pontiff. Before he did so the news arrived of the death of Innocent III, which took place at Perugia on the 16th of July, and of the election on the day following of Cardinal Savillia as his successor, under the title of Honorius III. This seemed indeed a severe blow to the hopes of the young order, for Innocent had been a sure and faithful friend, and it might well cause no small anxiety to have to treat with a new Pontiff for the confirmation of an unknown and untried institute.

He, however, set out, leaving Bertrand of Garrigues to govern the convent in his absence, whilst he himself made his third visit to the Roman capital. He arrived there in the month of September, and found the Pope still absent at Perugia; this caused him some delay, and during the interval he lived a poor and unknown life, having no other lodging at night than in the churches. It seemed at first as if many difficulties would stand in the way of the success of his enterprise; for the new Pontiff was engaged in various troublesome negotiations, and his court was full of dissensions. Dominic's resource was constant prayer; and in spite of all obstacles, he obtained the two bulls confirming the foundation of the order on the 22nd of the following December. The confirmation of the Order of Friars Minor was made at the same time, St. Francis being at that time in Rome; and by very many the meeting between him and Dominic is said to have taken place at this period, and not on the occasion of their former visit.

The first bull given by Honorius is of considerable length: it grants a variety of privileges and immunities, and confirms the order in the possession of all the lands, churches, and revenues with which it had been endowed by Fulk and other benefactors. The second bull is much shorter, and we insert it for the sake of a remarkable expression which it contains prophetic of the future destinies of the order: "Honorius, bishop, servant of the servants of God, to our dear son Dominic, prior of St. Romain at Toulouse, and to your brethren who have made or shall make profession of regular life, health and apostolic benediction. We, considering that the brethren of the order *will be the champions of the Faith and true lights of the world*, do confirm the order in all its lands and possessions present and to come, and we take under our protection and government the Order itself, with all its goods and rights."

It was at Santa Sabina, then the apostolic palace, that these two bulls were given on the same day. In neither of them, however, did the new Order receive the title which had been originally given to it by Innocent III, and which was so dear to Dominic, that of Preachers. In a third bull, however, dated the 26th of January, 1217, the omission is made up. It begins as follows: "Honorius, bishop, servant of the servants of God, to his dear son the prior and brethren of St. Romain, *Preachers* in the country of Toulouse, health and apostolic benediction."

Meanwhile Dominic, whose mission at Rome was accomplished as soon as the two first bulls had been granted, was anxious to return to Toulouse, but was detained at Rome by the command of the Pontiff, who had conceived a high esteem and affection for him. Day and night, therefore, he commended his children and their work to God, and specially in those watches which he still continued to keep in the churches, which were his only lodging. That of the Holy Apostles was the one he loved the best, and it was whilst fervently praying for his order at their tomb that he was granted a second vision to encourage and console him.

This was the appearance of the Apostles St. Peter and St. Paul, the first of whom gave him a staff, and the second a book, saying these words: "Go and preach, for to this ministry thou art called." Then he seemed to see his children sent forth two and two into the world, preaching to all nations the word of God. Some writers add that the Holy Spirit was seen to rest on his head in the form of a fiery tongue, and that from that time he was singularly confirmed in grace, and freed from many temptations; others, that he ever afterwards bore about with him the book of the Gospels and of the Epistles of St. Paul. In all his journeys, too, he constantly carried a stick, an unusual thing which he probably did in memory of this vision. His delay at Rome, if tedious to himself, was greatly profitable to others. Lent found him still there; and during that holy season he took occasion frequently to exercise his office of preaching.

His success induced the Pope to appoint him to explain the Epistles of St. Paul in the sacred palace before the court and cardinals. An ancient author of the noble house of Colonna, himself a Dominican, tells us that "Many came from all parts to hear him, both scholars and doctors, and all gave him the title of Master." Other authors, among whom is Flaminius, relate that the origin of this appointment of St. Dominic was as follows: He was, they say, greatly displeased, on the occasion of his visits to the palace, to see the followers of the cardinals idling about the antechambers, playing at games of chance, whilst their masters were engaged on the business of the Church; and that he suggested to the Pope whether some means could not be devised for entertaining them religiously and usefully, by the explanation of the Scriptures.

The Pope, agreeing to his views, laid the charge on himself, and instituted the office of Master of the Sacred Palace, which continues even to our own day and is always conferred on one of the Dominican order. This office is not simply a titular one; its duties are considerable and of no small importance, including the censorship of all books published in Rome; and its possessor has been described as the Pope's theologian, acting as his domestic adviser in all matters of a theological character.

Another of those dear and honorable friendships which so embellish the life of Dominic was formed during this visit to the Roman capital. Ugolino Conti, cardinal bishop of Ostia and afterwards successor to Honorius under the title of Gregory IX, already the friend and protector of Francis and of the Friars Minor, now first made the acquaintance of his brother and rival in sanctity. He was advanced in age, but a man of warm and enthusiastic feelings who ever counted the close personal ties which bound him to those two great men as among the greatest privileges of his life.

It was at his house that Dominic met another younger friend, William de Montferrat, who was spending Easter with Ugolino. The charm of the saint's intercourse, which indeed seems to have been of a very peculiar and winning kind, so captivated him that he was induced to take the habit of his order. He has left us the account of the whole matter in his own words: "It is about sixteen years," he says, "since I went to Rome to spend Lent there, and the present Pope, who was then bishop of Ostia, received me into his house. At that time Brother Dominic, the founder and first master of the order of Preachers, was at the Roman court, and often visited my lord of Ostia. This gave me an opportunity of knowing him; his conversation pleased me, and I began to love him. Many a time did we speak together of the eternal salvation of our own souls, and those of all men. I never spoke to a man of equal perfection, or one so wholly taken up with the salvation of mankind, although indeed I have had intercourse with many very holy religious. I therefore determined to join him, as one of his disciples, after I had studied theology at the University of Paris for two years, and it was so agreed between us; and also, that after he had established the future discipline of his brethren, we should go together to convert, first the pagans of Persia or of Greece, and then those who live in the southern countries."

Once more we find here the keynote of Dominic's soul, the salvation of souls, which "wholly took him up"; and how large and magnificent was that thought, of going *first* to convert Persia and Greece, and then on to the southern world! He had the very soul of chivalry under his friar's tunic; and we can well imagine the charm which such vast and glowing thoughts, clothed in the eloquence which was all his own, must have exerted over the minds of those who listened to him. He endeavored also to persuade Bartholomew of Clusa, archdeacon of Mascon and canon of Chartres, one of his own penitents, to enter the new order, for he clearly discerned that such was God's vocation to his soul. Bartholomew, however, turned a deaf ear to all he said, and Dominic predicted that many things would befall him in consequence of his resistance to grace, which things, he himself assures us, did really afterwards happen to him; but what they were does not appear.

Among the incidents of his life at Rome during this visit, we find mention of several active works of mercy, both spiritual and corporal. Outside the walls of the city there resided at that time certain recluses, commonly called *Murati* from their habitation. They were a community of hermits; each lived in a poor little cell separate one from the other, in which they were enclosed, never leaving them; being moved to this singular life by a particular spirit of mortification and solitude. Almost every morning, after celebrating Mass and reciting the Divine office, Dominic went to visit them, conversing with them on holy subjects, and exhorting them to perseverence. He was also accustomed to administer to them the Sacraments of penance and the Eucharist, and was in short what would be now called their director. When not engaged in these duties or in the public exercise of preaching, he was to be found in the churches, where he spent his nights.

CHAPTER 11

Dominic returns to Toulouse. He disperses the Community of St. Romain. His address to the people of Languedoc. Future affairs of the Order in that country.

It was not until the May of 1217 that Dominic was able to return to Toulouse. His return was very welcome to his children; yet their joy was, if we may so say, a little sobered, when almost immediately on his arrival, after gathering them together and addressing to them a fervent exhortation on the manner of life to which they now stood pledged, he announced his intention of breaking up the little community as yet but just formed and scattering its members to different countries. The plan seemed the height of imprudence; all joined in blaming it and endeavoring to dissuade him from it.

But Dominic was inexorable; the vision which he had seen beside the tomb of the Apostles was fresh in his eye; their voice yet sounded in his ear. Fulk of Toulouse, de Montfort, the archbishop of Narbonne, and even his own companions urged him to pause, but nothing would stir him from his purpose. "My lords and fathers," he said, "do not oppose me, for I know very well what I am about." He felt that their vocation was not to one place, but for all nations; not for themselves alone, but for the Church and the world. "The seed," he said, "will fructify if it is sown; it will but moulder if you hoard it up." Some little time he gave them to consider if they could submit to his determination, with the alternative otherwise of abandoning the order. But his followers, whatever had been their feelings on the subject, had too profound a veneration for his person and character to oppose their judgments to his and soon

yielded the point. The event showed how entirely his resolution had been guided by the spirit of God.

Meanwhile, in the preparation which he made for this
dispersion of his children, he showed how great was his anxiety and spirit of their rule. The convent of Toulouse he
designed to be the model which was to be followed in all
later foundations, and made several regulations to render
it more perfect in its arrangements. He thought it well that
the brethren should from time to time meet together for
mutual consent and encouragement. With this idea he caused
two large additional rooms to be built, one for containing
the habits of the community, the other for the brethren to
assemble in; for until now they, like the Cistercians, had
had no rooms but their cells and the refectory. These two
additions to their little convent added materially to the comfort of those who were to be left to inhabit it, and were
doubtless the more welcome to them as proofs of the watchful thoughtfulness of their father.

He was very earnest in enjoining upon them the strict
observance of that part of St. Austin's rule which forbids
all private appropriation of the smallest article. Even in the
church itself he desired that the spirit of holy poverty should
never be forgotten; and though he constantly insisted on
its being kept a mirror of cleanliness, yet he forbade all
elegancies and curiosities, and even ordered that the sacred
vestments should not be made of silk. As to the cells of the
brethren, the poverty he enjoined was absolute: a little cane
bedstead and a miserable bench were the only furniture
he allowed. They had no doors, in order that the superior
might always be able to see the brethren as he passed along;
the dormitory resembled, as closely as possible, that of a
hospital.

Blessed Jordan tells us that it was whilst engaged in these
regulations that the Holy Father had the vision which foretold to him the death of the Count de Montfort. He seemed
to see an immense tree, in whose branches a great quantity
of birds had taken refuge; the tree was luxuriant and

beautiful, and spread out its arms over the earth: suddenly it fell, and the birds all took flight, and Dominic was given to understand that this represented the fall of him who had been known in a special manner as the protector and "father of the poor." This was accomplished in the following year, when the two Raymonds regained possession of Toulouse, and the Count de Montfort fell at the siege of that city.

It is probable that his knowledge of the approaching return of war hastened Dominic in the execution of his designs. He fixed the feast of the Assumption for the assembly of all his brethren at Notre Dame de Prouille, previous to their departure for their different missions; and these missions were to include Paris, Bologna, Rome, the two convents of Toulouse and Prouille, and Spain; whilst he himself was letting his beard grow, with the intention that when things were fairly put in train in Europe, of setting out to the countries of the infidels. And all this was to be accomplished with sixteen followers: such was the largeness of Dominic's confidence in God.

On the appointed day, the little company all met to keep the festival of the Assumption with an unusual solemnity in the church of their mother-house of Prouille. It must have been a deeply touching spectacle to all present, and to Dominic himself one of profound and singular emotion. Great numbers of persons from the surrounding country, who knew the circumstances which had gathered the brethren together, came to witness the ceremony of the day; among them was de Montfort himself, and several prelates, all anxious to ascertain the final determination of St. Dominic as to the destination of his little flock. It was he himself who offered the Holy Sacrifice and who, still habited in the sacred vestments, preached to the assembled audience in language some of which is still preserved to us. We are compelled, from the severity of his tone, to draw conclusions unfavorable to the people of Languedoc; for it was them whom he thus addressed: "Now for many years past," he said, "have I sounded the truths of the Gospel in your ears, by my preaching, my entreaties, and my prayers, and with tears in my eyes. But, as they are wont to say in my country, the stick must be used when blessings are of no avail. Lo! princes and rulers will raise all the kingdoms of this world against you; and woe be unto you! they will kill many by the sword, and lay the lands desolate, and overthrow the walls of your cities, and all of you will be reduced to slavery; and so you will come to see that where blessings avail not, the stick will avail."

These dismal announcements were too truly fulfilled when the army of the French king was sent against the people of Toulouse; and they seem to indicate that the evils under which the unhappy country had so long labored had produced an effect which not even the twelve years' labor of an apostle had been able to counteract: it was a solemn farewell which framed itself, almost unintentionally, into words of prophetic warning. He then turned to his own brethren and reminded them of the first origin of their order, the end for which it was instituted, and the duties to which they stood pledged. Above all, he exhorted them to confidence in God, and a great and unflinching courage, always to prepare for wider and wider fields of labor and to be ready to serve the Church in whatever way they might be called to work for the conversion of sinners, heretics, or infidels. His words had an extraordinary effect on those who listened; any lingering feelings of dissatisfaction they might have felt were dispelled by this appeal to the heroism of their natures. Like soldiers harangued by a favorite leader on the battlefield, they seemed all kindled with a spark of his own chivalrous ardor, and were impatient to be led on to the enterprise which awaited them.

But another ceremony yet remained to be performed. When Dominic had concluded his address, the sixteen brethren knelt before him and made their solemn vows in his hands, binding themselves to the three obligations of the religious state; for until then they had been bound to him by no other tie than their own will. The nuns of Prouille, in like manner, all made their profession on the same day, adding the fourth vow of enclosure. When this ceremony was over, he declared to each of them the quarter to which they were destined. The two fathers who had until then had the direction of the convent of Prouille were to return there as before, whilst Peter Cellani and Thomas of Toulouse were to continue at St. Romain. A large section of his little company were appointed for the establishment of the Order in Paris; these were Matthew of France, Bertrand, Oderic, Manez the Saint's brother, with Michel Fabra and John of Navarre, the last of whom had but just received the habit, and our own countryman Lawrence. Stephen of Metz he reserved as his own companion, and the four remaining Spaniards were sent to Spain.

Before they separated to their different parts, Dominic determined to provide for the future government of the Order in case of his death or removal, for he still cherished the secret design of himself departing for the countries of the infidels and finding perhaps a martyr's crown among them. It was the old dream planned so long ago with Diego of Azevedo, and never laid aside. He therefore desired them to make a canonical election among themselves of someone who should govern the Order in his absence or in case of his death. Their choice fell on Matthew of France, who received the title of *Abbot*, a designation never continued in the Order; after his death the brethren were content with the title of *Master* for him who held the chief authority, whilst the other superiors were called priors and sub-priors, names chosen as best befitting the humility of their state. This election being finished Dominic committed the bull of confirmation to the keeping of the new abbot, that it might be solemnly published in the capital of France, and gave them a parting exhortation to keep their vows and be diligent in founding convents, preaching God's word, and following their studies; and so dismissed them with his blessing.

One of them, and one only, showed evident signs of reluc-
tance to obey. This was the newly-clothed brother, John
of Navarre. He strongly shared in the sentiments of those
ecclesiastics who solemly condemned the holy patriarch for
imprudence. He ventured, before departing, to ask for a
little money for his expenses on the way. The request seemed
reasonable; but Dominic's discernment saw clearly the secret feelings of distrust and discontent which prompted it.
He sharply reproved him, and set before him the example
of the disciples whom their Lord sent forth, "having neither scrip nor purse"; then, quickly exchanging severity for
the paternal tenderness which was more natural to him,
he threw himself at his feet, and with tears in his eyes besought him to lay aside his cowardly fears, and to arm himself with a generous trust in God's Providence. But John
still continuing stubborn in his view, and unconvinced of
the practicability of travelling two hundred miles without
funds, Dominic desired them to give him twelve pence, and
then dismissed him.

We are told that some Cistercians who were present expressed their surprise in no measured terms, that he should
send out these ignorant, unlettered boys to preach and teach;
their criticism was something more than free—it was even
contemptuous. Dominic bore the officious remarks with the
equanimity which he never failed to exhibit on such occasions, the virtue for which the Church has so worthily desig-
nated him "the rose of patience." "What is it you say, my
brothers," he replied with his accustomed sweetness; "are
you not a little like the Pharisees? I know, nay I am certain,
that these 'boys' of mine will go and come back safe, but
it will not be so with yours."

As for himself, when his little flock was dispersed, he
still lingered awhile at Toulouse, and before he left he gave
another token of his disinterestedness and magnanimity. The
two brethren of St. Romain became entangled in some disputes with the procurators of the bishop's court about the
portion of tithes granted to the Order by Fulk of Toulouse.

Dominic settled the matter by causing an instrument to be executed in accordance with the views of the procurator, without further controversy; this paper is dated the 11th of September, 1217. He left for Italy soon after its execution, but not till he had received several new sons into his Order; amongst these were Poncio Samatan, afterwards the founder of the convent of Bayonne; Raymond Falgaria, a noble of the neighborhood and successor to Fulk in the bishopric of Toulouse; and Arnold of Toulouse, first prior of the convent of Lyons. From this time we shall not have much occasion to speak of Languedoc; for, in following the future course of St. Dominic's life, we shall be led forward to other countries; the bright star which had risen in Spain, and spent its long meridian in France, was to shed its setting splendor over the fields of Italy.

Simon de Montfort perished the following year under the walls of Toulouse, as foreseen by Dominic. His death, like his life, was that of a brave and Christian knight. The victorious arms of the two Raymonds had stripped him of the greater part of the provinces with which he had been invested; and, urged to a last effort for their recovery, he laid siege to Toulouse with a force wholly unequal to the enterprise.

It was sunrise on the 25th of June when word was brought him of an ambuscade of the enemy. He received the message with tranquillity; and arming himself with his usual composure, he went to hear Mass before going to the field. Another dispatch arrived in the middle of the ceremony; they had attacked his machines of war, would he not hasten to their defense? "Leave me!" was his reply, "I stir not till I have seen the Sacrament of my redemption!" Yet once again another messenger rushed into the church; the troops could hold out no longer; he would surely come to their aid. He turned to the speaker with a stern and melancholy air: "I will not go," he said, "till I have seen my Saviour." He knew his last hour was at hand; the sadness of deep disappointment was in his heart, but he surely made that day a solemn offering and resignation to God of the life whose human hopes had failed. When the priest elevated the sacred Host, de Montfort knelt and uttered the words *"Nunc dimittis."* Then he went out to the scene of combat. His presence had its wonted effect on his followers, as well as on his enemies. The men of Toulouse fled back to the city, pursued by the victorious crusaders; but a stone from the wall struck their gallant leader to the ground; and smiting his breast with his hand, he expired, recommending his soul to God, and with the name of Mary on his lips.

His friendship towards the Order of Friars Preachers survived in his family. One of his daughers, Amice, or, as the Italians sweetly name her, Amicitia, the wife of the Seigneur de Joigny, bore so peculiar a love to the children of Dominic that she used all her endeavors to induce her only son to take the habit. He, however, followed the army of St. Louis to the Holy Land; but whilst detained in the island of Cyprus, he was taken with a mortal sickness, and on his deathbed, remembering his mother's prayers, he sent for the friars and received the habit from their hands. When the tidings were brought her she gave thanks to God, and on the death of her husband resolved to enter the Order herself. She was constantly repeating the words, "If I cannot be a Friar Preacher, I will at least be one of their sisters"; and she succeeded, after much opposition, in founding the convent of Montaign, where she herself took the habit and died in odor of sanctity about the year 1235.

Toulouse, the nursery of the Dominican Order, continued to be closely linked with its history for many a year, though after the death of de Montfort we hear less of the triumphs of its champions than of the sufferings of its martyrs. Among these we find some hardly to be passed over without notice, such as the blessed Francis of Toulouse, one of the first who received the habit and whom Taegius calls one of the most intrepid preachers of his time: he fell into the hands of the heretics, who tormented him in every way that more than pagan barbarity could suggest; but he preached through it all, and proclaimed the Catholic Faith. Then they plaited a crown of thorns and placed it on his head; and Francis received it joyfully, counting himself unworthy to be made partaker in one of the sufferings of his Lord; and still, as the blood streamed down his face, "he confessed and denied not," but boldly preached the word of God and the Faith of His Church. Then they shot him to death with arrows; and so, standing like Sebastian with his face to his enemies, and with that glorious crown upon his brow, he went to Christ. This was in 1260; a few years previously Toulouse had witnessed the confession of others of the Order, among whom was William of Montpellier and his companions.

They were all of the convent of Toulouse, and Count Raymond, the successor to the dominions and the heresy of the Raymond of Dominic's time, enraged at their boldness and success among his subjects, tried first to starve them into submission. He gave orders that none, under pain of death, should bring any meat or drink to the convent, or hold any communication with it, and posted guards about its boundaries to see his orders enforced. But angels set his guard at defiance, and were seen going to and fro with provisions so that no man durst hinder them. Then he drove them from the town, stripped them of all things they possessed and condemned their houses to be burned: this did not disturb them; they went on their way, singing the Creed and the *Salve Regina* with joyful countenances as they left the city gates. But though forced to retire, they soon returned to the province and everywhere carried, as before, the light of truth among the people; so that in 1242 Raymond determined on yet more violent measures. Being then at his country house of Avignette and seated at his ease at the window of his private room, William, with ten other companions, some of his own order, some of that of the Frairs Minors, were brought before him and severely tortured in various ways—Raymond looking on and enjoying the scene. And whilst his eyes were satisfied with the spectacle of their sufferings, there was not wanting music for his ears, if indeed it were of a kind that such a soul as his could understand. Under the very knives of their torturers, the dying martyrs raised a sweet harmony with their failing breath; they sang clear and loud the canticle *Te Deum*, and taught their murderers, even with their expiring voices, that the triumph of that hour belonged to their victims, and not to them. This happened on the vigil of the Ascension, 1242.

CHAPTER 12

The October of the year 1217 saw Dominic crossing the Alps on foot for the fourth time, on his way to Rome, in company with Stephen of Metz. A considerable obscurity hangs over this journey. According to an account sent to Rome by the fathers of the convent of Saints John and Paul at Venice, it was at that city that he first stopped, having, as is said, the intention of carrying out the design already spoken of—namely, to embark for the East and preach the Gospel to the Saracens in the Holy Land.

Whilst there he preached publicly on several occasions, with such effect that several of the inhabitants demanded the habit, and the authorities of the Republic granted to him and these new brethren the little oratory of St. Daniel. The words of this document are as follows: "In the year of Our Lord 1217, the holy father Dominic came to Venice with a few other brethren and received from the Republic the oratory then called St. Daniel, but which after his canonization was called the chapel of St. Dominic, and since the year 1567, down to the present day, has been called the chapel of the Rosary. In this oratory, which was at first very small, St. Dominic erected a little convent for his brethren, and in the place now called the novitiate may still be seen, in the windows and walls, the remains of this ancient fabric."

Whether indeed this relation may be trusted, insofar as concerns the foundation of the convent at Venice, seems a matter of doubt; yet there appears every probability that the Saint did visit the city at that time with the intention of embarking for the Holy Land; an intention which, it

is well known, he entertained whilst yet at Toulouse. What
the circumstances were which induced him to abandon it
does not appear; nor is there any certain account preserved
of his manner of passing the months which intervened between his departure from Toulouse and his arrival at Rome
at the close of the year 1217. We find, however, that he
stopped at Milan on his way and was there courteously entertained by the Canons Regular of San Nazario, who
received him as one of their own order, for he and his brethren still wore the Augustinian habit; nor did they change
it until after the vision granted to Blessed Reginald, of which
we shall speak further on.

In default of exact details concerning this fourth journey
to Rome, we will present our readers with the picture which
has been so faithfully left us of Dominic's mode of performing all his journeys, and leave them by its means to fill up
the blank and to follow him thus in their mind's eye as he
crossed the Alps on foot and made his way through the plains
of Lombardy, and, as some have not hesitated to add,
through the valleys of Switzerland and the Tyrol, preaching as he went. It will help us to a more intimate acquaintance with him, and set him before us with a more personal
reality, as we enter on the most important period of his life.

Dominic always travelled on foot, with a little bundle
on his shoulder and a stick in his hand. As soon as he was
a little out of the towns and villages through which he passed,
he would stop and take off his shoes, performing the rest
of his journey barefoot, however rough and bad the roads
might be. If a sharp stone or thorn entered his feet he would
turn to his companions with that cheerful and joyous air
which was so peculiar to him, and say, "This is penance,"
and such kind of sufferings were a particular pleasure to
him. Coming once to a place covered with sharp flints, he
said to his companion, Brother Bonvisi, "Ah! miserable
wretch that I was, I was once obliged to put on my shoes
in passing this spot." "Why so?" said the brother. "Because
it had rained so much," replied Dominic. He would never

let his companions help to carry his bundle, though they often begged him to suffer them to do so.

When he looked down from the heights which they were descending, over any country or city which they were about to enter, he would pause and look earnestly at it, often weeping as he thought of the miseries men suffered there, and of the offences they committed against God. Then, as he pursued his journey and drew nearer, he would put on his shoes, and kneeling down, would pray that his sins might not draw down on them the chastisement of Heaven. For there was in his character a singular mixture of that frank and joyous *bonhomie*, so invariably to be found in a high and chivalrous mind, with the tenderness of a melancholy which had in it nothing morose, but was rather the consequence of a profound reverence for the purity of God, the outrages against whom, as they hourly came before him, were felt with an exquisite sensibility.

He seldom looked about him, and never when in towns or other places where he was not alone. His eyes were generally cast down, and he never seemed to notice anything curious or remarkable on the way. If he had to pass a river he would make the Sign of the Cross, and then enter it without hesitation and was always the first to ford it. If it rained or any other discomfort disturbed him on the road, he encouraged his companions, and would begin singing in a loud voice his favorite hymn, the *Ave Maris Stella,* or the *Veni Creator.* More than once at his word the rain ceased, and the swollen rivers were passed without difficulty.

He constantly kept the fasts and abstinences of his rule, and the silence prescribed by the constitutions until prime; and this silence he insisted on being also observed by the others; though, as regarded the fasts and abstinences, he was indulgent in dispensing with them for the brethren whilst they were travelling; an indulgence he never extended to himself. Then, as they went along, he would beguile the way with talking of the things of God, or he instructed his companions in points of spiritual doctrine, or read to them; and this kind of teaching he enjoined on the other brethren when travelling with younger companions.

Sometimes, however, he was used to say, "Go on before, and let us each think a little of our Divine Lord." This was the signal that he wished to be left to silent meditation. At such times he would remain behind, to escape observation, and would very soon begin to pray aloud, with tears and sighs, losing all thought of the road he was following, or the possible presence of others. Sometimes they had to turn back and search for him, and would find him kneeling in some thicket or lonely place without seeming to fear wolves or other dangers. The dread of personal danger indeed formed no part of Dominic's character. His courage, though always passive, was essentially heroic. Over and over again he had been exposed to the assaults of his enemies and warned of their intentions against his life; but such things never so much as made him change his road and alter the plan of his journey in any particular; he always treated the subject with silent indifference. When his prayers were ended, his brethren, who often watched him on such occasions, would see him take out his favorite book of the Gospels, and first making the Sign of the Cross, pursue his road, reading and meditating to himself.

However long and fatiguing was the day's journey, it never prevented him from saying Mass every morning whenever there was a church to be found; and most frequently he would not merely say, but sing it; for he was one who never spared his voice or strength in the divine offices. We are constantly reminded of the heartiness of the royal psalmist, in the character left us of Dominic's devotion. "I will sing to the Lord with all my strength," was the language of David; "I will sing to the Lord as long as I have any being." And Dominic had no indulgence for any indolence or self-sparing in the praises of God. He always rendered Him the sacrifice, not of his heart only, but of his lips; and called on all his companions to do the same, for he felt it a good and joyful thing to praise the Lord.

It must be acknowledged that his wonderful bodily constitution was no little assistance in this matter to the fervor of his soul. In his animal nature, no less than in the cast of his mind, there was much of the gallant spirit of a soldier; he never felt that fatigue, or indisposition, or other little ailments and difficulties, could be an excuse for doing less for God. Therefore when he stopped for the night at some religious house, which he always preferred doing when it was possible, he never failed to join them in the singing of matins; and he gave it as his reason for choosing to stop at a convent, in preference to other lodgings which he might have accepted, saying, "We shall be able to sing matins tonight." At such times he generally chose the office of waking the others. These passing visits to the convents, either of his own or of other orders, were always full of profit to their inmates. They made the most of the few hours of his stay, and Dominic never thought of pleading for the privilege of a weary traveller. If the convent were under his own government, his first act was to call together the religious, and make them a discourse on spiritual things for "a good space"; and then if any were suffering from temptations, melancholy, or any kind of trouble, he was never tired of comforting and advising them till he had restored to them the quiet and joy of their souls.

Very often these little visits were so delightful to the religious who entertained him that on his leaving them in the morning they would accompany him on his way to enjoy a little more of his discourse; for the fascination of his conversation was universally felt to be irresistible. But if there were no such houses to receive him, he left the choice of the night's lodging to his comrades, and was all the better pleased if it chanced to be incommodious; he made it a rule, before entering, always to spend some time in the nearest church. When people of high rank entertained him he would first quench his thirst at some fountain, lest he should be tempted to exceed religious modesty at table, and so give occasion of scandal; a prudence which, in a man of such austerity of life, gives us a singular idea of his humility. When ill, he would eat roots and fruits rather than touch the delicacies of their tables; and even when canon of Osma, he never touched meat; he would take it and hide it in his plate, not to be observed. Sometimes he begged his bread from door to door, thanking his benefactors for their scanty alms on his knees, and with uncovered head. His sleep was taken on the floor, and in his habit; and very often those who slept near him could hear that the night was spent in prayers and tears, and "strong crying" to God for the salvation of souls.

Thus journeying, he would stop and preach at all the towns and villages in his way: what kind of preaching this was, we may easily guess. "What books have you studied, father," said a young man to him one day, "that your sermons are so full of the learning of holy Scripture?" "I have studied in the book of charity, my son," he replied, "more than in any other: it is the book which teaches us all things."

"With all his strength," says blessed Jordan, "and with the most fervent zeal, he sought to gain souls to Christ without any exception, and as many as he could; and this zeal was marvellously, and in a way not to be believed, rooted in his very heart." His favorite way of recommending to man the truths of God was the sweetness of persuasion; and yet, as his parting address to the people of Languedoc shows us, he knew (according to his own expression) "how to use the stick."

Finally, to cite once more the words of the writer just quoted, "Wherever he was, whether on the road with his companions, or in the house with the guests or the family of his host, or among great men, princes or prelates, he always spoke to edification, and was wont to give examples and stories whereby the souls of those who heard him were excited to the love of Jesus Christ, and to contempt of the world. Everywhere, both in word and deed, he made himself known as a truly evangelical man."

The same testimony was borne by those who were

examined on his canonization: "Wherever he was," they say, "whether at home or on a journey, he ever spoke *of* God or *to* God; and it was his desire that this practice should be introduced into the constitutions of his order." We must, however, conclude these brief notices, so precious in the personal details they have preserved to us of some of his characteristic habits, and once more take up the thread of his story, which finds him for the fourth time under the walls of the eternal city.

CHAPTER 13

The convent of St. Sixtus. Rapid increase of the Order. Miracles and popularity of St. Dominic. The visit of the angels.

Dominic was received at Rome with renewed evidences of affection and favor from Pope Honorius, who showed every disposition to forward the view with which he had returned thither, namely, the foundation at Rome of a convent of his Order. The church granted to him by the Pontiff for this purpose was chosen by himself; it was one already full of ancient and traditionary interest, which its connection with the rise of the Dominican Order has certainly not lessened. There is a long road that stretches out of Rome, following the course of the ancient Via Appia, which, deserted as it now is by human habitation, you may trace by its abandoned churches and its ruined tombs.

In the old days of Rome, it was the patrician quarter of the city; the palace of the Caesars looks down upon it, and by its side stand the vast ruins of Caracalla's baths, with the green meadows covering the site of the Circus Maximus. This circumstance of its being formerly the place of popular and favorite resort accounts for the abundance of Christian remains which mingle with the relics of a pagan age, and share their interest and their decay. For here were formerly the houses of many of noble and some of royal birth; and when their owners confessed the Faith and died martyrs for Christ, the veneration of the early Church consecrated those dwellings as churches, to be perpetual monuments of names which had else been forgotten. But in time the population of Rome gathered more and more to the northern side of the Caelian Hill, and the Via Appia has long been left to a solitude which harmonizes well enough with its original destination, for it was the Roman street of tombs. There, mixed with the ruined towers and melancholy pagan memorials of death, where the wild plants festoon themselves in such rich luxuriance and the green lizards and snakes enjoy an unmolested home, stand these deserted Christian churches, never open now save on the one or two days when they are places of pilgrimage for the crowds who flock to pray at shrines and altars which at other times are left in the uninterrupted silence of neglect.

Among these is one dedicated to St. Sixtus, pope and martyr, and the tomb of five others, popes and martyrs like himself. If the English traveller visit it now, on one of those days of which we speak when its doors are opened to the devotion of the faithful, and should chance to address himself to any of the white-robed religious whom he may find there and who seems to be its masters, he will be startled with the sound, so sweet, and alas! in a place of holy association, so strange to his ears, the accent of his own English tongue. The church of San Sisto is, in fact at this time, the property of the Irish Dominican convent of San Clemente, a circumstance not without its interest to ourselves.

This was the church chosen by Dominic for his first foundation at Rome, and Honorius did not hesitate to grant it to him, together with all the buildings attached. These had been erected by Innocent III with the intention of gathering together within their walls a number of religious women who were at that time living in Rome under no regular discipline. The design had never been carried out, and Dominic was ignorant of it when he applied for and obtained the grant of the church. His first care was to reduce the house to a conventual form, and to enlarge it so as to be capable of receiving a considerable number of brethren. To do this he was obliged to solicit the alms of the faithful, which were indeed abundantly supplied; the Pope himself liberally contributing to a work in which he felt no common interest.

Meanwhile Dominic labored at his usual trade of preach-

ing. Whilst the walls of his convent were daily rising above
the ground and growing into shape, he was busy forming
a spiritual edifice out of the hearts and souls of those whom
his eloquence daily won from the world to join themselves
to God. In our own day we are often tempted to talk and
think much of our great successes, and the extraordinary
impulse given to our religious life. It is a style known only
to those among whom that life is still but feeble, and would
doubtless have sounded strange in the ears of our fathers;
and nothing is better fitted to humble and silence our foolish boasting, than a glance at the results of a religious impulse in the ages of faith. It is nowhere painted to our eyes
in more vivid and magnificent colors than in the period
of this Church's history.

Many influences certainly paved the way for what in these
days would be called the "success" of Dominic and Francis.
As we have before said, they were wanted by their age: the
world was restlessly heaving with the excitement of new
feelings which stirred men with emotions they neither understood nor knew how to use. We need not therefore wonder at the enthusiasm with which they flung themselves into
the ranks of the two leaders whom God had sent them.

For, after all, great men are not the exponents of their
own views or sentiments. Be they saints, or heroes, or poets,
their greatness consists in this—that they have incarnated
some principle which lies hidden in the hearts of their fellow-
men. All have felt it; they alone have expressed and given
it life; and so when the word is spoken which brings it forth
to the world, all men recognize it as their own; they need
no further teaching and training in this thought, for unconsciously to themselves they have been growing into it
all their lives; and the devotion with which they follow the
call of him who guides them is, perhaps, the strongest sentiment of which human nature is susceptible; made up not
merely of admiration, or loyalty, or enthusiasm, but in addition to all these, of that gratitude which a soul feels towards that greater and stronger soul whose sympathy has

set its own prisoned thoughts at liberty, and given them the power and the space to act. Then like some pent-up and angry waters, that have long vexed and chafed themselves into foam and beaten aimlessly against the wall that kept them in, when the free passage is made, how impetuously they rush forth! At first agitated and confused, but gathering majesty as they flow, till the torrent becomes a river, and the river swells into a broad sea, the dash of whose long united waves no barrier can resist. This is what we call a popular movement.

Europe has seen such things often enough, as well for good as for evil; but she never saw one more universal or more extraordinary than the first burst into existence of the mendicant orders. Francis had been first in the field, and the first chapter of his order saw him in the midst of five thousand of his brethren. But the fields were white with the harvest, and the Friars Minor were not to be the only gatherers of it. In three months Dominic had assembled round him at Rome more than a hundred religious with whom to begin his new foundation. His convent of St. Sixtus had to be even yet more enlarged; and here he may now be said to have carried out for the first time the entire observance of that rule of life which was commenced at St. Romain.

This period of his life is every way remarkable; it sets him before us in a new character. Hitherto we have caught but broken and imperfect glimpses of him in his life of solitary and unappreciated labor. But now at length we see him manifested to the world, ruling over a numerous community, and sending them out to be in their turn the apostles of their day. Many details of his character come out to our view which till now have lain concealed; and as if to make him known in the eyes of men in an especial manner, God was pleased at this time to confirm his teaching and authority by many supernatural signs.

The first of these was on the occasion of an accident which happened during the erection of the convent. A mason, whilst excavating under part of the building, was buried by a mass of the falling earth. The brethren ran to the spot too late to save him, but Dominic commanded them to dig him out, whilst he betook himself to prayer. They did so, and when the earth was removed, the man arose alive and unhurt. This miracle, however much it confirmed the faith and devotion of his own followers, was little known or talked of beyond the walls of his convent; but it was followed by another of more public notoriety.

Dominic was accustomed at this time to preach in the church of St. Mark, where he was listened to with enthusiasm by crowds of all ranks who flocked to hear him. Among them one of his most constant auditors was a certain Roman widow, Guatonia or Tuta di Buvalischi; and one day, rather than miss the preaching, she came to St. Mark's, having left her only son at home dangerously ill. She returned to her house to find him dead. When the first anguish of her grief was over, she felt an extraordinary hope rise within her that by the mercy of God and the prayers of His servant Dominic, her child might yet be restored to her. She therefore determined to go at once to St. Sixtus; and firm in her faith she set out on foot, whilst her women servants carried the cold and lifeless body of the boy behind her.

St. Sixtus was not yet enclosed, on account of the unfinished state of the convent, and she therefore entered the gates without difficulty and found Dominic at the door of the chapter-house, a small building standing separate from the church and convent. Kneeling at his feet, she silently laid the dead body before him, whilst her tears and sobs of anguish told the rest. Dominic, touched with compassion, turned aside for a few moments, and prayed; then, coming back, he made the Sign of the Cross over the child, and taking him by the hand, raised him, and gave him back to his mother—alive, and cured of his sickness.

Some of the brethren were witnesses of this miracle, and gave their evidence in the process of canonization. Dominic strictly charged the mother to keep the fact a secret, but she disobeyed him, as the women of Judea had before disobeyed One greater than *him*. Her joy was too abundant, and out of its abundance her heart and lips were busy; and so the whole story was quickly spread through Rome, and reached the ears of Honorius, who ordered it to be publicly announced in the pulpits of the city.

Dominic's sensitive humility was deeply hurt: he hastened to the Pontiff and implored him to countermand his order. "Otherwise, Holy Father," he said, "I shall be compelled to fly from hence, and cross the sea to the Saracens; for I cannot stay longer here." The Pope, however, forbade him to depart: he was obliged to remain and receive what is ever the most painful portion of the saints, the public honor and veneration of the populace. And certainly they evinced it with a warmth which English hearts may find it difficult to understand. They were Catholics and Romans, and so thought little of human respect or of anything save the giving free vent to that almost passionate devotion which is the hereditary characteristic of their race.

So great and little, old and young, nobles and beggars, "they followed him about" (to use the words of contemporaneous authors) "wherever he went, as though he were an angel, reputing those happy who could come near enough to touch him, and cutting off pieces of his habit to keep as relics." This cutting of his habit went on at such a pace as to give the good father the appearance of a beggar, for the jagged and ragged skirt scarcely reached below his knee. His brethren on one occasion endeavored somewhat harshly to check some of those who crowded round him, but Dominic's good nature was hurt when he saw the sorrowful and disappointed looks of the poor people. "Let them alone," he said; "we have no right to hinder their devotion."

A memorial of these circumstances may still be seen in that same church of St. Mark of which we have spoken. Once a year, on the festival of its patron saint, there is an exhibition in that church of saintly treasures which few sanctuaries can rival and none surpass. There, amid the relics

of apostles and martyrs in jewelled and crystal shrines and
elaborate carvings, you may see, enclosed in a golden reli-
quary, a little piece of torn and faded serge. Priests are there
holding up these precious objects one by one for the veneration of the kneeling crowd, and they hold this also for you
to look at and to kiss, whilst they proclaim aloud, "This
is part of the habit of the glorious Patriarch St. Dominic,
who, in the first year of his coming to Rome, was wont
to preach in this church." And fancy is quick to suggest
that this precious morsel may be one of those so unceremoni-
ously torn from him by the crowds who flocked about him
on that very spot.

Other miracles are related as having occurred during the
time of his residence at St. Sixtus, and we give them here,
as no more exact date is assigned. Giacomo del Miele, a
Roman by birth and the syndic of the convent, was attacked
by sickness which increased so rapidly that he received Extreme Unction and was desired by the physician to prepare
for death. The brethren were greatly afflicted, for he was
a man of singular ability for his office, and much beloved.
Dominic was overcome by the tears of his children: desiring
them all to leave the cell, he shut the door, and, like Elias
when he raised the Sunamite's son, extended himself on the
almost lifeless body of the dying man and earnestly invoked
the Divine mercy and assistance. Then, taking him by the
hand, Giacomo arose entirely recovered, and Dominic delivered him to his companions, who knew not how to contain and express their joy.

Among the "Murati," whom we mentioned in a former
page, and whom he still continued to visit and direct, there
were some who lived a life of extraordinary mortification
and were entirely enclosed in little cells built in the walls,
so as that none could enter or communicate with their inhabitants, food and other necessaries being given to them
through a window.

One of these recluses was a woman named Buona, who
lived in a town near the gate of St. John Lateran; another,

Lucy, in a little cell behind the church of St. Anastasia.
Both of them suffered from incurable and most terrible dis-
eases, brought on by the severity of their mode of life. One
day, after Dominic had administered the Sacrament of Penance and the Holy Eucharist to Buona through her little
window and exhorted her to patience under her dreadful
sufferings, he blessed her with the Sign of the Cross, and
went away; but at the same instant she found herself perfectly cured. Lucy was likewise restored in a similar manner, as Brother Bertrand, who was present on the occasion,
attested.

But perhaps the most interesting of all these miraculous
events is one still daily commemorated in every house of
the Dominican order. We are assured that a similar event
happened *twice* during the period of his residence at St.
Sixtus; but we shall only give the account of one of these
circumstances, as related at length in the narrative of Sister
Cecilia: "When the Friars were still living near the church
of St. Sixtus, and were about one hundred in number, on
a certain day the blessed Dominic commanded Brother John
of Calabria and Brother Albert of Rome to go into the city
to beg alms. They did so without success from the morning
even till the third hour of the day. Therefore they returned
to the convent, and they were already hard by the church
of St. Anastasia when they were met by a certain woman
who had a great devotion to the Order; and seeing that
they had nothing with them, she gave them a loaf; "For
I would not," she said, "that you should go back quite empty-
handed."

As they went on a little farther they met a man who asked
them very importunately for charity. They excused themselves, saying they had nothing themselves; but the man only
begged the more earnestly. Then they said one to another,
"What can we do with only one loaf? Let us give it to him
for the love of God." So they gave him the loaf, and immediately they lost sight of him. Now, when they were to
come to the convent, the blessed father, to whom the Holy

Spirit had meanwhile revealed all that had passed, came out to meet them, saying to them with a joyful air, "Children, you have nothing?" They replied, "No, father;" and they told him all that happened, and how they had given the loaf to the poor man. Then said he, "It was an angel of the Lord: the Lord will know how to provide for His own: let us go and pray."

Thereupon he entered the church, and having come out again after a little space, he bade the brethren call the community to the refectory. They replied to him saying, "But, holy father, how is it you would have us call them, seeing that there is nothing to give them to eat?" And they purposely delayed obeying the order which they had received. Therefore the blessed father caused Brother Roger the cellarer to be summoned, and commanded him to assemble the brethren to dinner, for the Lord would provide for their wants. Then they prepared the tables, and placed the cups, and at a given signal all the community entered the refectory. The blessed father gave the benediction, and everyone being seated, Brother Henry the Roman began to read. Meanwhile the blessed Dominic was praying, his hands being joined together on the table; and, lo! suddenly, even as he had promised them by the inspiration of the Holy Ghost, two beautiful young men, ministers of the Divine Providence, appeared in the midst of the refectory, carrying loaves in two white cloths which hung from their shoulders before and behind. They began to distribute the bread, beginning at the lower rows, one at the right hand, and the other at the left, placing before each brother one whole loaf of admirable beauty.

Then, when they were come to the blessed Dominic and had in like manner placed an entire loaf before him, they bowed their heads and disappeared, without anyone knowing, even to this day, whence they came or whither they went. And the blessed Dominic said to his brethren: "My brethren, eat the bread which the Lord has sent you." Then he told the servers to pour out some wine. But they replied,

"Holy Father, there is none." Then the blessed Dominic, full of the spirit of prophecy, said to them, "Go to the vessel, and pour out to the brethren the wine which the Lord has sent them."

They went there and found, indeed, that the vessel was filled up to the brim with an excellent wine, which they hastened to bring. And Dominic said, "Drink, my brethren, of the wine which the Lord has sent you." They ate, therefore, and drank as much as they desired, both that day, and the next, and the day after that. But after the meal of the third day, he caused them to give what remained of the bread and wine to the poor, and would not allow that any more of it should be kept in the house. During these three days no one went to seek alms, because God sent them bread and wine in abundance. Then the blessed Father made a beautiful discourse to his brethren, warning them never to distrust the Divine goodness, even in time of greatest want. Brother Tancred, the prior of the convent, Brother Odo of Rome, and Brother Henry of the same place, Brother Lawrence of England, Brother Gandion and Brother John of Rome, and many others were present at this miracle, which they related to Sister Cecilia and to the other sisters who were then still living at the monastery of Santa Maria on the other side of the Tiber; and they even brought to them some of the bread and wine, which they preserved for a long time as relics.

Now the Brother Albert, whom the blessed Dominic had sent to beg with a companion, was one of the two brethren whose death the blessed Dominic had foretold at Rome. The other was Brother Gregory, and a man of great beauty and perfect grace. He was the first to return to Our Lord, having devoutly received all the Sacraments. On the third day after, Brother Albert, having also received the Sacraments, departed from this darksome prison to the palace of Heaven.

Allusion is made in the concluding part of this narrative to a circumstance which took place a little later. One day,

Dominic, being full of the Holy Spirit, was holding chapter and was observed by all present to be very sad. "Children," he said, "know that within three days, two of you now present will lose the life of your bodies, and two others that of their souls." Within the time described, the two brothers named above died, as we have related; and two others, whose names are not given, returned to the world.

We said that the circumstance of the angel's visit to the refectory of St. Sixtus, so beautifully related by Sister Cecilia, is still daily commemorated in the houses of the Order. And it is so; for from this time the custom was adopted of beginning to serve the lowest tables first, and so going, up to the table of the prior; a custom which was afterwards made a law of the Order, being introduced into the constitutions.

CHAPTER 14

The monastery of Santa Maria in Trastevere. Dominic is appointed to
reform and enclose the community. His success. Their settlement at
St. Sixtus. The restoration to life of the Lord Napoleon. Sister Cecilia.

Some mention was made in the last chapter of a design
entertained by Pope Innocent III to appropriate the church
of St. Sixtus to a number of religious women then living
in Rome without enclosure, and some even in the private
houses of their relations. The design of collecting them together under regular discipline had been found fraught with
difficulty, and had failed; even the papal authority, aided
by the power and genius of such a man as Innocent, had
been unable to overcome the wilfullness and prejudice which
opposed so wise a project.

Honorius, who no less than his predecessor ardently desired
to see it carried out, resolved to commit the management
of the whole affair to Dominic. He could not refuse; but
aware of the complicated obstacles which lay in the way,
he made it a condition that three other persons of high
authority might be united with him in a business which,
he probably felt, was far harder than the foundation of many
convents—namely, the reform of relaxation, and the union
under one head and into one body of a number of individuals
who owned no common interest or authority.

These religious had for a considerable time been badly
governed; perhaps, we should rather say, they had not been
governed at all. They claimed exemption from the ordinary
rules, were members of powerful families, and their relatives, among whom many of them lived, urged them on
to resist every encroachment on their liberty as an act of
tyranny. And indeed, in the then existing state of things,

they could not be said to be absolutely compelled to obedience: the matter was one rather demanding address than
authority.

But if ever man possessed the art of persuasion it was
the blessed Dominic, whom, as it is said, "none did ever
resist"; or rather persuasion with him was not art, but nature. It was the effect of that admirable union of patience,
prudence, and firmness, tempered with the charm of a sweet
and tranquil gaiety, which gave so wonderful a magic to
his intercourse; and his powers were never more severely
tested than on this occasion.

The coadjutors given him by the Pope were the cardinals
Ugolino, Bishop of Ostia, the venerable friend of St. Francis;
Stephen of Fossa Nuova; and Nicholas Bishop of Tusculum.
The very first steps which the cautious commissioners took
raised a storm of obloquy. The cardinals had enough to do
to quiet the nuns and bring them to listen to the Pope's
proposals. But those who held out had a strong party in
their favor. The gossip of Rome was on their side; and there
was a tempest of busy angry tongues all declaiming against
tyranny and aggression, and talking great things about innovation on ancient custom.

"And truly," says Castiglio, with a touch of Spanish humor,
"the custom was so very ancient, that it could scarce keep
its legs. Moreover," he adds, "we know well that for relaxation and liberty there will always be ten thousand persons
ready to do great things, but for virtue not one willing to
stir a step." However, as we have said, the nuns had the
popular clamor on their side, and they used their advantage
with considerable address. They had but to receive visitors
all day long, and keep up the excitement of their friends
by perpetual talking, and the Pope and cardinals would be
held at bay.

The most refractory of these religious were some who were
living at that time in the monastery of Santa Maria in Trastevere, in which was kept a celebrated picture of our Blessed
Lady, said to have been painted by St. Luke. This picture

was a particular favorite with the Roman people. Tradition said that it had been brought to Rome, many centuries before, from Constantinople; that it was the same that had been borne processionally by St. Gregory in the time of the plague, on that Easter day when the words of the *Regina Caeli* were first heard sung overhead by the voices of the angelic choirs. After that Sergius III had caused it to be placed in the Lateran Basilica, but in the middle of the night it found its own way back to the majestic old church which seemed its chosen resting place. The possession of this picture was no inconsiderable addition to the power and popularity of the nuns; without it they were determined never to stir, and there seemed great difficulties in the way of removing it.

Dominic's plan was simply to carry out that previously designed by Pope Innocent, and collect all the nuns of the different convents that had no regular discipline, as well as the others living out of enclosure, into one community; to whom he proposed giving up his own convent of St. Sixtus, receiving instead that of Santa Sabina of the Aventine Hill. His first visit was a failure; the very mention of enclosure and community life was received by a very intelligible assertion that they neither were nor would be controlled by him, the cardinals, or the Pope. But Dominic was not so easily daunted. He used all the skill and address of manner with which God had endowed him; and on his second visit he found means to win over the abbess, and after her all the community, with one solitary exception, to the wishes of the Pope.

There were, however, conditions proposed and accepted. These were that they must be suffered to carry their picture with them to St. Sixtus, and should it come back to the Trastevere of itself, as in the days of Pope Sergius, that they should be held free to come back after it. Dominic consented; but, saying this clause, he induced them to profess obedience in all else to himself; and they having done so, he gave them as their first trial a prohibition to leave their

convent in order to visit any of their friends or relatives;
assuring them that in a very short time St. Sixtus should
be ready to receive them.

After this it seemed as though the affair were pretty well
settled; "but" (to use the words of the grave and judicious
Polidori) "the instability of human nature, and especially
of the female sex, easy to be moved by whatsoever wind
may blow, did very soon make the contrary to appear." The
wise regulation which Dominic had made was evaded, and
the vituperating tongues were busier than ever. There were
no terms too strong to use in denouncing the proposed migra-
tion to St. Sixtus. It would be the destruction of an ancient
and honorable monastery; they were about blindly to put
themselves under an intolerable yoke of obedience, and to
whom?—to a *new man*, a *"frate,"* whose order nobody had
ever heard of before—a scoundrel (*ribaldo*), as some were
pleased to term him; they must certainly have been be-
witched. The nuns began to think so too, and many repented
of their too hasty promise.

Whilst this new disturbance was going on, Dominic was
relating the success of his mission to the cardinals. But the
fresh disorders which had arisen were revealed to him by
the Holy Spirit even at the moment that they occurred. He
resolved to let the excitement exhaust itself a little before
taking any new measure; and a day or two afterwards
proceeded to the convent, where, having said Mass, he assembled all the religious in chapter, and addressed them
at considerable length. He concluded with these words: "I
well know, my daughters, that you have repented of the
promise you gave me, and now desire to withdraw your
feet from the ways of God. Therefore, let those among you
who are truly and spontaneously willing to go to St. Sixtus
make their profession over again in my hands."

The eloquence of his address, heightened by that strange
and wonderful charm of manner to which all who knew
him bear witness, whilst none can describe it, was victorious. The abbess instantly renewed her profession (with the

same condition respecting the picture), and her example was followed by the whole community. Dominic was well satisfied with their sincerity; nevertheless he thought it well to add one precaution against further relapse. It was a simple one, and consisted of taking the keys of the gate into his own custody, and appointing some of his own lay brothers to be porters, with orders to provide the nuns with all necessaries, but to prevent their seeing or speaking with relatives or any other person whatsoever.

On Ash Wednesday, which fell that year on the 28th of February, the cardinals assembled at St. Sixtus, whither the abbess and her nuns also proceeded in solemn procession. They met in the little chapter-house before mentioned, where Dominic raised to life the widow's child. The abbess solemnly surrendered all office and authority into the hands of Dominic and his brethren; whilst they, on their part, with the cardinals, proceeded to treat concerning the rights, government, and revenues of the new convent.

Whilst thus engaged, the business of the assembly was suddenly interrupted by an incident which is best told in the language of one of the eye-witnesses: "Whilst the blessed Dominic was seated with the cardinals, the abbess and her nuns being present, behold! a man entered, tearing his hair and uttering loud cries. Being asked the cause, he replied, 'The nephew of my lord Stephen has just fallen from his horse, and is killed!' Now the young man was called Napoleon. His uncle, hearing him named, sank fainting on the breast of the blessed Dominic. They supported him; the blessed Dominic rose, and threw holy water on him; then, leaving him in the arms of the others, he ran to the spot where the body of the young man was lying, bruised and horribly mangled. He ordered them immediately to remove it to another room, and keep it there. Then he desired Brother Tancred and the other brethren to prepare everything for Mass. The blessed Dominic, the cardinals, friars, the abbess and all the nuns then went to the place where the altar was, and the blessed Dominic celebrated the Holy Sacrifice with an abundance of tears. But when he came to the elevation of Our Lord's Body, and held it on high between his hands, as is the custom, he himself was raised a palm above the ground, all beholding the same, and being filled with great wonder at the sight. Mass being finished, he returned to the body of the dead man; he and the cardinals, the abbess, the nuns, and all the people who were present; and when he was come, he arranged the limbs one after another with his holy hand, then prostrated himself on the ground, praying and weeping. Thrice he touched the face and limbs of the deceased, to put them in their place, and thrice he prostrated himself. When he was risen for the third time, standing on the side where the head was, he made the Sign of the Cross; then, with his hands extended towards heaven and his body raised more than a palm above the ground, he cried with a loud voice, saying, 'O young man, Napoleon, in the name of our Lord Jesus Christ, I say unto thee, arise.' Immediately, in the sight of all those who had been drawn together by so marvelous a spectacle, the young man arose alive and unhurt, and said to the blessed Dominic, 'Father, give me to eat'; and the blessed Dominic gave him to eat and to drink, and committed him, joyful and without sign of hurt, to the cardinal his uncle."* It must be acknowledged, there is a wonderful grandeur in this narrative. We realize at once the alarm and emotion of the bystanders and the supernatural calm and tranquility of the saint, who was acting under the Spirit of God. Never, perhaps, was any miracle better attested, or more accurately described; and as we shall hereafter see, it bore abundant fruits.

Four days after, on the first Sunday in Lent, the nuns took possession of their convent. They were forty-four in all, including a few seculars, and some religious of other convents. The first who spontaneously threw herself at Dominic's feet and begged the habit of his Order was the

---

*Narrative of Sister Cecilia.

same Sister Cecilia whose narrative has been just quoted. She was then but seventeen, of the house of Cesarini, and distinguished for the great qualities of her soul, even more than for the nobility of her birth. Meager as is the account left us concerning her, we scarcely feel the want of further details, for her character is sufficiently evidenced in the little which is preserved. She had a soul large enough to appreciate that of Dominic. Child as she was, she had been quick to recognize, and value at their true worth, the qualities of that mind which had brought into order the tempestuous and disorganized elements of the community of the Trastevere.

Then she became an eye-witness of that great miracle which we have just related in her own beautiful language; and the admiration which she had already felt for him was raised to a devotion as fervent as it was lasting. We are told that Dominic communicated to her the most hidden secrets of his heart; and we feel in reading the narrative which she has left, so noble and touching in its biblical simplicity, that she was worthy of such a confidence. Her example was followed by that of all the nuns; all received the habit of the new Order, and took the vow of enclosure.

Dominic waited until nightfall before he ventured to remove the picture so often named; he feared lest some excitement and disturbance might be caused by this being done in broad day, for the people of the city felt a jealous unwillingness to suffer it to depart. However at midnight, accompanied by the two cardinals Nicholas and Stephen and many other persons, all barefoot and carrying torches, he conducted it in solemn procession to St. Sixtus, where the nuns awaited its approach with similar marks of respect. It did not return; and its quiet domestication in the new house completed the settlement of the nuns. They were soon after joined by twenty-one others from various other houses, and thus was formed the second house of religious women living under the rule of St. Dominic.

CHAPTER 15

Affairs of the Order in France. First settlement of the brethren at the convent of St. James at Paris. Foundation at Bologna. Character of the religious houses of the Order. Settlement of the Friars in Spain and Portugal. Brothers Tancred and Henry of Rome.

Before we proceed to give any account of the settlement of St. Dominic at the convent of Santa Sabina, whither he removed after that of St. Sixtus had been given up to the nuns, as just related, it will be necessary for us to speak of several events which had taken place since his departure from Toulouse in the autumn of the preceding year. Various were the discouragements and difficulties which had attended the first outset of the missionaries sent from Prouille. Dominic of Segovia and Michel de Uzero had returned from Spain without having been able to succeed in establishing themselves in that country, and had joined their brethren in Rome.

The little community destined for the French capital had scarcely fared better, and might possibly have abandoned their project in a similar manner, had it not been for the presence of the Englishman Lawrence. "For as they drew near to that great city, they went along in great doubt and affliction, because in their humility they greatly feared to preach in so celebrated a university, where there were so many famous doctors and masters versed in sacred science; but God, in order to encourage them, revealed to his servant Lawrence all that should hereafter happen to this mission, and all the favors which God and the Blessed Virgin would show them in their house of St. James, and all the bright stars, as well of sanctity as of learning, that should rise from thence to illuminate not the Order only, but the entire Church; which revelation, as it greatly comforted the soul of brother Lawrence, so he in like manner declared it to his companions, to animate them also; and they believing it, for the opinion which all had of the sanctity of that servant of God, conceived a lively faith. Wherefore they joyfully entered into the city, where all things happened as he had predicted."*

Notwithstanding this "Joyful entry," they spent ten months in extreme distress. None of them were known in Paris except Matthew of France, who in his youth had studied at the university; and Lawrence very shortly after was summoned to Rome, where he was present, as we have seen, before the removal of the Friars from St. Sixtus. It was not until the August of 1218, nearly a year after their departure from Prouille, that John de Barastre, one of the king's chaplains and a professor of the university, having been struck by the singular effects of their preaching and their patient endurance of so much poverty and suffering, persuaded his colleagues to grant them the little church of St. James, then attached to a hospital for poor strangers, afterwards the most celebrated house of the Order. But besides the missionaries whom he had already sent from Prouille, Dominic had not been long in Rome before he began to dispose of some of the followers who had so soon gathered there about his standard. It seems certain that it was whilst still inhabiting St. Sixtus that John of Navarre (who had returned with Lawrence from Paris), Brother Bertrand, Brother Christian, and Peter, a lay brother, were dispatched to lay the first foundation of the Order in Bologna.

Their preaching soon attracted general attention; they are said to have been the first religious who had ever been heard to preach publicly in Bologna, and the astonishment and admiration felt for their eloquence was increased when it was understood that they were the children of Dominic, whose name was not unknown to the Bolognese. Two houses

---

*From a short notice of blessed Lawrence in Marchese's *Diario Domenicano,* drawn from ancient writers.

were soon given to them, with the accompanying grant of
a neighboring church, called Santa Maria della Mascarella.
They were soon after joined by the two brethren who had
returned from Spain and a few others whom Dominic dispatched from Rome; but they had to struggle with many
difficulties.

As soon as they could they began to arrange their house
into a conventual form, building a very humble refectory
and dormitory; for it seems to have been always felt as a
first and indispensable requisite in these early foundations
of the Order to have a religious house, in order to carry
out their rule in a religious spirit, and this even at a time
when the community consisted of no more than four or five
persons. That this was done from a deep conviction of the
utility and necessity of such external observances, and not
from a love of show or a desire to build great establish-
ments, is evident if we look at the way in which it was
done. "As well as they could" (we are told in the account
of this Bolognese foundation), "considering the confined
space, they made a dormitory and refectory, with other necessary offices; their cells were so small that they were not
more than seven feet long and four feet two inches wide,
so that they could scarce contain a hard and narrow bed
and a few other things; but they were more content with
this poor habitation than if they had possessed the largest
and most magnificent palaces."*

Here they led "a life of angels"; and "so wonderful was
their regular observance, and their continual and fervent
prayer; so extraordinary their poverty in eating, in their beds
and clothes, and all such things, that never had the like
been seen before in that city." They continued to live in
this way, without making much progress, and in spite of
their first favorable reception, enduring many affronts and
persecutions, until the end of the year 1218, when as we
shall see, a fresh impulse was given to their enterprise by

---

*Michel Pio of Bologna.

the arrival among them of one man, the celebrated Reginald of Orleans.

Certainly if we wish to form an idea of the true spirit of the Order, we cannot do better than dwell on what is preserved to us concerning the manner of these first foundations. Throughout all of them we shall find the same characteristics. The great missionary work of preaching and saving souls was the first thing thought of: everything gave way to that. They were scattered abroad right and left, as soon as they had given themselves to the work, for Dominic never departed from the inflexible law which he had laid down at Prouille: "We must *sow* the seed, and not hoard it up." Doubtless there must often have been hard sacrifice and struggles with nature in this; his children were separated from him as soon as they had learnt to love him; and, to use the expression of blessed Jordan, in speaking of his departure from Bologna on a late occasion, "they wept to be so soon taken from their mother's breast."

"But all these things," he adds, "happened by the will of God. There was something marvelous in the way in which he was wont to disperse the brethren here and there through all parts of the Church of God, in spite of all the representations often made to him, and without his confidence being once disquieted by a shadow of hesitation. One might have said he knew beforehand their success, and that the Holy Spirit had revealed it to him; and indeed who would dare to doubt it? He had with him to begin but a small number of brethren, for the most part simple and illiterate, whom he sent through the world, by twos and threes, so that the children of the world, who judge according to human prudence, were wont to accuse him of destroying what he had begun, rather than of building up a great edifice. But he accompanied those whom he sent forth with his prayer; and the power of God was granted to them to multiply them."

But though this was the first thought, it was never so followed out as to induce the neglect of the fundamentals of religious observance. The Friars Preachers were to sacrifice all comfort and all human ties for the work of God; they were to endure poverty, humiliation, and detachment of heart in its most painful form; but one thing they were not to sacrifice, and that was the character of religious, and the habits of regular observance. Whilst they begged their bread and lived on alms, the first thing on which those alms were expended was the rude and imperfect conversion of their poor dwellings into a religious shape.

We feel at once how different such a plan of proceeding is from our modern notions; and the difference is more important than appears at first sight. "Let us have essentials," is the favorite expression of our own day; "let us only do our work; the external forms are of secondary importance." But the language of the saints and the men of faith was rather, "Let us have the religious spirit, for without it our work will be of no avail"; and in their deep and living humility they acknowledged that they were powerless to retain this spirit, made up as it is of prayer and recollection and continual self-restraint, without certain external helps and hindrances which modern theorists feel themselves privileged to despise. Every part of the Dominican rule and constitutions breathes of this principle; whilst the salvation of souls is ever placed before us as the end and object of the Order, the formation of the religious man himself is provided for by regulations of the most astonishing minuteness; and as a part, and an essential part, of these, there is given us the beautiful ordering of the religious house.

We do not mean to assert that this necessary connection between the outward form and the inward spirit is anywhere stated in express terms, for there was not much talk about theories and general principles among men in the Middle Ages; yet, perhaps unconsciously to themselves, they ever acted under a deep prevailing sense of this sacramental character of our being. They believed that not in soul alone, but also in body, the whole nature was to be made subject to Christ; and with the simplicity of antique wisdom, they condescended to provide for this by making laws, not only

for their work and their prayer, but even for their houses
and their dress. The religious man was ever to be surrounded
by an atmosphere redolent with sanctity; he was to reflect
a light of holiness cast on him by the very walls of his dwelling. Nothing, therefore, was neglected by which they could
be invested with this peculiar character. They were the mold
in which souls were insensibly to receive a shape that separated them from the world.

The amateurs of ecclesiastical architecture tell us that,
in its purest form, no ornament will ever be found introduced
for ornament's sake; there was always a use and significance
in the most fanciful and grotesque of those elaborate designs. And so in the conventual house, common and necessary things were not exchanged for what was fanciful or
extraordinary; but a religious form and coloring was given
to the whole. Thus the man who was being trained to the
life of religion was placed where he saw nothing that did
not harmonize with that one idea.

His refectory was as unlike a dining room as possible:
it was as much a room to pray in, as to eat in. There, ranged
in a single row behind the simple wooden tables that stood
on either hand, sat the same white-robed figures beside
whom he stood in the choir, and with an air scarcely less
modest and devout. At the top was the Prior's seat; there
were neither pictures nor ornaments on the wall, only a
large crucifix above that seat, to which all were to bow
on entering; for even in hours of relaxation the religious
man was to be mindful of the sufferings of his Lord. There
was no talking or jesting as in the feasting of the world,
for the refectory was a place of inviolable silence; but from
a little pulpit one of the brethren read aloud (as we have
seen brother Henry represented doing in the scene at St.
Sixtus), that, to use the words of the old rule of St. Austin,
"Whilst the body was refreshed, the soul also might have
its proper food." The house was to be poor and simple, having "no curiosities or notable superfluities, such as sculp-
ture, pavements, and the like, save in the church," where

some degree of ornament was allowed to do reverence to
the Presence of God. The dormitory too had its own character; the cells were all alike in size and arrangement, for
here all were equal. They were separate, that everyone might
be silent and alone with God; yet partly open, that the
watchful eye of the superior might never be shut out. Even
the dormitory passage itself had something holy; for it was
ordained that "to promote piety and devotion to the Blessed
Virgin, the especial Patroness of the Order, an altar with
her image should be erected in the dormitory of every convent," and here the lamp was kept burning through the night.

Each of these places had its own sweet tradition. Angels,
as we have seen, have before now served in the Dominican
refectories; nor, as we gaze on such a scene, do we feel they
were out of place; and the dormitories have been blessed
no less than the choir with the sweet presence of Mary, who
through those open doors has given her benediction to the
sleeping brethren, and sprinkled them with her dear maternal hand. Surely these houses were as the gate of Heaven.
All about them were holy sentences, preaching from the
walls; poverty reigned everywhere, but clad in the beauty
and majesty of that spirit of *order*, which has been fitly
termed, "the music of the eye." All things were in common,
and common things were made to speak of God; yet there
was neither gloom nor melancholy, but rather a glad and
cheerful aspect, tempered by the pervading tone of silence
and recollection; so that the beholder might well exclaim,
"How good and joyful a thing it is for brethren to dwell
together in unity!"

At the risk of being tedious on a subject which may not
perhaps be felt to be of general interest, we would but suggest how often we must feel, in reading the earlier devo-
tional writers, that many of their most charming passages
could only have been inspired in a house of this character.
The author of the following sentences had certainly caught
their spirit nowhere but in a religious refectory: "He that
reads words of holy wisdom to his brother, offers choice

wine to the lips of Jesus. He that at table gives up to his brother the better portion, feeds Jesus with the honey of charity. *He that during refection reads to his brethren correctly and distinctly,* serves up a heavenly cup to the guests of Jesus; but if he reads ill, he takes away the relish of the food; and if he stammers, he stains the cloth which covers the table of Jesus. He that goes to the common refectory with his brethren to hear spiritual reading, eateth and drinketh with Jesus and His disciples; and if he lay up in his heart the word of God which he hears, he reposes with St. John, during supper, on the breast of Jesus."*

Writing in a day and in a country where our holy and beautiful houses have long ago been swept away and the ideas that raised them have become lost like historical antiquities, we well know how difficult it is to realize the true significance of the monastic rules. They and all their accompaniments are looked on as, at best, but dreary fancies which have had their day, but could never stand the test of utility. "To what purpose is this waste?" is the continual cry of England over the relics of her old religion. Nevertheless our fathers had their purpose, and did not deem it waste; and we are desirous of directing our reader's attention to the particular care evinced in this matter by the founder of the Dominican Order, because, if we do not mistake, it illustrates one prominent characteristic of his own mind, as well as of the institution which was its offspring, and which bore and ever retains the likeness of its father.

The life of a saint like St. Dominic is not made up alone of journeys and foundations and the dates of his birth and death; his living soul is to be found in the rule whose most striking features were the impression of his own hand: and it is not a little remarkable that, together with that free and pliable spirit which is one of its distinguishing characters, there should be this invariable adhesion to the externals of monastic and community life. The same rule was

---

*Thomas à Kempis, *Garden of Roses*, ch. 17.

observed in all the foundations of the Order, and this of
course by the particular direction of its founder; and the
fact reveals more of his mind and feeling than whole volumes
of commentary. It exhibits him to us in that mixed character of contemplation and action, the union of which is the
basis of the Dominican life: we see him at once, "the Jacob
of preaching and the Israel of contemplation"; and we see
also what in his eyes constituted the essentials of such a
life, and the indispensable means for attaining it.

In Spain blessed Peter had succeeded in founding a convent at Madrid, of which foundation, however, no particulars are preserved. Two of his companions, as we have seen,
returned to rejoin Dominic at Rome, whilst the third, Suero
Gomez, went on to his native country of Portugal, where
he became known to the Infanta Donna Sancha, who gave
him a little solitary oratory on Monte Sagro, about six miles
from Alancher, dedicated to Santa Maria *ad Nives*. Here
he built a miserably poor convent, or rather hermitage,
formed of stones and straw cemented together with mud,
"according to the manner of those first days of fervor in
the Order." He lived in this singular dwelling alone for some
time, but very soon numbers of all ranks flocked to him
to receive the habit from his hands; and "though they were
so many, and of such character and nobility as might have
done honor to any order in the Church, yet did he not abate
one iota in the rigors which he had learnt from his holy
master, and which were established as laws in the constitutions."* Every day he preached in the city, which soon became renowned for its sanctity of manners. He was a true
son of Dominic, "thinking only how to sow the Divine word,
and caring nothing for his own body"; and so, little by little,
the mud hermitage was frequented like a place of pilgrimage,
and the crowds who thronged there to see and hear one
whom they reckoned rather as an angel or apostle than as
a common man, compelled him to enlarge his dwelling in

---

*Michel Pio.

order to receive them; so that in the following year, when
Dominic himself visited the spot, he found a spacious and
well-ordered convent, the mother-house of the Order in Portugal. Suero was in every way a remarkable man: his adherence to the rule, even in the minutest particular, was
almost a proverb. In 1220, when he went to Bologna to
attend the first general Chapter, he performed the whole
journey on foot, carrying only a stick and his breviary, and
so begged his way the entire distance. He became afterwards the first Provincial of Spain.

It only remains for us to add a few words concerning
some of the brethren whose names have already been mentioned as having joined the order at Rome. Tancred, the
prior of St. Sixtus, had been called in a singular way. He
was a German, and a courtier of the Emperor Frederic II.
Being at Bologna when the first brethren arrived there, he
was one day made sensible of a singular and powerful impression on his soul, urging him to reflect on the great question of eternity in a manner wholly new to him. Disturbed
and agitated, he prayed to the Blessed Virgin for direction;
and in the night she appeared to him, saying these words:
"Go to my household." He awoke in doubt as to their meaning, but in a second dream there appeared to him two men
dressed in the habit of the Order, the elder of whom addressed him, saying, "Thou hast asked of Mary to be directed
in the way of salvation: come with us, and thou shalt find
it." In the morning he begged his host to direct him to the
nearest church, that he might hear Mass. As he entered,
the first figure he met was that of the old man he had seen
in his vision; the church was in fact Santa Maria, in Mascarella, and the friar was none other than the Prior Roger.
Tancred's mind was soon made up as to his future course;
and, abruptly severing his engagements with the court, he
proceeded to Rome, where he took the habit. Henry of Rome,
who has also been mentioned, entered the Order against
the earnest remonstrances of his family. As they expressed
a determination to carry him back by force if he would

not return, Dominic sent him out of Rome, with some companions, by the Via Nomentana. His relatives pursued him as far as the banks of the Anio. Seeing there was no chance of escape, Henry raised his heart to God, and invoked His help through the merits of His servant Dominic; and the waters of the little stream suddenly increased to so large and rapid a torrent, that the horses of his pursuers were unable to pass. After this he returned undisturbed to St. Sixtus.

After the sisters had removed to that convent, thirty of the friars were left there under the government of Tancred, but in a distinct and separate house; for the convent at Santa Sabina was not yet able to contain them all. Brother Otho, also a Roman by birth, was appointed the prior and director of the nuns.

CHAPTER 16

Dominic at Santa Sabina. The vocation of St. Hyacinth. Reginald of Orleans. The Blessed Virgin bestows on him the habit of the Order.

It is said that all lives have their chapter of poetry; if so, the poem of Dominic's life is now opening before us. No period of his history is at once so rich in legendary beauty, and so full of ample and delightful details, as that of his residence at Santa Sabina—the church which, as we have already said, had been granted to him and his brethren by Pope Honorius when they abandoned St. Sixtus to the nuns of the Trastevere. It was attached to the palace of the Savelli, of which family Honorius was a member; and we are told that the change of residence was particularly welcome to the friars, inasmuch as the neighborhood was at that time more thickly populated than that of St. Sixtus, and the church was one of popular resort. This character has long since departed from it; and the tide of population, retreating every year further and further to the west, has left the Aventine hill once more to its silent and solitary beauty. Built on the brow of that hill, as it rises abruptly above the Tiber, the convent of Santa Sabina stands between the ancient and the modern city. On one side it looks over a long vista of churches and palaces, until the golden glow of the horizon above Monte Mario is cut by the clear sharp outline of that wonderful dome which rises over the tomb of the apostles.

Turn but your head, and you gaze over a different world. Heaped all about in fantastic confusion, there are the arches of gigantic ruins, and the broken walls and watch towers standing among the vineyards; and beyond them is the wide Campagna stretching like a sea into the dim horizon, spanned by the long lines of the aqueducts, that seem as though they reached the very base of those distant mountains which stand round the Eternal city as "the hills stand about Jerusalem." St. Sixtus is not far off—you may find your way down to it through the green and pleasant lanes that wind among the almond trees; everything here seems full of Dominic; and when the story of his life has become dear and familiar to us, the whole of the Aventine seems consecrated as his shrine.*

It was here, then, that the friars removed as soon as the nuns had taken possession of their former residence; and they had not long settled in their new convent when some very remarkable additions were made to their numbers. Ivo Odrowatz, the Polish Bishop of Cracow, was at that time in Rome, having in his company his two nephews, Ceslaus and Hyacinth, both of them canons of his cathedral and

---

*The convent of Santa Sabina remains little altered since the time of St. Dominic, and many memorials of him are still preserved within its walls. Among others is an orange tree said to have been planted by his hand, which is shown in the quadrangular enclosure. A few years since, this tree sent out a young and vigorous sucker, which grew and flourished, and in the course of the year 1854 produced flowers and fruit. It was remarked that this took place during the novitiate of Père Lacordaire and his companions, to whom is due the restoration of the French province; and the little incident was hailed as significant of that universal restoration and return to youthful vigor and the beauty of regular discipline whose impulse since that period has been manifested throughout the entire order.

A singular discovery has recently been made with the enclosure of this convent. "About three months ago" (says Cardinal Wiseman in his lecture on "Rome, Ancient and Modern," delivered January 31, 1856), "the good religious wished to make an alteration in their garden, and reduce it more into the English style. They were, of course, their own workmen; and it was not long before their industry was repaid. They met with an opening, into which they entered, and found an ancient Christian hall elegantly painted in arabesque. Having cleared it out, they found an entrance into another chamber. In this way they went forward from room to room; so that when I last heard, about a fortnight ago, they were arrived at the tenth apartment. The discovery has excited immense interest, no suspicion having been entertained of such a monument existing there. One room is covered with names of about the third or fourth century, only one of which had then been deciphered. But this excavation is further important in another way. For the first piece of antiquity discovered was a portion of the wall of Tullius, the early king of Rome; and this recurring at a distance from a portion found, a few years ago, in the Jesuit's neighboring vineyard, in planting new vines, decides the direction of the wall, and the boundary of the primitive city."

men of singular virtue. They had all been present in St.
Sixtus on the occasion of the raising of the young Napoleon
to life; and when, by means of Cardinal Ugolino, they became personally acquainted with Dominic, the deep impression made on their minds by that scene was increased
by his saintly and winning manners. Ivo urged him to send
some of his brethen to the northern countries, but the difficulties of the language seemed to offer an insuperable obstacle
to this plan; Dominic, however, suggested that were some
of his own followers to take the habit, it would be the best
way of carrying out his wishes.

A few days after this Hyacinth and Ceslaus, with two
others, Henry of Moravia and Herman, a noble German,
presented themselves at Santa Sabina, and throwing themselves at the feet of the Saint, begged to be allowed to enter
the Order. They were joyfully received, and their progress
was as rapid as it was extraordinary. Doubtless, in those
days of early fervor, the growth of souls planted in a very
atmosphere of sanctity was quicker and more vigorous than
now; and we are led to exclaim, "There were giants in those
days," when we find these four novices, within six months
after their first admission, ready to return to their own country to be the founders and propagators of the Order. They
travelled back with the Bishop of Cracow, preaching as they
went. Separation, that law of the Dominican institute, was
the lot that awaited them also. Hyacinth and Ceslaus pursued their way to the north, where they divided the land
between them. Ceslaus planted the order in Bohemia, whilst
the apostolate of Hyacinth extended over Russia, Sweden,
Norway, Prussia and the northern nations of Asia. Dominic's
old dream of a mission to the Cumans became realized in
the labors of this the greatest of his sons, and in him the
order of Friars Preachers took possession of half the known
world.

Henry proceeded to Styria and Austria and founded many
convents, especially that of Vienna. An account of singular
beauty is left of his death. He fell sick in the convent of

Wrateslavia; and finding his last hour draw near, he fixed his eyes on a crucifix before him and sang sweetly while he had strength. After a little space he was silent, yet smiled, and put his hands together, and showed in his eyes and his whole face a great and inexplicable joy. Then, after a brief time, he spoke, and said, "The demons are come, and would fain disturb and trouble my faith, but I believe in God the Father, and the Son, and the Holy Ghost"; and with these words on his lips he gently expired.

Herman, the fourth of this society, was left at Friesach to govern a convent founded in that place. He was a man of extraordinary devotion, though of small learning. In consequence of his simplicity and ignorance he was often despised and ridiculed by his companions; and, seeking comfort from God in prayer, he obtained the gift of so much understanding of the holy Scriptures that, without study of any kind, he was enabled to preach not only in German, but also in Latin, with extraordinary eloquence and success.

But another disciple was to be gathered into the Order during this same year whose career, if shorter than any of those we have mentioned, was scarcely less brilliant; and who was destined to exercise a considerable influence over some of the most important of the early foundations. Indeed, there were singular marks of a Providential ordering of things in what seemed the accidental assembling at Rome that year of so many men whose hearts were ready for the work which was preparing for them there. Among these he of whom we are about to speak was not the least distinguished. Reginald, deacon of the church of Orleans, had come there, in company with the bishop, with the intention of visiting the holy place and thence passing on in pilgrimage to Jerusalem. He was already known as a profound doctor in canon law, and held the chair of that science in the University of Paris. But brilliant as was his intellect and the renown which it had procured him, it did not satisfy him; for he had within him something greater than genius, and a thirst which the world's applause could not satiate.

Whilst the world of Paris was busy with his fame, there had come upon him a desire to abandon all things for Christ, and to take refuge from popular applause in some state where he could spend his life for the souls of others, while his own should be made a sharer in the very poverty and nakedness of the crucifix. His pilgrimage to Rome and Jerusalem was undertaken under this idea: it formed part of his plan for breaking loose from the ties of his present life, and searching for the better part to which he felt he was called and chosen.

The result must be told in the words of blessed Humbert: "He prepared himself for this ministry, therefore, though he knew not in what way he was to carry it out; for he was ignorant that the Order of Friars Preachers had as yet been instituted. Now it chanced that in a confidential discourse with a certain cardinal he opened to him his whole heart on this matter, saying to him that he greatly desired to quit all things in order to go about preaching Jesus Christ in a state of voluntary poverty. Then the cardinal said to him, 'Lo! there is an order just risen up, whose end is to unite the practice of poverty with the office of preaching; and the master of this new order is even now present with us in the city, who also himself preaches the word of God.' Now when Master Reginald heard this, he hastened to seek out the blessed Dominic, and to reveal to him the secret of his soul. Then the sight of the saint, and the graciousness of his words, captivated his heart, and he resolved to enter into the Order.

"But adversity, which proves so many holy projects, failed not in like manner to try his also. He fell sick, so that the physicians despaired even of saving his life. The blessed Dominic, grieving at the thought of losing a child ere as yet he had scarcely enjoyed him, turned himself to the Divine mercy, earnestly imploring God (as he himself has related to the brethren) that He would not take from him a son as yet but hardly born, but at least to prolong his life, if it were but a little while. And even whilst he yet prayed, the Blessed Virgin Mary, Mother of God and Mistress of the World, accompanied by two young maidens of surpassing beauty, appeared to Master Reginald as he lay awake and parched with a burning fever; and he heard the Queen of Heaven speaking to him, and saying, 'Ask me what thou wilt, and I will give it to thee.' And as he considered within himself, one of the maidens who accompanied the Blessed Virgin suggested to him that he should ask nothing, but should leave it to the will and pleasure of the Queen of Mercy, to the which he right willingly assented. Then she, extending her virginal hand, anointed his eyes, ears, nostrils, mouth, hands, reins, and feet, pronouncing certain words meanwhile appropriate to each anointing. I have heard only those which she spake at the unction of his reins and feet: the first were, 'Let thy reins be girt with the girdle of chastity'; and the second, 'Let thy feet be shod for the preaching of the Gospel of Peace.' Then she showed to him the habit of the Friars Preachers, saying to him, 'Behold the habit of thy order,' and so she disappeared from his eyes. And at the same time Reginald perceived that he was cured, having been anointed by the Mother of Him who has the secrets of salvation and of health. And the next morning, when Dominic came to him, to ask him how he fared, he answered that nothing ailed him, and so told him the vision. Then both together did render thanks to God, who strikes and heals, who wounds and who maketh whole."

Three days after this Dominic again came to his room, bringing with him a religious of the Hospitallers of St. John. And as they sat all three together, the same scene was repeated in the sight of all. We are told by some that on her former appearance the Blessed Virgin had promised this repetition of her previous visit, and that Reginald had mentioned this fact to St. Dominic. He now conjured him and his companion to keep the whole of the circumstances secret until after his death; and he did this out of humility. Dominic complied with his request; and in announcing to the brethren his intention of changing the form of their habit, he did not give the reason which had caused the change until after Reginald's death.

Until this time the habit of the regular canons had continued to be worn by all the brethren; it was now changed for that which had been shown by Mary to Reginald, and which Dominic had himself seen on the second occasion of her appearance. The linen surplice was laid aside, and in its place was used the long woollen scapular, which was the particular part of the habit she was seen holding in her hands. Thenceforward this has been the distinctive sign of religious profession among the Friars Preachers; and the words with which it is accompanied in the ceremony of the giving of the habit mark at once its origin, and the reverence with which its wearers are accustomed to regard it: "Receive the holy scapular of our Order, the most distinguished part of our Dominican habit, the maternal pledge from Heaven of the love of the Blessed Virgin Mary towards us."

This especial love of Mary for the Order of Friars Preachers is indeed a claim which we do not wonder at their making, when we consider the many ways in which it has been evinced. In those early days of the Order one of the popular names by which the brethren were known was that of "the Friars of Mary"; a title which reveals to us how filial was the devotion which they felt for the Mother who had clothed them with her own hands; and we shall find, among the traditions of Santa Sabina, other tales which show us the singular and tender nature of the protection she gave them.

Some of these traditions, illustrating as they do this period of Dominic's life, we will give in the following chapters, together with that sketch of what we may term his conventual habits, which has been left us by blessed Jordan and other early writers; and they will probably render us more familiar with his personal character than any other portion of his history. Meanwhile Reginald of Orleans departed for the Holy Land, whence he did not return until the conclusion of the year.

CHAPTER 17

Dominic's life at Rome. The rule of the Order. Description of his person and appearance. His prayer, and manner of life.

When Dominic was fairly settled at Santa Sabina, he saw himself surrounded by a multiplicity of cares and occupations, any one of which would have demanded the whole strength and time of an ordinary man. There was the government of two communities: that of his own convent, a company of novices gathered from all ranks and ages, unused to rule and discipline, and who had to learn the whole science of religion from his lips alone; while the training of the nuns of St. Sixtus was even a harder task, for with them there were long habits of negligence and relaxation to eradicate, before the spirit of fervor and observance could possibly be infused. How hard and difficult a thing it was, we may judge from the unwearied assiduity with which Dominic labored at his task. He visited them daily, instructing them in the most minute particulars of their rule; and sent to Prouille for eight of the more experienced religious of that house, one of whom, Sister Blanche, was appointed prioress. His long and patient care was not thrown away. Enclosure and the observance of a holy rule produced their usual marvels and transformed the undisciplined nuns of the Trastevere into mirrors of sanctity and grace. These two undertakings, carried on at the same time, called for a genius of government which few have ever possessed in a more remarkable degree than St. Dominic. But within his soul there lay vast resources and a certain fullness of spiritual light which never failed to guide him in the guidance of others; so at least we are led to affirm if we contemplate him alone and unaided in his gigantic tasks.

And if we are curious to know the means whereby he achieved them, we must seek for them in that rule which, if we mistake not, exhibits to us more of the character of his mind than we can gather from any other source. "The Christian perfection which he taught" (to use the admirable words of Castiglio) "consisted primarily indeed in the love of God and of our neighbor; but secondarily and accidentally in that silence and solitude, and in those fasts, mortifications, disciplines, and ceremonies, which are the instruments whereby we reach unto that high and most excellent end."

It would seem indeed as if these "ceremonies" he speaks of formed no insignificant part of Dominic's great idea of spiritual training. We read of his "diligent training of the nuns in the rules and ceremonies"; and again St. Hyacinth is said to have become a perfect master in "all the ordinances and ceremonies of the Order during his short novitiate." And if we examine the rule itself, we find in it very much of this outward training so deep and significant in its intention, and so great in its results. This arose partly from the sagacity which perceived how large an influence is exerted over the inner man by the subjugation of his external nature; partly also from a characteristic feature in Dominic's mind, the love of order. Whilst wholly free from the narrowness of mere formalism, his soul yet delighted in that harmony which is a chief element of perfection: it was as though his eagle eye had gazed on the ordering of the heavenly courts, and drawing from the image pictured on his soul, he strove to reflect something of their beauty in his convent choirs.

And so, perhaps, those bowings and prostrations of the white-robed ranks, which, when exactly performed, give so unearthly and beautiful an appearance to the worship of a religious choir may, at the same time as it harmonized the souls of the worshippers into recollection, have been intended to recall and symbolize those scenes on which doubtless his own spiritual vision had so often rested, and the repeated foldings of those many wings, and the casting of the golden crowns upon the ground.

Let us now see what was the rule of his own life at this period, and the impression which his intercourse and example left on the minds of those who observed him; and first we will give the portrait they have delineated of his outward appearance. It must have been very noble, if we may judge from the description of Sister Cecilia: "He was about the middle stature, but slightly made; his face was beautiful, and rather sanguine in its color; his hair and beard of a fair and bright hue, and his eyes fine. From his forehead, and between his brows, there seemed to shine a radiant light which drew respect and love from them that saw it. He was always joyous and agreeable, save when moved to compassion by the afflictions of his neighbors. His hands were long and beautiful, and his voice was clear, noble, and musical. He was never bald, and he always preserved his religious crown or tonsure entire, mingled here and there with a very few white hairs."

Next we find an equally minute and interesting description of his dress. Gerard de Frachet, who wrote by command of blessed Humbert so early as 1256, speaks thus: "Everything about the blessed Dominic breathed of poverty: his habit, shoes, girdle, knife, books, and all like things. You might see him with his scapular ever so short, yet did he not care to cover it with his mantle, even when in the presence of great persons. He wore the same tunic summer and winter, and it was very old and patched, and his mantle was of the worst." It was this same spirit of poverty that induced him never to have any cell or bed of his own. He slept in the church. If he came home late at night from his expeditions drenched with rain, he would send his companions to dry and refresh themselves, but himself would go as he was to the church. There his nights were passed in prayer; or, if overcome with fatigue, he would sleep leaning against the altar steps, or lying on the hard stones. On one part of the pavement of the church of Santa Sabina there is still preserved an inscription indicating one of the stones as that whereon he was accustomed to lie at night. If, when he travelled, they stopped where there was no church, he slept anywhere—on the floor, or on a bench or sitting in his chair, and always dressed in his habit as during the day.

Thrice every night he disciplined himself to blood; the first time for himself, the second for sinners, the third for the souls in Purgatory. His prayer was in a manner continual. There was neither place nor time in which he did not pray, but especially in those night hours which he spent alone with God in the church. Very often they watched him, unknown to him, and saw the way in which, when he believed himself entirely alone, he poured out all the fervor of his soul without control. After compline, when the others were dismissed to rest, he remained behind, visiting each altar in turn and praying for his Order and for the world. Sometimes his tears and prayers were so loud as to wake those who slept near; and though very often these exercises lasted until the hour of matins, he never failed to assist at the office with the spirit and alacrity which were so remarkable in him. He was most zealous for the exact performance of what he considered the primary duty of a religious, and would go through the choir from one to another, calling on them to sing with attention and devotion, and in a loud and distinct tone. He never passed an altar whereon was the figure of Our Lord without a profound inclination to recall the sense of his own nothingness. He taught his brethren to do the same at the repetition of the *Gloria*, as a homage to the Most Holy Trinity, and was wont to quote the words of Judith, "The prayer of the meek and humble shall ever please Thee." He was accustomed likewise to pray, in imitation of Christ in the garden, with his face on the ground; and in this posture he would remain for a long space, repeating passages from the Psalms of the most profound abnegation and accompanied with many tears, so that the place was often wet where his face had leaned.

Some of his favorite ejaculations are preserved. "O God, be merciful to me a sinner!" He was heard exclaiming: "I have sinned, and done amiss." Then, after a little space, "I am not worthy to behold the height of Heaven, because of the multitude of my iniquities, for Thy wrath is irritated against me, and I have done evil in Thy sight. Yea, my soul cleaveth to the ground; quicken me according to Thy word." To move his disciples to a similar mode of prayer, he would cite the example of the holy kings throwing themselves at the feet of Christ, and would say, "Come let us adore, and fall down before God, and weep before the Lord who made us." "If you have no sins of your own to weep for," he would say to the younger novices, "weep after the example of the prophets and Apostles, and of the Lord Jesus; and grieve for the sinners who are in the world, that they may be brought back to penance." Another of his favorite devotions was to keep his eyes fixed on the crucifix, and meanwhile to genuflect a hundred times or more; and so he would pass many hours, uttering ejaculations from the Psalms; or he would kneel silently, and as if unconscious of aught save the presence of God; and then his face, and his whole person, and his very gestures, seemed as though he would penetrate the distance that separated him from his Beloved; now beaming with a holy joy, and now sorrowfully bathed in tears.

At other times he was seen to stand upright before the altar with his hands clasped before his breast, as though holding a book, out of which he had the air of reading; then he would press them over his eyes, or raise them above his shoulders. In these postures he had the appearance of a prophet, now listening or speaking with God and the angels, now thinking within himself on what he had heard. He would stand also with his arms stretched out in the form of a cross, and would so pronounce steadily and at intervals sentences like these: "O Lord God of my salvation, I have cried before Thee day and night. I have cried unto Thee, O Lord; all the day long have I stretched out my hands to Thee. I have stretched out my hands unto Thee: my soul

gaspeth to Thee as a land where there is no water." This
was when he prayed for any special grace or miracle, as
on the raising of Napoleon; and at such times his face
breathed an air of indescribable majesty, so that the
bystanders remained astonished, without daring to question him of that which they beheld with their own eyes:
often, in rapture, he was seen raised above the ground; his
hands then moved to and fro as though receiving something
from God, and he was heard exclaiming, "Hear, O Lord,
the voice of my prayer, when I cry unto Thee, and when
I hold out my hands to Thy holy temple."

As soon as the hours and the grace after dinner were ended,
he would retire alone to some secret place where, sitting
down and making the Sign of the Cross, he would meditate
on those things which he had heard read. Then taking out
that book of the Gospels which he always carried, he would
kiss it reverently and press it to his breast; and those who
observed him could mark how, as he read, he would seem
to fall into arguments with another, smiling or weeping,
beating his breast, or covering his face with his mantle, rising and again sitting and reading, as the passing emotions
of his soul sought for expression. Nor must we fail to notice
the singular devotion with which he daily celebrated the
holy sacrifice of the Mass, which he almost always sang.
At the Canon and the Lord's Prayer his tears fell in abundance; those who served his Masses noticed this, and bore
witness that it was always the case, and that with a tenderness of devotion which moved them also to weep with him.

Of his manner towards his subjects, we read that its un-
deviating rule was charity. He was their loving father, even
whilst he knew how to reprove and correct them. The following are the words of Rodolph of Faenza: "He was ever
kind, cheerful, patient, joyful, merciful, and the consoler
of his brethren. If he saw any of them fall into a fault,
he would seem as though he did not at the time observe
it, but afterwards, with a serene countenance and with gentle
speech, would say, 'Brother, you have done wrong, but now

repent'; and so did he bring all to penance. And yet, though he told them of their faults with such humble words, he could gravely punish them."

"He punished transgressors of the rule with severity, and yet with mercy," says John of Navarre, "and greatly did he grieve when he had to punish any." Brother Frugerius, another of the eye-witnesses of his life, says, "He was rigid himself in the observation of the rule, and would have it observed also by others; yet did he punish transgressors with meekness and sweetness. He was kind and patient in trouble, joyful in adversity, loving, merciful, and the consoler of his brethren, and of all men."

To which testimony Brother Paul of Venice adds, "So sweet and just was he in correction that none could ever be troubled by a punishment or reproof received from him." Another of his disciples adds, "Although, like a father, he could use the rod of correction; yet also, as a mother, he could give the breast of consolation; and so sweet and efficacious was his way of comforting those who came to him that none went away without solace and relief. And if he saw his brethren at any time sad or afflicted, he would call them to him and condole with them, and ofttimes deliver them by his prayers."

We may draw the reader's attention to the striking similarity of the character sketched by so many different hands. Indeed, when we read over "The Acts of Bologna," as these evidences for his canonization are entitled, we are immediately struck with the exact resemblance they bear to one another. We see, as it were, the portrait of one whose features were too marked not to be instantly caught by the painter: they were the outlines of the most perfect form of charity. And the mother of his charity was a profound humility. "Never did I see a man so humble in all things as was Brother Dominic," is the language of one of the witnesses on his canonization; "he despised himself greatly, and counted himself as nothing; he was the example to his brethren in all things—in words, gesture, food, clothing, and manners. He was generous, too, and hospitable, and gladly gave all he had to the poor. He passed his nights without sleep, praying for the sins of others."

And blessed Jordan, on the last-mentioned quality (zeal for souls), says, "It was the trait in which he most desired to resemble his Lord." With the beautiful eulogy which is given by this holy writer, the worthy successor and biographer of his great patriarch, we must conclude this chapter: "The goodness of his soul and the holy fervor with which he acted were so great that none could doubt him to be indeed a chosen vessel of honor adorned with precious stones. He had a particular firmness of spirit, always equal, save when moved to pity and compassion. The peace and quietude of his heart was manifest in his gentleness and his cheerful looks. And he was so firm and resolute in the determinations he had taken after just reflection that never, or almost never, did any succeed in making him change his mind. The holy joy which shone in him had something singular about it, which drew all men's affections to him so soon as they had looked upon his face. He embraced all in a great charity, and so was loved of all; and his rule was to rejoice with them that rejoiced, and to weep with them that wept. He was all love for his neighbor, all pity for the poor; and the simplicity of his conduct, without a shadow of insincerity either in word or deed, made him dear to all."

With this portrait in our mind, sketched by the very eye-witnesses of his daily life, we shall now proceed to give some of those legends attached to the period of his residence at Rome, to which we have before referred.

CHAPTER 18

Attacks of the devil. Legends of St. Sabina and St. Sixtus.

On the second Sunday in Lent, being the first after the settlement of the nuns at St. Sixtus, Dominic preached in their church, standing, as it is said, "at the grating"—that is, so as his discourse should be heard both by them and by the congregation assembled in the public part of the church. As he did so, a possessed woman who was in the midst of the crowd interrupted the sermon: "Ah, villain!" cried the demon, speaking through her voice, "these nuns were once all mine own, and thou hast robbed me of them all. This soul at least is mine, and thou shalt not take her from me, for we are seven in number that have her in our keeping." Then Dominic commanded her to hold her peace, and making the Sign of the Cross he delivered her from her tormentors in the presence of all the spectators.

A few days after this she came to him and throwing herself at his feet, implored to be allowed to take his habit. He consented to her request and placed her in the convent of St. Sixtus, where he gave her the name of Amata, or, as we are used to call her, Amy, to signify the love of God displayed in her regard. She afterwards removed to Bologna, where she died in the odor of sanctity, and lies buried in the same tomb with Dominic's two other holy daughters, Cecilia and Diana, the latter of whom was foundress of the convent of women in that place.

In speaking of this and other examples of the malice of the demon which are narrated in the history of St. Dominic, we cannot but observe something perhaps a little distinctive about them. Never do we find one instance in which Satan was permitted the least power to vex or trouble him. Never, as with so many other saints, was he suffered to do him bodily harm or to assault him with grievous temptations. The evil one appears to us always baffled and contemptible, as in the power of one who is his master, the very Michael among the Saints. Yet, though always petty, and as it were ridiculous, he ceased not in his efforts to thwart and disturb him, and chiefly directed his malice against the friars and the sisters of St. Sixtus, grievously trying them by perpetual distractions, as though he hoped thereby at least to diminish something of the fervor of their devotions. Once indeed he made a more serious attempt against Dominic's life.

One night, as Dominic prayed in the church of Santa Sabina, a huge stone was hurled at him by an invisible hand from the upper part of the roof which all but grazed his head and even tore his hood, but falling without further injury to the saint was buried deep in the ground beside him. The noise was so loud that it awoke several of the friars, who came in haste to the spot to inquire the cause; they found the fragments of the broken pavement and the stone lying where it fell; but Dominic was kneeling quietly in prayer, and seemed as if unconscious of what had happened.

Another story of a similar character is told as follows: "The servant of God, who had neither bed nor cell of his own, had publicly commanded his children in chapter that in order that they might wake the more promptly to rise to matins, they should retire to bed at a certain hour, in which he was strictly obeyed. Now, as he himself abode before the Lord in the church, the devil appeared before him in the form of one of the brethren, and though it was past the prohibited time, yet did he remain in the church with an air of particular devotion and modesty. Wherefore the Saint, judging it to be one of the friars, went softly up to him, and desired him to go to his cell, and sleep with the others.

"And the pretended friar inclined his head, in sign of humble obedience, and went as he was bid; but on each of the two following nights, he returned at the same hour and in the same manner. The second time, the man of God rose very gently (although, indeed, he had reason to be somewhat angry, seeing he had at table during the day reminded all of the observance of that which had been enjoined), and again desired him to go away. He went; but, as we have said, returned yet a third time. Then it seemed to the Saint that the disobedience and pertinacity of this brother was too great, and he reproved him for the same with some severity; whereat, the devil (who desired nothing else save to disturb his prayer and stir him unto wrath, and move him to break the silence) gave a loud laugh, and, leaping high into the air, he said, 'At least I have made you break the silence, and moved you to wrath!' But Dominic calmly replied, 'Not so, for I have power to dispense; neither is it blameworthy wrath when I utter reproofs unto the evil-doers.' And the demon, being so answered, was obliged to fly."

On another occasion, as he was by night walking about the convent of St. Sabina, guarding his flock with the vigilance of a good shepherd, he met the enemy in the dormitory, going like a lion seeking whom he might devour; and recognizing him, he said, "Thou evil beast, what doest thou here?" "I do my office," replied the demon, "and attend to my gains." "And what gains dost thou make in the dormitory?" asked the Saint. "Gain enough," returned the demon. "I disquiet the friars in many ways; for first, I take the sleep away from those who desire to sleep in order that they may rise promptly for matins; and then I give an excessive heaviness to others, so that when the bell sounds, either from weariness or idleness they do not rise; or, if they rise and go to choir, it is unwillingly, and they say their office without devotion."

Then the Saint took him to the church, and said, "And what dost thou gain here?" "Much," answered the devil; "I make them come late and leave soon. I fill them with disgusts and distractions, so that they do ill whatsoever they have to do." "And here?" asked Dominic, leading him to the refectory. "Who does not eat too much or too little?" was the reply; "and so they either offend God or injure their health." Then the Saint took him to the parlor, where the brethren were allowed to speak with seculars and to take their recreation. And the devil began maliciously to laugh, and to leap and jump about, as if with enjoyment, and he said, "This place is all my own; here they laugh and joke, and hear a thousand vain stories; here they utter idle words, and grumble often at their rule and their superiors; and whatsoever they gain elsewhere they lose here."

And lastly they came to the door of the chapter-room, but there the devil would not enter. He attempted to fly, saying, "This place is a hell to me: here the friars accuse themselves of their faults, and receive reproof and correction, and absolution. What they have lost in every other place they regain here." And so saying, he disappeared, and Dominic was left greatly wondering at the snares and nets of the tempter; whereof he afterwards made a long discourse to his brethren, declaring the same unto them, that they should be on their guard.

But if, at the risk of wearying the reader, we have given these instances of the infernal malice, it is time for us to present him with other and more lovely pictures, as they are left us in the relation of Sister Cecilia. The first, as is fitting, shall be of the maternal love of Mary. Before reading it, we must remember that Dominic never had cell or bed of his own, and slept, when he slept at all, in the church or the dormitory. "One night, Dominic having remained in the church to pray, left it at the hour of midnight and entered the corridor where were the cells of the brethren. When he had finished what he had come to do, he again began to pray at one end of the dormitory, and looking by chance towards the other end, he saw three ladies coming along, of whom the one in the middle appeared the most beautiful and venerable. One of her companions carried a magnificent vessel of water, and the other a sprinkler, which she presented to her mistress, and she sprinkled the brethren and made over them the Sign of the Cross. But when she had come to one of the friars, she passed him over without blessing him; and Dominic having observed who this one was, went before the lady, who was already in the middle of the dormitory near to where the lamp was hanging. He fell at her feet, and though he had already recognized her, yet he besought her to tell him who she was. At that time the beautiful and devout anthem of the *Salve Regina* was not *sung* in the convents of the friars or of the sisters at Rome; it was only recited, kneeling, after compline. The lady who had given the blessing said therefore to Dominic, 'I am she whom you invoke every evening, and when you say *'Eia ergo advocata nostra,'* I prostrate before my Son for the preservation of this Order.' Then the blessed Dominic inquired who were the two young maidens who accompanied her, and she replied, 'One is Cecilia, and the other Catherine.' And the blessed Dominic asked again why she had passed over one of the brethren without blessing him; and he was answered, 'Because he was not in a fitting posture'; and so, having finished her round, and sprinkled the rest of the brethren, she disappeared.

"Now the blessed Dominic returned to pray in the place where he was before, and scarcely had he begun to pray when he was wrapt in spirit unto God. And he saw the Lord, with the Blessed Virgin standing on His right hand; and it seemed to him that Our Lady was dressed in a robe of sapphire blue. And looking about him, he saw religious of every order standing before God; but of his own he did not see one. Then he began to weep bitterly, and he dared not draw nigh to Our Lord or to His Mother; but Our Lady beckoned him with her hand to approach. Nevertheless, he did not dare to come until Our Lord also in His turn had made him a sign to do so. He came, therefore, and fell prostrate before them, weeping bitterly. And the Lord commanded him to rise; and when he was risen, He said to him, 'Why weepest thou thus bitterly?' And he answered,

"I weep because I see here religious of all orders except mine own.' And the Lord said to him, "Wouldst thou see thine own?' And he, trembling, replied 'Yes, Lord.' Then the Lord placed His hand on the shoulder of the Blessed Virgin, and said to the blessed Dominic, 'I have given thine Order to My Mother.' Then He said again, 'And wouldst thou really see thine Order?' And he replied, 'Yea, Lord.' Then the Blessed Virgin opened the mantle in which she seemed to be dressed, and extending it before the eyes of Dominic, so that its immensity covered all the space of the heavenly country, he saw under its folds a vast multitude of his friars.

"The blessed Dominic fell down to thank God and the Blessed Mary, His Mother, and the vision disappeared, and he came to himself again and rang the bell for matins; and when matins were ended, he called them all together and made them a beautiful discourse on the love and veneration they should bear to the most Blessed Virgin, and related to them this vision. It was on this occasion that he ordered his friars, wherever they might sleep, always to wear a girdle and stockings."

Another story we give in the words of the same writer: "It was the constant habit of the venerable Father to spend the entire day in gaining souls, either by continual preaching or hearing confessions or in other works of charity. And in the evening he was accustomed to come to the sisters and give them a discourse or a conference on the duties of the Order, in presence of the brethren; for they had no other master to instruct them. Now one evening he was later than usual in coming, and the sisters did not think he would come at all, they having finished their prayers and retired to their cells. But, lo! suddenly they heard the little bell which the friars were used to ring to give the sisters a signal of the approach of the blessed Father. And they all hastened to the church, where, the grating being opened, they found him already seated, with the brethren, waiting for them. Then he said, 'My daughters, I am come from fishing, and the Lord has this night sent me a great fish.' He spoke of

Brother Gandion, whom he had received into the Order; he was the only son of the Lord Alexander, a Roman citizen, and a man of consequence.

"Then he made them a long discourse which gave them great consolation. After which, he said, 'It will be well, my children, if we drink a little.' And calling Brother Roger, the cellarer, he bade him go and bring a cup and some wine. And the friar having brought it, the blessed Dominic desired him to fill the cup to the brim. Then he blessed it and drank first, and after him also the other friars who were present. Now they were of the number of twenty-five, as well clerks as laics; and they drank as much as they would, yet was not the wine diminished. When they had all drunk, the blessed Dominic said, 'I will that my daughters drink also.' And calling Sister Nubia, he said to her, 'Come in thy turn, and take the cup, and give all the sisters to drink.' She went therefore, with a companion, and took the cup, full up to the brim, without a drop having been poured out. And the prioress drank first, and then all the sisters, as much as they would, the blessed Father saying to them, 'Drink at your ease, my daughters.' They were a hundred and four, and all drank as much as they would; nevertheless the cup remained full, as though the wine had just been poured into it; and when it was brought back, it was still full. This done, the blessed Dominic said, 'The Lord wills me now to go to Santa Sabina.' But Brother Tancred, the prior of the brethren, and Odo, the prior of the sisters, and all the friars, and the prioress, with the sisters, tried to detain him, saying, 'Holy Father, it is near midnight, and it is not expedient for you to go.'

"Nevertheless he refused to do as they wished, and said, 'The Lord wills me to depart, and will send His angel with me.' Then he took for his companions Tancred and Odo, and set out. And being arrived at the church door, in order to depart, behold! according to the words of the blessed Dominic, a young man of great beauty presented himself, having a staff in his hand, as if ready for a journey. Then the blessed Dominic made his companions go on before him, the young man going first, and he last, and so they came to the door of the church of Santa Sabina, which they found shut. The young man leaned against the door, and immediately it opened; he entered first, then the brethren, and then the blessed Dominic. And the young man went out, and the door again shut; and Brother Tancred said, 'Holy father, who was the young man who came with us?' And he replied, 'My son, it was an angel of God, whom He sent to guard us.' Matins then rang, and the friars descended into the choir, and were surprised to see there the blessed Dominic and his companions, for they knew that the door had been left shut."

Such are some of the legends of these times. Traces of them may yet be found on the spots they have enriched with their associations. Over the door of Santa Sabina, a half-defaced fresco commemorates this visit of the angel; within, is still preserved the fragment of the stone which was hurled at Dominic in prayer; and the spot on the pavement where he was wont to take his scanty rest is marked by a Latin inscription. The room, too, where Hyacinth and Ceslaus received the habit is yet shown, and the picture that hangs over the choir tells the story of their singular vocation. This church and convent have never passed from the hands of the Order, and the freshness of their association with the legendary history of its founder is unimpaired.

St. Sixtus is no longer inhabited, though still the property of the Order. The malaria drove the nuns from its walls so long ago as the year 1575; since which time they have been established at a new house on the Quirinal, bearing the name of "San Dominico e Sisto." But amid its desertion and ruin one monument of its ancient history yet remains. That little chapter-house, on whose threshold the widow's son was raised to life and where Dominic and the sisters were assembled when the news came of the death of young Napoleon, yet stands—one of the very few buildings in the ancient ecclesiastical style which are yet left in Rome. A fate has awaited this almost solitary relic of Christian architecture which we cannot but trust may have results worthy of its historic interest.

In it has been made the first attempt to restore the early ecclesiastical style, which has been seen in Rome for three centuries. It has been recently arranged as a chapel, and its walls decorated with frescoes in the antique manner, descriptive of the life of Dominic. It may have been nothing but a change; yet one feels it was a happy and appropriate change that the first steps towards a revival of Christian art should have been made in this monument of the Dominican Order, and by the hands of a Dominican artist.*

In 1667 the two convents of St. Clement and St. Sixtus were granted to the Irish Dominicans, driven out of their own land by the persecutions of the times. "Inasmuch as our province of Ireland," says Father Antony Monroy, the master-general of the Order at that time, "has endured long and cruel persecutions, so that its sons have neither house nor place where they may lay their head, we judge them worthy of all commiseration." The brief continues by formally ceding to them these two convents "as a refuge for the miserable province of Ireland," and also as a place of education; and they have ever since been assigned to the brethren of that nation.

Some years ago the church and buildings of St. Sixtus were covered with paintings and inscriptions commemorative of the many miracles and incidents of St. Dominic's life which had taken place within their walls; and the pulpit was shown from which he was accustomed to preach and propagate the Rosary among his audience; but many of these are now destroyed or removed. No lapse of years or injury of time could however efface the memory of the Saint on that spot, and in the diploma wherein Clement VIII restored the locality to the Dominican Order, after it had for some time been alienated, he prefaces the donation by a long summary of those wonderful events which have made it worthy to be enumerated among the holy places of Rome. The diploma is dated the 19th of January, 1611.

---

*Père Hyacinth Besson.

CHAPTER 19

Dominic leaves Rome. He visits Bologna on his way to Spain. Incidents of his journey. He preaches at Segovia. Foundations there, and at Madrid. His continual prayer.

It was in the autumn of 1218 that Dominic prepared to leave Rome, in order to visit the places where his children had been forming so many new settlements during the short year which had passed since their first dispersion at St. Romain. That memorable year had seen them well-nigh planted throughout Europe; and he felt that the rapid increase of the Order rendered his own presence and inspection of the young houses a thing no longer to be delayed.

It is said also that a feeling of humility was one of the motives which urged him to leave Rome: his preaching and the fame of his miracles had gained him a reputation from which he shrank.

We therefore find him in the month of October leaving the city gates with his stick, his little bundle, and his copy of the Gospels, in company with a few of his own religious— a Franciscan, Brother Albert, soon after joining them on the road—whilst Hyacinth and his three companions set out at the same time for the north. Dominic's steps were directed towards Bologna, where the brethren were still in their first convent of Santa Maria della Mascharella, suffering many inconveniences and discouragements, against which they continued to struggle until the month of December following, when, as we shall have occasion to show, the arrival of Reginald of Orleans gave a fresh spirit to their undertaking.

Dominic's visit lasted but for a few days; yet we can easily imagine the joy and comfort which it diffused among them. In the course of his stay the same miracle which had previously taken place in the refectory of St. Sixtus was here renewed; the brethren were fed by angels, and the story is told with such a peculiar quaintness by the good Father Ludovico Prelormitano that we cannot resist inserting the account in his own words: "After that our most sweet father St. Dominic had finished the arduous business committed to him by the Holy Pontiff at Rome, he came to Bologna, and lodged at the Mascharella, where the friars still abode, not being able yet to go to St. Nicholas by reason of the rooms being yet too fresh and damp. And it happened on a day that, by reason of the multitude of the brethren, there was no bread, except a few very little pieces; and the blessing being given, the good father raised his eyes and his heart to God; and lo! (*januis clausis*) the doors being closed, there appeared two beautiful youths with two baskets of the whitest loaves, and giving one thereof to each friar, they so multiplied, that abundantly (*ad saturitatem*) there remained enough for three days. And this great miracle happened twice at Rome and twice at Bologna.

"The second time, after the loaves, they gave a good handful of dried figs. And the brother who made oath of the same to Pope Gregory IX added and said, 'That never had he eaten better figs.' Then replied the Pontiff, 'Grammercy to Master Dominic, for they were not gathered in your garden'; as though he had said, 'God did at that time produce them.' And the number that ate was more than a hundred friars. *Benedictus Deus!*"

He adds, "I have been in the cells which the said friars built, and accurately measured them, in the year 1528: they were four feet and a half wide, and scarcely six long. And the rector of Santa Maria Mascharella, my very dear friend, told me that every year, on the same day when the holy angels brought the heavenly bread, most sweet odors were perceived in the space then occupied by the refectory, which lasted forty hours." The table on which the miraculous loaves were placed was left at Santa Maria when the friars removed to St. Nicholas, and was still to be seen, guarded by iron bars in the wall, at the time when Father Prelormitano wrote.

But Dominic soon left Bologna; his journey being now principally directed towards that native country which he had not seen for sixteen years. Two anecdotes alone are left us of his journey. It is said that on quitting Bologna in company with the Franciscan before mentioned, they were attacked by a fierce dog, who tore the poor friar's habit, so that he was unable to proceed on his journey and sat down by the wayside in some despair. Dominic applied a little mud to the rent garment, and this new kind of mending perfectly succeeded; when the mud dried, the habit was discovered perfectly joined together.

The other story is thus amusingly told by Castiglio: "Having one day come to an inn with several companions, the hostess was much disturbed at the small gains she saw herself likely to make by them; for they being many, and eating little, she saw herself put to much trouble to little purpose. Wherefore, as the servants of God conversed together on spiritual things, as was their wont, she went about grumbling and blaspheming saying all the evil words that came into her mind; and the more the holy father St. Dominic sought to appease her with fair speeches, the more violent she became, not being willing to hear reason. At length, being wholly disturbed by the noise of this virago, St. Dominic spoke to her and said, 'Sister, since you will not leave us in peace for the love of God, I pray Him that He will Himself silence you'; the which words were no sooner uttered than she lost the power of speech, and became entirely dumb. She continued so until the Saint's return from Spain, when, as he stopped at the same inn, she threw herself at his feet to implore his pardon, and he restored to her the use of her tongue, with a warning that she should use it in future to the praise of God."

It was probably in the course of this journey that the following incident occurred at the city of Faenza, as given in the ancient memoirs preserved in the convent of that place. Albert, the bishop of Faenza, was so charmed by his eloquence and the fascination of his discourse, that he would not allow him to lodge anywhere but in the episcopal palace. This did not, however, prevent Dominic from pursuing his ordinary course of life; every night he rose at the hour of matins, as was his custom, and proceeded to the nearest church to assist at the Divine Office. The attendants of the bishop noticed this; and on watching him secretly to observe how he was able to leave the palace without rousing the inmates, they observed two beautiful youths who stood by the door of his chamber with lighted torches, and so led the way for him and his companions, every door opening for them as they went along; and in this way they were every night conducted in safety to the church of St. Andrew, whence, after the singing of matins, they returned in like manner. When this was made known to Albert, he himself watched and became an eye-witness of the fact; and in consequence he procured the above church to be the foundation of a convent of the order. A memorial of the circumstance is preserved in the name given to the ground lying between the palace and St. Andrew's church, which is still called "The Angels' Field."

Doubtless many cities of northern Italy received like passing visits from Dominic, but no certain traditions concerning them have been preserved. We can, therefore, but follow him in imagination as he made his way over the plains of Lombardy, and crossing the Alps found himself once more in the convent of St. Romain at Toulouse. The number of the brethren was greatly increased, but their prospects, together with those of the Church generally in those parts, had received a serious check by the death of the Count de Montfort and the renewed persecutions of the heretics. Dominic remained a while with them to encourage them, and nominated Bertrand of Garriga, who had just returned from Paris, their superior. He then continued his journey to Spain; and we find that before Christmas he was at

Segovia, in Old Castile.

One circumstance occurred on his way which must not be omitted. The brethren who travelled in his company, discouraged perhaps by the hardships of the journey and yet more by those which they witnessed in the young houses of Bologna and Toulouse, broke out into murmurs and even determined to quit the habit and return to the world. Some writers tell us that these religious were not those who came from Italy with the Saint, but some young Castilian novices who had been attracted to him by the fame of his eloquence and miracles, and whose fervor cooled as soon as they made a closer acquaintance with the austerity of his rule; and this seems the more probable conjecture.

However that may be, their discontent was soon discovered by Dominic: he did his best to deter them from their purpose, but in vain; three only remained with him, the others having put their hand to the plough, looked back, and left him. Turning sadly and gently to those who remained faithful, Dominic addressed them in the words of Our Lord on a like occasion: "Will ye also go away?" And the memory of this incident has been preserved in a touching passage of the Constitutions of the Order, introduced at a later period, with an evident allusion to these circumstances. "Whenever novices," it is said, "wish to return to the world, we command all the religious freely to let them go, and to return them all that they have brought. Nor must they give them any vexation on this account, after the example of Him, who, when some of His disciples went back, said to those that remained, 'Will ye also go away?' "* The greater number of those who had abandoned him shortly afterwards returned to their obedience.

The city of Segovia, where Dominic first stopped, is not far from Osma. His return to those familiar scenes, so thick with memories of his friendship with the bishop Diego and the long quiet years of his early life before the call of God

---

*Const. F. F. Praed. d. i. c. 14.

had drawn him before the world, must have been full of
singular emotion to a heart so tender and sensitive as his
own. Perhaps it was something of this natural affection for
old scenes, linked to such dear associations, that made him
fix on this neighborhood for his first foundation on his return to his native land. Only a few particulars of his residence there have been preserved. He lodged at the house
of a poor woman, who contrived to get possession of a coarse
hair shirt which he had worn and had laid aside to exchange
it for one of yet harsher material. Some time afterwards
the house caught fire, and everything was burned excepting
the box which contained this precious relic. This hair shirt
was long preserved among the relics of the monastery of
Valladolid.

Dominic had not been long in the city before he began
his usual work of preaching, and with more than usual success. Possibly the familiar language of his mother-tongue
and the sight of those Spanish hills, after the long years
of exile and separation, gave a fresh inspiration to his words.
It seemed, too, that God was willing that special tokens
of His miraculous powers should accompany the preaching
of His servants. A long drought had afflicted the country
of Segovia and reduced the inhabitants to the utmost distress. One day, as they gathered together outside the walls
to hear the preaching, Dominic, after beginning his discourse, as if suddenly inspired by God exclaimed, "Fear nothing, my brethren, but trust in the Divine mercy. I announce
to you good news, for today even God will send you a plentiful rain, and the drought shall be turned into plenty." And
shortly after, his words were fulfilled, for such torrents of
rain fell that scarcely could the assembled crowd make their
way to their own homes. The spot where this took place
is still shown, and the event is commemorated by a little
chapel which has been erected in his honor.

On another occasion, as he preached before the senate
of the city, he spoke thus: "You listen to the words of an
earthly king, hear now those of Him who is eternal and

divine." One of the senators took offence at the freedom
of his words, and mounting his horse, rode off, exclaiming
contemptuously, "A fine thing, forsooth, for this fellow
(*ciarlatino*) to keep you here all day with his fooleries. Truly,
it is time to go home to dinner!" Dominic looked at him
sorrowfully: "He goes, as you see," he said, addressing the
others, "but within a year he will be dead." And, indeed,
not many months after the occurrence, he was slain on that
very spot by his own nephew.

Dominic's preaching soon rendered him very popular
among the Segovians. They were proud of him as a fellow
countryman, and flocked together to listen to him wherever
he appeared. We are told that he never spoke in public without first prostrating in prayer before a little image, and
repeating the versicle, *"Dignare me laudare te, Virgo sacrata,"*
&c.

It is with him also, according to Père Croiset, that the
custom among preachers of introducing the *Ave Maria* at
the beginning of their sermon, first arose. In a short time
a number of new disciples were gathered together at Segovia, the foundations of a convent were laid, under the title
of the Holy Cross; and one of his followers, named Corbolan and known as "Blessed Corbolan the Simple," was appointed prior. This convent was erected close by the little
river Eresma, on whose banks Dominic was accustomed to
address the multitudes. Close by may still be seen another
spot consecrated by the memory of his presence. It is a grotto
deep sunk in the rock, where he was wont nightly to retire
from the presence of his followers to give himself up to the
free exercise of prayer and the presence of God. Its walls
(as those testified who secretly watched him at these times)
were often wet with his tears and his blood. This grotto
now forms part of the chapel erected in his honor, and is
attached to the church. It was visited by St. Theresa, who
declared that she received such grace and consolation in
her visit to it that she could have desired to spend her life
within its recesses.

As soon as the convent of Segovia was founded, Dominic proceeded to Madrid. The house already founded there by Brother Peter, originally sent thither from Toulouse, was without the town. It was very poor, having a little church like a hermitage, and a narrow dormitory without division. Dominic resolved to convert it into a monastery of women, for he considered its revenues and endowments unsuitable for his brethren. This, therefore, was the third convent of sisters which he founded. Nor was his care of them inferior to that he had before bestowed on Prouille and St. Sixtus. A beautiful letter is still preserved in which he addresses them on their duties and vocation.

We give part of it as another illustration of the importance he evidently attached to those external aids whereby the strictness and entireness of the rule should be perfectly observed: "Brother Dominic, Master of the Preachers, to the Mother Prioress, and all the convent of the Sisters of Madrid, health and amendment of life by the grace of God. We rejoice, and thank God for your spiritual progress, and that He has drawn you from the mire of the world. Combat still, my daughters, against your old enemy by prayer and watching; for he only shall be crowned who has striven lawfully. Hitherto you have had no house suitable for following all the rules of our holy religion, but now there will be no excuse; since now, thanks be to God, you have a building where regular observance can be exactly kept. Therefore I desire that silence may now be kept in all the places enjoined by the Constitutions, in the choir, refectory, dormitories, and wherever you live according to rule...We send our dear brother Manez, who has labored so much for your house, and has fixed you in your holy state, to order all things as shall seem good to him, to the end that you may live holily and religiously."

The people of Castile received Dominic with extraordinary marks of honor; Castiglio gives us a long list of donations granted by the magistrates of Madrid to his Order, bearing the date of May, 1219. His sermons were listened to by crowds of the inhabitants, among whom a wonderful change was effected in a short time. This change was so great and striking that, in the words of Castiglio, "he could not be satisfied with weeping, by reason of the marvellous and heavenly contentment which he felt for the clear and manifest favors of God, and his tenderness towards sinners." The preaching of the Rosary, as usual, was his great instrument for the conversion of the people, and many wonders were wrought by the extension of its devotion. When at length he prepared to return to Toulouse, the regret of the citizens knew no bounds; "for his manner and conversation," continues Castiglio, "had marvelously captivated the souls of all, and they felt themselves raised on high to great and heavenly desires, whilst their affections were likewise drawn to him by a singular tenderness." There must, indeed, have been something peculiarly sweet and familiar in the intercourse between him and these converts of Madrid; for we find him writing to the Pope to declare their fervent and devout dispositions; and Honorius in consequence sent a brief conveying his special benediction both to them and to the people of Segovia.

Several other convents were already founded in Spain, but it is uncertain what share St. Dominic himself had in their establishment. Nor is there any universal agreement among authors as to the cities he visited, though it seems certain that he made some stay at Palencia, the scene of his early university life. We have an interesting memorial of his visit in the will of Antony Sersus, who leaves a certain sum for candles for the confraternity of the Holy Rosary, founded in that place by "the good Dominic of Guzman," as he terms him.

We find by this how very early a date may be claimed for the confraternities of the Rosary, which indeed were founded in almost every city wherein Dominic preached, especially in the north of Italy. For still, as he passed from place to place, his work was ever the same: he preached without rest and intermission, and many of the miracles attributed to him by popular tradition are given to us associated with stories of the propagation of the Rosary. His time was never his own: he had long since made it over to God for the salvation of souls; his idea of the vocation of a Friar Preacher was one of utter self-abandonment, and so whenever he appeared abroad he was followed by crowds, attracted by the odor of his sanctity, who were accustomed to say that penance was easy when preached by Master Dominic.

Yet, though never alone, his life of prayer was uninterrupted; the secret of that perpetual communion with God in the midst of exterior distractions, so admirably displayed in the life of the great spiritual daughter of his Order, St. Catherine of Siena, when she spoke of the interior cell of the heart wherein she was wont to retire, was well known to him: it was there he found his rest; and the habit of prayer had knit his heart so close to God that nothing had the power of separating him from that center, "wherein," says Castiglio, "he reposed with a marvelous quiet and tranquillity. Never did he lose that repose of soul which is essential to the spirit of prayer; but in all his labors and disquiets, in the midst of hunger, thirst, fatigue, long journeys, and continued interruption from others, his heart was free and ready to turn to God at all hours, as though it were conscious of none else but Him. Therefore many consolations were granted to him that are not given to others; and of this we have evidence in his words, his zeal, and all his actions, wherein there appeared a certain grace and sweetness of the Holy Ghost, showing how dearly favored was his soul."

In fact, St. Dominic was pre-eminently a man of prayer; it is the feature above all others which we find traced upon his life. By night or by day, whether alone or with others, silent in contemplation, or surrounded by the distractions of an active apostolic vocation, his heart never stirred from the true and steady center it had so early found in God; and in this one fact lay the secret of all the graces which adorned his most beautiful soul. It was the source of that interior tranquillity which fitted him to be called "the rose of patience," as well as of the exterior and gracious sweetness to which all have borne testimony, and which with him was nothing else than the fragrant odor proceeding from the abiding presence of God.

CHAPTER 20

Return to St. Romain. He proceeds to Paris. Jordan of Saxony. Interview
with Alexander, King of Scotland. Return to Italy.

We find Dominic once more among the brethren of St.
Romain in the April of the year 1219. His presence was joyfully welcomed, nor was it among his own brethren only
that his coming always seemd to diffuse a spirit of gladness:
if we may credit an ancient writer, "even the Jews and Gen-
tile Saracens, whereof there were so many in Spain, held
him dear, all save the heretics, whom he was wont to con-
quer and silence by his preachings."*

And now, once more, Toulouse heard for awhile the mighty
eloquence of that voice which had before carried the Gospel
of peace over the hills and villages of Languedoc. Such crowds
flocked to hear him that St. Romain could not contain them:
it was in the cathedral church of St. Stephen, before the bishop
and chapter, that he was obliged to deliver his sermons; and
their fruit was an abundance of conversions. Here again he
gave himself without reserve to all the labors of his apostolic
calling. All day long he was in the city, or in the surrounding
country, preaching and instructing the people; and the night
was devoted to prayer and sharp austerities. Here, too, all
his care and devotion was lavished on his brethren and children, whom he strove to form to sanctity. Prouille and St.
Romain were to him now, what St. Sixtus and Santa Sabina
had already been at Rome; and another miracle of the mul-
tiplication of the loaves is said to have taken place in the
refectory of St. Romain.

Bertrand of Garrega was his companion in the journey

*John of Spain.

to Paris, which next lay before him. Some of his younger disciples were also with him, and it was in tenderness to their weakness and fatigue that he is said to have miraculously changed some water into wine, a trait of his characteristic thoughtfulness and compassion "for," says Gerard de Frachet, "they had been tenderly nurtured in the world."

On the road they turned aside to visit the sanctuary of Roquemadour, near Cahors, where they spent the night praying in the Church of Our Lady. The next day as they journeyed along, singing litanies and reciting the Psalms of the divine office, two German pilgrims overtook them; and being greatly attracted by the devotion of their exterior, they followed closely behind them. When they came to the next village, their new friends begged them to sit down and dine with them; and they continued this conduct for four consecutive days.

On the fifth day Dominic said to Bertrand, "Brother Bertrand, it grieves me to reap the temporal things of these pilgrims, without sowing for them spiritual things: let us kneel down and ask God to grant us the understanding of their language, that we may speak to them of Christ." They did so, and during the rest of their journey were able to converse with them without difficulty. When they drew near Paris, they separated, and Dominic charged Bertrand to keep the matter secret till his death, "lest" as he said, "the people should take us for saints, who are but sinners."

Jordan of Saxony tells us another anecdote of this journey which he heard from the lips of Bertrand himself: it was that, being threatened with a violent tempest of rain, they walked on in the midst of it, Dominic making the Sign of the Cross as he went along, and none of them were touched by the floods of water that fell around them.

On another occasion, when the rain had drenched them through and through, they stopped for the night at a little village, and his companions went to the inn fire to dry their clothes whilst Dominic, as usual, made his way to the church, where he spent the night before the altar. In the morning the habits of the others were still wet, but his were perfectly dry; the fire of charity that burned within had communicated itself also to his exterior.

We have already noticed the foundation of the convent of St. Jacques, at Paris; in spite of all obstacles, the numbers of the brethren had now increased to thirty, and the presence of Dominic was a fresh encouragement to them. His stay among them was very short, but marked by two characteristic proceedings. His first act was to "set in order a regular house, with cloisters, dormitory, refectory, and cells for study";* for it must be remembered that the brethren were in close connection with the university, where they followed the course of divinity and philosophy with the other students. Dominic's next step was to carry out his usual law of dispersion: Limoges, Rheims, Poitiers and Orleans were all chosen as the scenes of new foundations; and the little band, so hardly gathered together, were no sooner collected than they were scattered abroad.

Peter Cellani, the citizen of Marseilles who had been the first benefactor and disciple of the Order, was chosen for Limoges; but he ventured to plead his ignorance and incapacity for preaching. "Go, my son," was the heroic answer of his leader, "go, and fear nothing: twice every day will I remember thee before God, and do not thou doubt. Thou shalt gain many souls to the Lord, and He will be with thee." Peter obeyed with the simplicity so natural to him, and was used afterwards to say that in all his difficulties he had never invoked God and St. Dominic without obtaining relief. Whilst at Paris, Dominic had the happiness of giving the habit to his old friend William of Montferrat, whose two years of study at the university were now complete. His first acquaintance was also made with Jordan of Saxony, then also a young student of the university. The

---

*These words are from Martene's history, and are an additional evidence of what we have before alluded to as one of the primary conditions of a religious community, according to the system of St. Dominic; namely, the *"regular house."*

story of his vocation to religion is of singular beauty. He was accustomed every morning to rise for the matin service of Notre Dame; and, whatever might be the season or the weather, nothing ever detained him in his bed.

One morning, fearing he was late, he left his lodging in great haste and hurried to the church door, which he found shut, for the hour was still early. As he stood waiting to enter, a beggar solicited an alms, and Jordan felt about him for his purse; but in his haste he had left it in his room, and he had nothing to give. Sooner, however, than refuse an alms for the love of God, he stripped off a rich belt mounted in silver, which he wore after the fashion of the times, and gave it to the poor man. As he entered the church and knelt for a moment before the great crucifix, he saw the same belt hanging round the neck of the figure, and at that moment a voice within him called him powerfully to the closer service of God. This call, and the desire to which it gave rise, pursued him without rest, and when he heard of the fame of Dominic, he resolved to lay the whole state of his soul before him. His counsel and direction restored his peace; but he did not take the habit until Reginald of Orleans finally won him to the Order by his eloquence.

Another interesting incident of Dominic's visit to Paris, as connected with the history of the Order in our own island, is his interview with Alexander II, king of Scotland. This monarch was then at the French capital for the purpose of renewing the ancient alliance of his crown with the royal house of France. The Princess Blanche, mother to St. Louis, had a particular esteem for St. Dominic and often invited him to her court, and there probably the Scottish king first met with the patriarch of the Friars Preachers. We know nothing of the particulars of their interview; but we are assured that he eagerly pressed the Saint to send some of his brethren to Scotland, and promised them his fatherly and royal protection. At what exact period this request was granted seems a little doubtful;* but it is certain that Alexander did build several convents for the fathers in his kingdom, and always bore a singular love to the Order. Eight religious were sent into Scotland, headed by one Father Clement, afterwards bishop of Dublin; and no less than eight monasteries were founded in that country during the reign of this prince.

The period of his short visit being expired, Dominic once more took the road to Italy, accompanied only by William de Montferrat and a lay brother who had come with him from Spain. All these long journeys were performed on foot, in the fashion of poor pilgrims; and their rapidity, and the short rest he allowed himself, fill us with admiration for the energy and courage which they evince. His joyous and manly temperament of spirit bore him on in spite of all fatigues and dangers, and in those days foot-travelling over wild and uncultivated countries must have been plentiful in both. Passing through Burgundy, he arrived at Chatillon on the Seine, where he was charitably lodged by a poor ecclesiastic; but Dominic richly repaid his kindness, for whilst he was yet in the house, the news was brought him that his host's nephew had fallen from a high roof and was being brought home dead.

Dominic went to meet him, and restored him to his parents alive and well. Other miracles of healing also marked his stay in the place, from whence he proceeded on to Avignon, where a little trace of his sojourn may yet be seen in a well, bearing an inscription to the effect that in 1219 the founder of the Friars Preachers blessed this water, which has since restored health to many sick persons.

All Dominic's companions were not quite such good travellers as himself. We find that as they were making their way through the passes of the Lombard Alps, the strength and courage of poor Brother John, the Spanish lay brother, entirely failed him: overcome with hunger and fatigue, he

---

*The Melross Chronicle assigns the year 1230 as the earliest date of the establishment of the Order in Scotland.

sat down, unable to proceed further. The good father said
to him, "What is the matter, my son, that you stop thus?"
And he replied, "Because, father, I am dying of hunger."
"Take courage, my son," said the Saint; "yet a little further,
and we shall find some place in which we may rest."

But as Brother John replied again that he was utterly
unable to proceed any further, Dominic had recourse to his
usual expedient of prayer. Then he bade him go to a spot
he pointed out, and take up what he should find there. The
poor brother dragged himself to the place indicated and
found a loaf of exquisite whiteness which, by the Saint's
orders, he ate, and felt his strength restored. Then, having
asked him if he were revived, Dominic bade him take the
remains of the loaf back to the place where he found it;
and having done so, they continued their route. As they went
on, the marvel of the thing seemed to strike the brother
for the first time. "Who put the loaf there?" he said; "I
was surely beside myself to take it so quietly! Holy father,
tell me whence did that loaf come?" "Then," says the old
writer, Gerard de Frachet, who has related this story, "this
true lover of humility replied; 'My son, have you not eaten
as much as you needed?' And he said, 'Yes,' 'Since, then,'
replied the Saint, 'you have eaten enough, give thanks to
God, and trouble not yourself about the rest.'"

And now Dominic was once more on the Italian soil, which
thenceforth he never quitted to the day of his death. It was
the summer of 1219; only eight months had elapsed since
he had quitted Rome, and within that space he had spread
his order through the whole extent of Spain and France.
His road was literally marked by new foundations: we may
trace it on the map by the convents that date their origin
from this time. Asti, Bergamo, and Milan all received him
with marks of honor; at Bergamo he was detained by a
severe illness, which even compelled him to discontinue his
abstinence and fasting; a fact noticed as almost unexampled in his life.

At Milan he was welcomed as the messenger of God; the

canon of St. Nazaire, in particular, received him with singular marks of affection, and three celebrated professors,
all citizens of that place, received his habit. In company
with these new brethren he set out for Bologna, where he
arrived about the month of August; but it is time for us
to give some brief account of the progress of that convent
since the period of his last visit to it in the preceding year.

CHAPTER 21

The Convent of Bologna. Effects of Reginald's preaching and government. Fervor of the Community of St. Nicholas. Conversion of Fathers Roland and Moneta. Dispersion of the brethren through the cities of Northern Italy. Reginald's novices. Robaldo. Bonviso of Placentia. Stephen of Spain. Rodolph of Faenza. Reginald is sent to Paris. Jordan joins the Order. Reginald's success—and death.

The progress of the brethren of Bologna at their little convent of La Mascharella had been slow, and their difficulties and discouragements very great, up to the time of the arrival amongst them of Reginald of Orleans. As soon as he returned from the Holy Land, he set out for Bologna, according to his previous agreement with St. Dominic, and arrived there on the 21st of December, 1218. His presence caused an immediate change in the position of the friars: he held the authority of vicar-general in Dominic's absence, and his extraordinary powers of government, added to the brilliancy of that eloquence which so remarkably distinguished him, infused a fresh spirit into the community, whilst crowds of those who had before treated them with contempt now crowded about their church in hopes of catching the words of the celebrated preacher.

There was a certain vehemence of spirit about Reginald that carried all before him; very soon the church was too small to contain his audience, and he was compelled to preach in the streets and public piazzas; the people came from all surrounding towns and country to hear him, and the age of the apostles seemed to have returned. The fire of his words produced an astonishing effect on the hearts of all who listened; and whilst a general change of manners was observed among all ranks, a vast number were kindled with a holy and impetuous enthusiasm, and feeling the call of God in their hearts, they turned their backs on the world, and eagerly demanded the habit of religion. "He was filled with a burning and vehement eloquence," says Brother Jordan, "which kindled the hearts of his hearers, as though with a lighted torch." Within six months Reginald received more than a hundred persons into the Order: among them were several of the most distinguished doctors and students of the university; and it came to be a common saying that it was scarce safe to go and hear Master Reginald, if you did not wish to take the friar's habit.

This rapid increase of the brethren soon rendered their habitation too small for them. Early in the spring of 1219, they removed to the church and convent of St. Nicholas delle Vigne, situated without the walls. Many miraculous signs had betokened the future sanctity of this place; angels had been heard singing over it by those who worked in the vineyards; and a kind of universal tradition had pointed it out as someday to be a place of prayer and pilgrimage. The life led within its walls, under the government of Blessed Reginald, was a worthy fulfillment of these auguries.

It was the strictest and most fervent realization of the rule of Dominic which has ever been seen. Many of the brethren closely imitated him in their nightly watchings and discipline, and in the devotions which were dear and peculiar to himself. At no hour of day or night could you enter the church without seeing some of the friars engaged in fervent prayer. After compline they all visited the altar, after the manner of their holy founder; and the sight of their devotion, as they bathed the ground with their tears, filled the bystanders with wonder. After singing matins very few returned to bed; most of them spent the night in prayer or study, and all confessed before celebrating the Holy Sacrifice. Their devotion to the Mother of God was of the tenderest kind. Twice every day they visited her altar, after matins and again at compline, walking round it three times, as they sang canticles in her honor, and recommended themselves and their Order to her love and protection. They held it a matter of conscience never to eat till they had first announced the word of God to some soul.

They also served in the hospitals of the city, adding the corporal to the spiritual works of mercy; and in spite of the excessive austerity of their lives, it is said such was the joy of their hearts, shining out in their countenances, that they seemed none other than angels in the habit of men.

The strict observance of the rule of silence practiced among them is illustrated by the following anecdote. One night a friar, being in prayer in the choir, was seized by some invisible hand and dragged violently about the church, so that he cried aloud for help. These disturbances, arising from diabolic malice, were very frequent in the beginning of the Order; and at the sound of the cry more than thirty brethren, guessing the cause, ran into the church and endeavored to assist the sufferer, but in vain; they too were roughly handled, and, like him, dragged and thrown about without pity. At length Reginald himself appeared, and taking the unfortunate friar to the altar of St. Nicholas, he delivered him from his tormentor. And all this while, in spite of the alarm and horror of the circumstances, not one of those present, who amounted in all to a considerable number, ventured to speak a single word, or so much as to utter a sound. The first cry of the vexed brother was the only one uttered during the whole of that night.

This admirable discipline was certainly attained and preserved by the practice of a somewhat rigid severity; yet its very sharpness attests the perfection which must have been reached by those who could have inflicted or accepted it. In the following anecdote, as given by Gerard de Frachet, the supernatural and passionless self-command exhibited by the chief actor robs the story of that austere character which might make an ordinary reader shrink, and clothes it with a wonderful dignity and sublimity. A lay brother had committed a slight infringement of the law of poverty, and on conviction of his offence refused to accept the penalty imposed. Reginald perceived the rising spirit of insubordi-

nation, and at once prepared to extinguish it. Causing the
delinquent to bare his shoulders, he raised his eyes to Heaven,
bathed in tears, and calmly and gently, as though presiding
in choir, pronounced the following prayer: "O Lord Jesus
Christ, who gavest to Thy servant Benedict the power to
expel the devil from the bodies of his monks through the
rod of discipline, grant me the grace to overcome the temptation of this poor brother through the same means. Who
livest and reignest, with the Father and the Holy Spirit,
for ever and ever, Amen."

Then he struck him so sharply that the brethren were
moved to tears, but the penitent was reclaimed, nor did
he ever again relapse into a similar fault. This sort of chastisement was a very ordinary means which he used to deliver
them from the assaults of the devil; yet we should err if
we attributed to him a harsh or tyrannical spirit. It was
a severity wholly compatible with the sweetness which
formed a peculiarity of his character; for the very tenderness of his love towards his children was the cause of that
severity he showed against the enemy of their souls. They
certainly never looked on it in any other light, for he was
beloved as a father, and the fame of his strict discipline
did not keep multitudes from embracing it as their surest
guide to Heaven.

The first who joined the Order after the arrival of Reginald
was Roland of Cremona, the public Reader of Philosophy
at the University. His coming was most opportune, for the
brethren were then still suffering from the old spirit of dis-
couragement; and in spite of the presence of Reginald among
them, some had even resolved on quitting the Order. They
were assembled in Chapter, engaged in earnest and sorrowful conference, when the door suddenly opened and Roland
appeared among them and impetuously demanded the habit.
Reginald, yielding to a sudden inspiration, took off his own
scapular and flung it over his shoulders. The incident seemed
to restore the spirit and courage of the whole assembly, and
the fame of Roland's conversion was the means of inducing

many of his former companions to take a similar step.

Another remarkable conversion was that of Brother Moneta, also a professor of the University, but a man who, until the coming of Reginald, had been wont to ridicule all religion and to live without any of its restraints. Hearing of the wonderful effects of the new preacher's eloquence, he feared to expose himself to its influence and kept away. One day, however, being the feast of St. Stephen, some of his scholars endeavored to carry him with them to hear the preaching. Not liking to refuse and yet unwilling to comply, Moneta proposed that they should first hear Mass at St. Procolus. They went, and stayed during three Masses till, unable to delay longer, Moneta was obliged to accompany the others to Santa Maria, where Reginald was then delivering his sermon. The doors were so crowded that they could not enter, and Moneta remained standing on the threshold. But as he stood there he could command a view of the whole scene, and every word reached his ear. A dense mass of people filled the church, yet not a sound broke the words of the preacher. He was speaking on the words of St. Stephen, the saint of the day: "Behold, I see heaven open, and Jesus standing at the right hand of God." "Heaven is open today also," he exclaimed; "the door is ever open to him who is willing to enter. Why do you delay? Why do you linger on the threshold? What blindness, what negligence is this! The heavens are still open!"

And lo! as he listened, Moneta's heart was changed and conquered. As Reginald came down from the pulpit he was met by his new penitent, who abandoned himself to his direction, and, after remaining in the world under probation for a year, he was received to the habit and became himself the founder of several convents. His after holiness equalled the irregularity of his former life. He died full of years and of merit, and, it is said, blind from his constant weeping. It was in his cell that the great patriarch breathed his last, as we shall hereafter relate.

Such was the position of the community of Bologna when

Dominic again appeared among them. His first act was to make a renunciation of certain endowments which had been made over to the convent by a citizen of the place. Dominic tore the contract in pieces with his own hands, declaring they would rather beg their bread than depart from their law of poverty. His next step was one which perhaps a little moderated the joy caused by his presence; it was another dispersion of the society so newly gathered together. Religious were sent to every one of the towns where, as he passed through on his late journey, he had prepared the way for their reception; and in a few weeks, Milan, Bergamo, Asti, Verona, Florence, Brescia, Faenza, Placenza and other cities of Tuscany and Lombardy received little companies of the new apostles.

There was, doubtless, a reason for this very extensive dispersion of the Order throughout the north of Italy; it may be found in the fact that that country was at the time overrun by the self-same destructive heresy of the Manicheans which had produced such desolating effects in France. This was the great enemy against which the Order of Friars Preachers had been raised to combat; and wherever it showed its head, Dominic knew that he and his faithful soldiers had a call to follow. If the community of Bologna was greatly reduced by those colonies sent to other cities, its numbers were soon made up by fresh acquisitions.

Among those clothed by the holy father was Brother Robaldo, who afterwards became distinguished for his success against the heretics in the city of Milan. A somewhat amusing story is told of him when preaching there. The Manicheans then filled the city in great numbers, and treated the Catholic missionaries with the utmost insolence. As Robaldo was one day in prayer before the high altar of the church, a band of these miscreants determined to divert themselves at his expense, and sent one of their number in to practice a joke upon him. "Father," said the heretic, "I well know you are a man of God, and able to obtain whatsoever you wish by prayer; I pray you, therefore, to make over me the Sign of the Cross, for I suffer from a cruel fever, and I would fain receive my cure from your hands." Robaldo knew well the malice of his enemy, and replied, "My son, if you have this fever, I pray God to deliver you; if you have it not, but are speaking lies, I pray Him to send it to you as a chastisement." The man instantly felt the approach of the malady he had feigned, and cried impatiently, "Sign me with the cross, I say, sign me; it is not your custom to send curses upon men, but cures." But Robaldo replied again, "What I have said, I have said; if you have it, may He deliver you; if not, you will surely have it."

Meanwhile the others stood at the door, laughing to see the saint, as they thought, made a fool of; but their merriment was soon silenced when they saw their companion return to them with every symptom of the fever he had before pretended. The result of these circumstances was his own conversion, and that of his entire family; and Robaldo, on his sincere penitence, restored him to health and received him and all his children into the communion of the Church.

Bonviso, of Placentia, was another of the novices clothed at Bologna by the great patriarch. Before he was professed he was sent to preach in his own country, and very unwillingly he went, for his humility made him fear lest he should fail, and bring disgrace on the Order. Dominic, however, encouraged him and said, "God's words will be in your mouth, my son; go without fear, and do my will"; and Bonviso never felt afterwards any difficulty in preaching. He was one of those who gave their evidence on the canonization of the Saint, and says that so long as he knew him he never slept save on benches or on the ground, and never in any particular place; but sometimes in the church, sometimes in the dormitory, and often in the burial place of the convent.

Stephen of Spain was another of the new disciples of the Order; his conversion was remarkable. He has himself described it, being at the time a student at Bologna. "Whilst I was there," he says, "Master Dominic arrived and preached to the students and others, and I went to confession to him, and I thought he loved me. One evening, I was sitting down to supper with my companions when two of the friars came to me and said, 'Master Dominic is asking for you,' and I replied that I would come so soon as I had supped. But they repeating that he expected me at once, I rose, and leaving everything as it was I came to St. Nicholas, where I found Master Dominic in the midst of a number of the friars. He turned to them and said, 'Show him how to make the prostration,' and they having shown me how to do it, I made it, and he instantly gave me the habit of a friar preacher. I have never thought of this without astonishment, reflecting by what instinct he could thus have called and clothed me, for I had never spoken to him of the matter; wherefore I doubt not he acted by some divine revelation." Stephen was another of the witnesses on the canonization whose evidence is preserved among the other "Acts of Bologna."

Another very distinguished member of the family of Bologna was Rodolph of Faenza, whom we notice here, though he entered the Order at an earlier period. Some affirm that he acted as confessor to St. Dominic; and it is said that the Saint, being at one period afflicted on account of the withdrawal of some who had at first given themselves to God, Rodolph was granted a vision wherein he saw Our Lord and His Blessed Mother, who laid their hands on his head and comforted him; after which they led him out to the shores of the river, and showed him a great ship, as it were, laden with brethren dressed in the habit, and said to him, "Seest thou all these, Brother Rodolph! They are all of thy Order, and are going forth to fill and replenish the world."

Rodolph acted as procurator to the convent, and on one occasion he made some trifling addition to the two dishes allowed by the rule; this greatly displeased Dominic, who himself never tasted but one; and, calling the procurator to his side he whispered, "Why do you seek to bribe the brothers with these pittances?" And yet we are assured the addition to their ordinary fare was of the plainest kind. "Dominic's own dinner," adds Rodolph, "was so spare, and so quickly finished that often, as he waited whilst the others dispatched their meal, he fell asleep for weariness, after his long vigils."

Such were some of the brethren of the convent of St. Nicholas. Its reputation for sanctity came to be so great that men spoke of it as a kind of harbor of salvation—as may be illustrated by the following beautiful story which is given us by Taegius and others. There was a certain cleric in Bologna of great learning, but devoted to worldly vanity and to other than a holy life. Now, one night he seemed suddenly to be in the midst of a vast field, and above him the sky was covered with clouds, and rain fell in great abundance, and there was a terrible tempest. He, therefore, desiring to escape from the hail and lightning, looked all around him to see if by any means he might find a place of shelter, but he found none. Then at the last he perceived a small house, and going to it he knocked, for the door was fast shut. And a voice spoke to him from within, saying, "What wantest thou?" And he said, "A night's lodging, because of the great storm that is raging." But the keeper of the house answered him, saying, "I am Justice, and this is my house; but thou canst not enter here, for thou art not just." Then he went away sad, and presently he came to a second house, and he knocked there likewise; and the keeper answered and said, "I am Peace, but there is no peace for the wicked, but only to them of good will. Nevertheless, because my thoughts are thoughts of peace, and not of affliction, therefore I will counsel thee what thou shalt do. A little way from hence dwelleth my sister, Mercy, who ever helpeth the afflicted: go, therefore, to her, and do even as she shall command thee." So he, continuing on his way, came to the door of Mercy, and she said to him, "If thou wouldst save thyself from this tempest, go to the convent of St. Nicholas where dwell the Friars Preachers; there thou shalt find the food of doctrine, the ass of simplicity, the ox of discretion; Mary who will illuminate, Joseph who will make perfect, and Jesus who will save thee." And he, coming to himself and thinking well on the words of Mercy, went quickly, and with great devotion received the holy habit.

The great talents and success of Blessed Reginald determined Dominic to remove him to Paris, in the hopes that he would do as much for the convent there established as he had done for that of Bologna. His departure was a severe grief to his brethren; they wept as though torn from the arms of their mother; but the expectations of their founder were fully realized in the short but brilliant career which awaited Reginald in the French capital. That marvelous eloquence whose vehemence was so irresistible, while at the same time so far removed from mere human impetuosity, soon drew all to hear him. When he preached, the streets were deserted; his holy life, too, so corresponded to his words that men looked on him as an angel of God. "All judged him to be one come down from Heaven," says an old writer; and indeed the students and citizens of Paris were best able to appreciate the worth of one whose sacrifice to the cause of religion they had witnessed with their own eyes. Matthew of France, the superior of the convent of St. James, who had himself been a student at Paris in former years, when Reginald was professor in the same university, asked him once how he, who had been used to so luxurious and brilliant a life in the world, had found it possible to persevere in the severe discipline of their Order. Reginald cast his eyes humbly to the ground. "Truly, father," he said, "I do not think to merit anything for that before the tribunal of God. He has given me so much consolation in my soul, that the rigors of which you speak have become very sweet and easy." And this, indeed, appeared in all he did, for whilst he was constantly distinguished for the exceeding austerity of his life, he did all things with such a ready and joyful spirit that he taught men the sweetness of the Cross by the very lightness with which he bore it.

Among the disciples whom he drew into the Order, and

who received the habit at his hands, was Jordan of Saxony. We have already spoken of his first vocation to religion, but he did not finally determine on taking the habit until overcome by the persuasions of Reginald. He brought with him a near and dear friend, Henry of Cologne, then canon of Utrecht. "A man," he says, "whom I loved in Christ, with an affection I never gave to any other; a vessel of perfection and honor, so that I remember not in all my life to have seen a more gracious creature." They lodged in the same house, and followed their studies together; and Jordan, whose mind was always full of the thoughts of that vocation which yet he himself had not as yet obeyed, often spoke of it to his friend and endeavored to persuade him to form a similar determination. Henry constantly rejected the idea; Jordan as constantly persevered in his arguments and persuasions. He has left us an account of the result, given in his most beautiful style: "I made him go to Blessed Reginald to confession, and when he came back, opening the prophet Isaias by way of taking counsel, I fell on the following passage: 'The Lord made me to hear his voice, and I did not resist him: I went not back.' And as I interpreted the passage, which answered so well to the state of my own heart, we saw a little further on the words, 'Let us keep together,' which, as it were, warned us not to separate from one another, but to consecrate our lives to the same object."

"Where are now those words, 'Let us keep together?'" wrote Henry some years after, in a letter to his friend. "You are at Bologna, and I at Cologne!" But this was the Dominican law of dispersion. A vision completed the conquest of Henry. He saw Christ sitting in judgment, and one by his side cried to him, and said, "You who stand there, what have you ever abandoned for God?" Filled with trouble at this saying, his soul was torn by a short and agonizing struggle. He desired, yet he could not resolve on the sacrifice. At length he sought Reginald, and yielding to the powerful impulse with which God was drawing his heart in spite of himself, he made his vows in his hands. When he returned to Jordan,

"I saw," says the latter, "his angelic countenance bathed in tears, and I asked where he had been, he answered, 'I have made a vow to God, and I will perform it.'"

They were both clothed together at the close of that Lent; but a singular revelation had previously declared to Jordan the death of Reginald and something of his own future destiny in the Order. On the night that blessed man departed to God, towards the commencement of the month of February, he saw in his sleep a clear and sparkling fountain suddenly spring up in the church of St. James, and as suddenly fail; and as he grieved, understanding the vision to predict the untimely death of Reginald, a clear stream of water took the place of the fountain and flowed on in immense waves till it filled the world. It was a fit emblem of his own future career, so abundant in its fecundity that he is said to have clothed a thousand novices with his own hand.

Among Reginald's disciples, during his life at Paris, may also be mentioned Robert Biliber Kilward, an Englishman, who afterwards became archbishop of Canterbury under Edward I and cardinal of the Roman Church. He was reckoned one of the greatest theologians of his age, as well as a distinguished minister of state; yet in all his dignities he never laid aside his religious dress or character, made his journeys on foot, and lived in the utmost simplicity of holy poverty, reckoning his profession, as a Friar Preacher, the greatest of all the dignities lavished on him by fortune.

Reginald's death took place in the early part of the March of 1220. When the physicians declared the hopelessness of his case, Matthew of France came to announce their decision to him, and to propose that he should receive the Sacrament of Extreme Unction: "I do not fear the assault of death," he replied, "since the blessed hands of Mary herself anointed me at Rome. Nevertheless, because I desire not to make light of the Church's Sacraments, I will receive it, and humbly ask that it may be given to me."

His body was laid in the church of Sainte-Marie-des-Champs, and though he has never been solemnly beatified,

the veneration which was paid him may be gathered from
the prayers and hymns in his honor which may be found
in the ancient office books of the Order. He was undoubtedly one of its greatest men, to whom there has hardly been
done sufficient justice. In him might be seen the rare union
of human genius and heroic sanctity; and even when the
supernatural element had taken possession of every capacity of his soul, it consecrated them without destroying any
of his fervor and richness of imagination, or the force and
impetuosity by which it manifested itself in his preaching,
and which gave him such a magical power over the hearts
of his hearers. These dazzling gifts once placed the world
at his feet, but he was happy above so many of his fellows
in that he made no other use of its homage and its smiles
than to offer them to God. None, perhaps, ever made a
nobler sacrifice, or felt that it cost him less; and he may
stand to all ages an example of the rarest of all the miracles
of grace, a soul of consecrated genius.

The spirit of a saint may be said to multiply itself, and
to survive in his disciples; and in the distinctive graces exhibited to us in them we have another means of estimating
the character of their founder, besides what is afforded us
by the study of his own life. Or rather we might say the
truest judgment will be formed by a comparison of the
founder and his disciples; and when we find any one trait
of the former caught up and repeated over and over again
in those who came after him, and whose supernatural life
was formed on the model of his own, we may safely conclude that the similarity is no accident, but the result of
some great principle which had struck deep root in his soul
and spread its branches far and wide over his followers.

Now if this be so, we can scarcely fail to be struck with
one peculiarity in the histories of these early companions
of Dominic which will surprise us, if we have any share
in the popular prejudice which attaches to his name. We
might have expected, along with much zeal and fervor, to
have found some traces of that stern fanaticism which is

attributed to him and his Order, betraying itself like an hereditary malady in the ranks of the Friars Preachers. But as we search for illustrations of bigotry or gloom, or of a fierce and bloody vindictiveness, we lose ourselves, as it were, in a garden of sweetness. Gathered from all states of life— knights, courtiers, professors, men of the world, penitents, and saints—the novices of Dominic, so soon as his spirit has breathed over them, display to our gaze amid many varieties, one trait of which has the indescribable peculiarity of a family likeness.

It is sweetness: that quality of which it is said, in the Book of Ecclesiasticus, "Accomplish your works with sweetness, and you shall draw the love and esteem of men." We see it first in the great founder himself, of whom it is said, "None did ever resist the charm of his intercourse, or went away from him without feeling himself the better." It spoke in his low sonorous voice; nay, it might be seen in the very splendor of his starry forehead, and in the beauty of that countenance which everyone who gazed on it described as full of joy and hilarity. And yet, we are told, he often and easily wept, but only when moved by the sufferings of others; nay, so tender was his heart that he could not think of human misery as he gazed over a distant city without being touched to tears.

This tenderness of spirit was the hereditary birthright of his children. There was Reginald of Orleans, winning men to penance against their will; and Henry of Utrecht, that "gracious creature," as Jordan calls him, with the joy of God painted on his angelic countenance, and whose voice breathed the odor of a childlike innocence. There was Jordan himself, whose simple *bonhomie* of character is perhaps as delightful as any of them; who could tranquillize disturbed consciences by a look, who was severe only to those who were severe to others, and whom we find taming and playing with the wild ferrets on the road as he journeyed, in the overflowing tenderness and kindness of his heart.

Of another we read that as he prayed in the garden, his looks were so gentle that timid birds would come and perch on his outstretched arms. And whole volumes might be written of their deaths. Of numbers it is related that they died singing. In the convent of Vincenza we find a brother who, after "singing versicles to the Blessed Virgin, with wondrous delightsomeness, signed to his companion to rejoice also with him, saying, 'Brother, do not think it strange, but it is impossible for me not to sing of the love of Mary.' Then after a while he opened his eyes again, and said oftentimes with much jubilation, 'Let everything that hath breath praise the Lord'; and so, with a smile, expired." Father William of Anicy, as he lay dying, was visited by the angels, who visibly appeared to the bystanders; and one of them bent over his bed and kissed his forehead, a grace he had deserved by his angelic life and conversation.

There was John of Gascony, "a very marvel of sanctity, who, like the swan, sang as he was a-dying; sweetly repeating with his last breath, 'Into Thy hands, O Lord, I commend my spirit. Alleluia! For Thou hast redeemed me O God of truth! Alleluia! Alleluia!' "

Then again we find other stories of their special earnestness in the work of peace. Fr. Robaldo, for instance, seemed to have a vocation for the healing of quarrels and feuds. He worked miracles to make men forgive one another; but perhaps his own angelic temper had a greater magic in it than his miracles. A young Milanese noble had been slain by his feudal enemy, and the two surviving brothers had vowed revenge. Robaldo, after having in vain endeavored to appease one of them, took him by the hand and commanded him not to move till he had promised peace. He instantly lost the power of motion, and whilst he stood thus his other brother came to the spot, uttering curses and imprecations, and binding himself by oaths never to rest till he had steeped his sword in the blood of the murderer. And yet neither of them could resist the sweetness of Robaldo, and it ended by his sending them to the house of their enemy to dine with him, and bringing all three next day to the convent church, to bury all their differences at the foot of the altar.

Then there was our own Lawrence; called blessed because of his blessed temper, and known through Spain and France as the reconciler of enemies. In short, turn where we will, we find the feet of these true preachers "shod with the preparation of the Gospel of peace." They were all shaped after one likeness, even that of their holy patriarch: "benign, merciful, patient, and sober, not giving cursing for cursing, but rather blessing those that cursed." Such are the words of Bonviso of Placentia.

These we repeat were no fanatics: the pages of our own history will furnish us, in the followers of Cromwell or Argyle, with a portrait of fanaticism never to be found among these Friars Preachers; and when we have been compelled to grant them the character of saints, it will perhaps startle us to know that many of these very men bore also the dreaded title of Inquisitors.

We must not close this chapter without noticing the foundation at Bologna of a convent of women, which was begun through the means of Diana of Andala, one of St. Dominic's spiritual daughters. Her extraordinary constancy and resolution overcame all the obstacles opposed by her friends; and eventually her own father became one of the most liberal supporters of the new house. Cecilia and Amy, the two sisters of St. Sixtus before named, were removed from thence to Bologna in 1223; and all three lie buried in the same grave, where their remains have been twice discovered, and honorably translated.

CHAPTER 22

Dominic journeys through Italy and returns to Rome for the fifth time. Increase of the Order. Character of the first fathers. Interview with St. Francis. Favors of the Holy See.

After Reginald's departure from Bologna, Dominic remained a while in the place, chiefly occupied in quieting the dissensions among the inhabitants which arose from the jealousy subsisting between the nobles and the citizens. Nor were his efforts unavailing: the Bolognese recognized him as their mediator of peace, and this was the first origin of that singular affection with which he was ever afterwards regarded in the city. Their confidence in him was increased by their conviction of his entire disinterestedness in the whole matter; for when their gratitude sought to show itself by gifts and donations, he constantly and inflexibly refused to receive the smallest offering beyond the pittance of daily alms which was begged from door to door. Indeed, his rigid regard of poverty was in no degree inferior to that observed by St. Francis: if there was food enough in the convent to suffice for the day, he never allowed more alms to be received for the next day; and very often he himself would undertake the office of begging in the streets, which he practiced with a peculiar pleasure.

He left Bologna in the October of the same year, and crossing the Apennines proceeded to Florence, whither some of the brethren had already been dispatched and had commenced their foundation. Here again the malice of the devil was overcome and made the means of extending the Order. A woman named Benita, who had been grievously tormented by the evil spirit and had led an irregular and irreligious life being converted and delivered from her possession by the prayers of Dominic, took the veil, and the name of Sister Benedicta.

From Florence he came to Viterbo, where the Pope was then staying, who received him with open arms. The recital of the progress which he and his brethren had made since his departure from Rome filled the Pontiff with delight. He testified his renewed affection and esteem by briefs, addressed to the prelates and ecclesiastical superiors throughout all the countries of Christendom, recommending the Order of Friars Preachers to their protection and respect. These briefs are dated the November and December of 1219.

Soon after their publication, Dominic returned for the fifth time to Rome, where he arrived in the commencement of the year 1220. A trifling circumstance is recorded connected with his return which may seem scarce worthy of notice, and yet discloses to us whole volumes of the character and disposition of this great man. He had brought with him, we are told, from Spain certain spoons of cypress wood for the nuns of St. Sixtus. Sister Cecilia thus describes this beautiful little incident: "Upon a certain time St. Dominic, returning from Spain, brought the sisters, as an affectionate little gift, some spoons of cypress, for every sister one. And upon a day, having finished his preaching and other works of charity, in the same evening he came to the sisters, that he might deliver to them these spoons from Spain." Amid all his journeys and fatigues, he had time and room enough in his heart for so simple a thought as this; and the comfort and pleasure of his children was still present to his mind. One of those spoons, carried over the hills of Spain and Italy in the bundle of the Saint during the long foot-journeys of so many months, was surely a precious relic.

He was soon busy in his old quarters at Santa Sabina and hard at work again, preaching to the Roman people. A great number of miracles and miraculous conversions are recorded as taking place at this time; and many of them we find spoken of as effected through the instrumentality of the Rosary. The stream of novices continued to flow as abundantly as ever into the cells of Santa Sabina, and the care of the Saint was bestowed on them with all his usual vigilance and tenderness. Their fervor, according to the testimony of Theodoric of Apoldia, was truly admirable. "When they looked on the beauty and purity of their institute," he says, "all their regret was not sooner to have embraced it."

A great care was ever taken of the novices, both as to their instruction and their health, for their zeal always had to be moderated. Instead of its being necessary to wake them for the midnight office, it was rather needful to seek for them in retired places, where they had hidden themselves to pray, and oblige them to take some rest. The abstinence they practiced was remarkable; many passed eight days without drinking, and mixed their food with cold water. They ever looked on preaching for the salvation of souls as the essential part of their institute. When they went to preach, according to Dominic's direction, they took with them only the Bible or the New Testament. When it was proposed to send missions among the barbarian nations or wheresoever there was a certainty of suffering, crowds offered themselves for the service; they had a holy eagerness for the salvation of souls and the chance of a crown of martyrdom.

It was at this time, according to the most probable conjecture of historians, that the interview took place between Dominic and Francis, in the palace of Cardinal Ugolino, which the Franciscan writers give as occurring at Perugia in the year 1219. After a spiritual conference of some duration, the cardinal asked them whether they would agree to their disciples accepting ecclesiastical dignities. Dominic was the first to reply: he said that it was honor sufficient for his brethren to be called to defend the Faith against heretics. The words of St. Francis were equally characteristic. "My children," he said, "would no longer be Friars Minors if they became great; if you would have them bring forth fruit, leave them as they are." Edified by their replies, Ugolino did not, however, abandon his own views; when he was elevated to the papacy, he promoted a great number of both

Orders to the episcopate, as many as forty-two of whom were of the Order of Friars Preachers.

We shall not pause to notice at any length the renewed favors of the Holy See, so liberally poured out in the shape of briefs and letters at this period, one of which, published in the commencements of this year, constituted Dominic the Superior or Master General of the entire Order—an office he had hitherto only held by tacit consent, and which was doubtless formally given him at this time with a view to the assembling of the brethren in the first general chapter, which was now in contemplation.

Whilst the preparations for this event were in hand, the friars were every day making further advances in Lombardy, and the great convent of St. Eustorgia was founded at Milan. The church had been granted to the Order through the intervention of Cardinal Ugolino; and before their coming, a certain hermit had been wont to declare to the people, saying, "Before long this church will be inhabited by friars called Preachers, who shall give light to the whole world; for every night I see bright lamps shining over it which illuminate the entire city." The canons also heard the sweet music of angelic choirs singing round the walls, and a great devotion had attached to the sanctuary in consequence. This convent became the headquarters of the Order in Lombardy, and it was ever foremost in its attacks on the heretics of the day.

The general chapter had been fixed for the Pentecost of 1220, just three years from what may be deemed the commencement of the Order. Its astonishing progress in that brief period seems to our eyes truly miraculous; perhaps the coldness of later days, could they have beheld it in vision, might have seemed as hard of credit or comprehension to the men of that heroic era. To ourselves the comparison can bring nothing but humiliation, whilst we contemplate a vigor, and, if we may so say, an impetuosity in the religious life of those days, which seems like the giant verdure of the forests of the New World beside our own stunted and degenerate growth.

And what is perhaps as worthy of our admiration is the simplicity and unconsciousness with which the facts of this extraordinary progress are given to us; we scarcely find a word, among those who were the eye-witnesses of what had been going on during those three years, expressive of any sense of success. The work was the work of God, and for their own share in it, each one, with a sincere humility, could have joined in the words of their holy founder as he stood in the midst of that first assembly of his children: "I deserve only to be dismissed from among you, for I have grown cold and relaxed, and am no longer of any use."

CHAPTER 23

First general Chapter at Bologna. Law of poverty. The Order spreads through Europe. Dominic's illness at Milan. Visit to Siena. Tancred. Apostolic journeys through Italy. Return to Bologna, and conversion of Master Conrad. John of Vicenza. Anecdotes.

It was on the 27th of May that the fathers of the Order met in the convent of St. Nicholas at Bologna. Jordan of Saxony, who has left an account of their proceedings, was himself present, having come from Paris three weeks before. But so little was there among any of them of a desire to seem great in men's eyes that very few details have been left regarding it, and many things are passed over in silence which would have been interesting to know. The numbers of friars present at the first chapter of his Order held by Francis have been carefully preserved; but no similar reckoning was made of the Friars Preachers: we know only that France, Spain, Italy, and even Poland had their representatives in that assembly.

Dominic was then fifty years of age, having lost nothing of that manly vigor of mind and body which ever distinguished him. If we seek amid the scanty materials which history has left us to find some token which may reveal to us the secret feelings of his heart at a moment so deep in its interest, we shall find that power and success and a government over other men which gave him a personal empire of souls extending over half Christendom had produced no change in the simplicity and humility of his heart. It tended Godward as it had ever done; and his first act was to implore permission to renounce a superiority of which he accounted himself unworthy. Some, perhaps, may be tempted to look on this as an easily assumed modesty, and to doubt how far he hoped or expected his resignation would be accepted. But the evidence of blessed Paul of Venice shows that even at this time the darling hope of his soul had never been abandoned; he still cherished the thought, so soon as the Order was firmly established, of carrying the light of the Gospel among the heathen. "When we shall have fully instructed our Order," he was wont to say, "we will go to the Cumans, and preach the Faith of Christ"; and, doubtless, this secret and deeply rooted idea was in his mind when he made the effort to rid himself of the government of his Order.

It is needless for us to say this resignation was unanimously rejected, and Dominic was compelled to retain an authority none other could have accepted in his lifetime. Yet he made it a condition that his power should be limited and controlled by the appointment of definitors, whose office extended over all the acts of the chapter, and even to the correction and punishment of the Master himself, in case of necessity.

Many of the laws, still forming part of the constitutions of the Order, were now established—those relating to abstinence and fasting, and many regarding the titles and authority of the local superiors. But the principal object of this chapter was the entire adoption of the rule of poverty, which had not been formally laid down by any statute. A renunciation was made of all lands and possessions until then retained, and it was resolved that nothing should be accepted in future save the daily alms on which they depended for support. The property of the monasteries of Toulouse and Madrid was respectively made over to the convents of women; and the Order was reduced to the severity of the apostolic standard.

If in the revolution of six centuries the change which has passed over the whole surface of society has necessitated a repeal of what, at the time, seemed a fundamental law, it need neither scandalize nor surprise us. Dear as was the rule of poverty to Dominic's heart, he never put it forth as the *end* of his Order: he judged it but a means, and at that age a chief and essential means, for the one unchanging object of the Institute of Preachers: the salvation of souls. And when the living authority of the Church in a later day dispensed the observance of the letter of a rule no longer adapted to that object, she adhered strictly to the spirit, and explained the principle on which this change was made in words* so luminous and conclusive that they leave nothing to be added on the subject. Dominic was anxious to provide for the preservation of another essential of his institute, the pursuit of sacred learning—and for this purpose proposed that all the temporal affairs of the convent should be left in the hands of the lay brothers, so as to set the others entirely at liberty for the purposes of prayer and study. This was overruled by the other fathers, experience having shown the danger of this custom in other orders; and Dominic did not press the proposal.

Some regulations were added about the cells, in respect to size and arrangement, and it was ordered that a crucifix and an image of the Blessed Virgin should be in each. The chapter was to be held yearly, at Paris and Bologna in turn: this regulation was afterwards done away, as the extension of the Order rendered so frequent an assembly impossible, and made it desirable to fix it at other cities according to circumstances. The arrangement was made at this time in consequence of the neighborhood of the two universities, a connection with which was held to be of the first importance.

We do not know what length of time was taken up by the proceedings of the chapter; but we find that early in the summer Dominic's attention was once more wholly given to the foundation and settlement of new convents. Brethren were sent also to Morocco and several of the infidel countries, as well as to Scotland, as some historians tell us. Luke, bishop

---

*See Const. F. Praed, d. ii. c.1; where the principles of religious poverty as professed by the Order are laid down with great exactness.

of Galicia, speaking of this period, says, "At that time one saw nothing but foundations of the Friars Preachers and Friars Minors springing up everywhere; and wherever heresy appeared, the children of Dominic," he adds, "were at hand to combat and subdue it." The Ghibeline influence of the German Emperors was doubtless a chief cause of that heretical tendency so widely diffused in the north of Italy, and there Dominic's chief efforts were directed. His residence at Bologna was constantly broken by excursions to the various cities of Lombardy, though we have no certain guide as to the exact order in which these visits were made. We find him again at Milan, in company with Brother Bonviso, in the course of the summer, and here he was again taken ill.

Bonviso has left an account of this illness, and remarks upon the patience and cheerfulness he displayed in the extremity of fever: "I never had reason to complain of him" (he says); "he seemed always in prayer and contemplation, to judge from his countenance; and so soon as the fever subsided, he began to speak to the brethren of God; he praised God and rejoiced in his suffering, as was his custom." He caused them to read to him, as he lay on his rough wooden bed, those Dialogues of Cassian and the Epistles of St. Paul, which had ever been his favorite books; and we feel that it is not fanciful to detect in this persevering attachment a token of that tranquil stability of mind which formed so distinctive a peculiarity of his nature.

It would be scarcely interesting to the reader to be detained with the mere names of foundations, or of the new disciples daily admitted to the Order. We shall endeavor to select a few among those which may be most worthy of our notice. The date of Dominic's visit to Siena has not been exactly preserved, though it may probably be referred to the present year. As he preached in one of the churches of that city, Tancredo Tancredi, a young noble of high birth and renown for learning stood amid the crowd. As he listened and gazed at the celebrated preacher, he saw another figure standing beside him in the pulpit, and whispering in his ear: it was the Blessed Virgin, who was inspiring the words of her faithful servant. The sight filled Tancred with admiration, but as the saint descended the pulpit stairs, that same glorious vision of Mary floated nearer and nearer to the spot where he stood. It pointed with its hand to the figure of the preacher, and a low sweet voice uttered in his ears, "Tancred, follow after that man, and do not depart from him." From that time Tancred became what he had been so sweetly called to be, a close and faithful follower of his great master. Many very beautiful records are left us of his life. He had a strange familiarity with the angels, who stood by him as he prayed. Once, as he was earnestly interceding in prayer for an obstinate sinner, the angelic friend beside him whispered, "Tancred, your prayer for that soul will be in vain." But the zeal and charity of this true Friar Preacher was not to be checked even by such a word as this: he only prayed the harder, as though he would be heard; and, lo! three days after, he saw the soul for whom he labored flying up safe to Heaven. We can scarce find a more beautiful or instructive anecdote of the might of prayer than this.

Immense numbers of all ranks were attracted by the ever-increasing fame of the new institute; many were men of learning and sanctity, many doubtless very imperfect and uninstructed; yet we are told St. Dominic did not hesitate to employ the latter equally with the former in the work of teaching, in the firm conviction that, when so engaged, God would speak by them as readily as by those better fitted, according to human judgment, for the task; and also, as it would seem, because such work formed a part of his method of training them. This labor of training went on incessantly, for it was his own hand that formed and directed all of those new disciples. We can scarcely estimate aright the prodigious labor which he assigned himself; we see him, as it were, in every city of Italy; and we find him in the same year busy at this engrossing work at Bologna, which was now his headquarters; and never did he relax, for all his engagements, that public office of preaching to which he held himself so solemnly bound.

Very strange must have been the scenes which were often witnessed in the churches where those discourses were delivered. Every day, and sometimes more than once, he preached whilst at Bologna. The people crowded round his pulpit, and often the multitude were forced to adjourn to the open air. They followed him afterwards to his convent door that they might still gaze at him or speak with him. On one of these occasions two young students addressed him, and one said, "Father, I am just come from confession; I pray you obtain from God the pardon of my sins." The saint, after a moment's thought, replied, "Have confidence, my son, for your sins are already pardoned." Then the other made the same request, but the answer was different: "Thou hast not confessed all," said Dominic; and the young man, entering into himself, discovered indeed a secret sin which had escaped his memory.

On another occasion, he had been preaching in one of the public places of the city when, the sermon being ended, a nobleman—the governor of St. Severino, who had been among the audience—pushed his way through the crowd and waited on his knees to receive his blessing as he came down from his pulpit. Nor did his admiration end here; that one sermon had gained for the Order the grant of a church and convent, and established the Friars Preachers in the marches of Ancona.

Every part of the country between the Alps and the Apennines was trodden by the unwearied feet of this great apostle. At Cremona, he met once more his friend and fellow laborer St. Francis, who was there, together with his spiritual daughter St. Clare. The three saints lodged in the same house, and an anecdote of their meeting has been preserved. The water of a well belonging to the house had become unfit for use, and the people of the place, bringing some of it in a vase, begged one of the two saints to bless it that it might recover its sweetness. A graceful contest arose, each wishing the other to undertake the miracle, but the humility of Francis conquered. Dominic blessed the water, which was immediately restored to its clearness and sweet savor.*

In the course of his wanderings, Dominic found himself one night before the gates of St. Colomba, a Cistercian house, but the hour was late and he would not disturb the inmates. "Let us lie down here," he said to his companion, "and pray to God, who will surely care for us." They did so, and both immediately found themselves transported to the interior of the convent. Thus we see it was ever with the same simplicity that Dominic journeyed; it was the poor mendicant friar, with his wallet on his back, and nothing save the light that gleamed on his noble forehead to distinguish him from other men who went barefoot up and down the hills and valleys of Italy, where we may now mark the magnificent foundations of St. Eustorgio of Milan, or Saints John and Paul of Venice, and that other convent which lies amid the wooded hills of Como, and a thousand others, all nurseries of saints.

The festival of the Assumption saw him once more at Bologna, where, on his return, he found matter for both sorrow and displeasure; for Rodolph of Faenza, the procurator of the convent, had in his absence made some additions to the building which the saint judged inconsistent with the profession of holy poverty. Before his departure he had himself left directions for the proposed alterations, and even a kind of plan or model to ensure the preservation of that rigorous observance of poverty which was so dear to him, and which he conceived to be the indispensable condition of religion. He gazed at the new building with tears flowing down his

---

*Such of our readers as are familiar with the Franciscan historians will doubtless be surprised at the omission in these pages of many other interviews between the two great patriarchs, noticed by those writers; but although far from wishing to decide on these as being wholly fictitious, we feel ourselves obliged to pass them over in silence, as they are not given by Dominican authorities, and are often difficult to reconcile with the chronology of the Order.

cheeks. "Will you build palaces whilst I am yet living," he said, "after such a fashion as this? Know then that if you do, you will bring ruin on the order; you have pierced my very heart." Such words did indeed pierce the hearts of those who listened; and during the remainder of his life none dared speak of finishing the building, on which not another stone was laid. And yet the cells he found so luxurious and unsuitable were after all but poor and narrow, and not much superior to those which had been before erected.

How rigid indeed was the poverty and humility of the structure, we may judge from another circumstance which occurred about this time. St. Francis also came to Bologna on a visit to the religious of his Order recently established in the city; but when he found them living in a large and spacious house, he was so indignant that he ordered them every one to quit it, and he himself took up his dwelling in the convent of the Friars Preachers, "which," says Father Candidus Chalippus, "he found more to his taste, and where he passed some days with his friend St. Dominic."

Shortly after the return of the latter to Bologna, a remarkable addition was made to the number of his disciples in the person of Conrad the German. He was a professor of the university, whom the brethren had long ardently desired to have amongst them. On the evening of the Assumption Dominic was in familiar conversation with a certain Cistercian prior, and said to him, "Prior, I will tell you a thing which you must keep secret till my death. Never have I asked anything from God, but He has granted it to me." "Then, father," said the prior, "I marvel that you do not ask the vocation of Master Conrad, whom the brethren desire so greatly to have among them." "The thing is difficult," answered Dominic; "nevertheless, if you will pray with me this night, I doubt not God will incline to our request." That night the prior kept watch in the church by his friend's side; and at the hour of prime, as they entoned the hymn, *Jam lucis orto sidere,* Conrad entered the choir and demanded the habit from the hands of the Saint.

Another of the disciples of this year was John of Vicenza, who deserves a more particular notice. Martin Schio, his father, intended him for the law, and sent him with this intention to Padua, then the great legal university. There, however, a more sublime vocation awaited him. Dominic passed through the city, and no church in the place being large enough to hold the crowds who flocked to hear him, he preached in the great piazza known as the Piazza della Valle. John was there, and that day's preaching put all thoughts of law out of his head. As soon as the sermon was ended, he went to find the preacher and begged to be instantly admitted among his followers and to receive the habit of his order. He made his novitiate at Bologna, but afterwards returned to the convent of Padua, where he became one of the most famous preachers of his time. He was called the apostle of Lombardy, and indeed Lombardy needed an apostle in those unhappy days, torn as it was by the wars, and desolated by the cruelties, of Frederic II and the tyrant Ezzelino.

John was a preacher of peace amid all the terrible calamities of those times. He left one memorial of himself in the salutation "God save you," which he introduced among the citizens of Bologna during a time of public commotion, to excite them to gentler and more courteous treatment of their opponents, and which soon spread through Europe and has lasted to our own day. The angels were seen whispering in his ear as he preached, and his words had ever the same burden, purity and peace. He was a fervent lover of the Rosary, and sometimes, as he preached this devotion, a bright rose would appear on his forehead, or a golden sunny crown would glitter over his head. He had a marvelous power over the fiercest animals; eagles were obedient to him, and a wild untamable horse became tractable at his bidding. His devotion to the memory of Dominic was very remarkable, and Father Stephen of Spain assures us that 100,000 heretics were converted by only hearing the account of his life and miracles as narrated by his devoted follower. The Pope at length appointed him on a mission of pacification to the north of Italy, and such was the success of his labors, especially after a discourse addressed to the populace on that very Piazza della Valle where he had first heard the eloquence of his holy father, that all the contending parties agreed to abandon their differences and accept of peace.

Ezzelino alone held out; and concerning him John had an awful vision. He saw the Almighty seated on His throne, and seeking for a scourge for the chastisement of Lombardy. Ezzelino was chosen as the instrument of His wrath, and surely a more terrible one was never found. At that time John had never seen him, and when first they met and he cast his eyes on him he wept, recognizing him as the man he had seen in his vision, and cried aloud, "It is he whom I saw—the scourge of Lombardy. Woe! woe to thee, unhappy country! for he shall execute judgment on thee to the uttermost." Nevertheless, even this monster was in some degree touched and softened by the preaching of Blessed John.

We can scarcely imagine a more wonderful and beautiful sight than that presented on St. Augustine's day in the Campagna of Verona, when the banks of the Adige saw 300,000 people met together, with the princes and prelates of half Italy, to swear a universal peace. There by the riverside rose an enormous pulpit sixty cubits high, that John, who stood in it to harangue and bless the vast assembly, might be seen by all. Ezzelino himself was there. A few weeks before, he had been burning and laying waste everything that was before him, and Mantua, Brescia and Bologna had all united in besieging the unhappy city of Verona. But one powerful and impassioned appeal of blessed John had changed the entire scene; and now the sun rose on that vast assembly, ranged in order according to their dignities, and in the midst of a profound silence he addressed them again from the words of Our Lord, "Peace I give you, my peace I give unto you";*

---

*These words are engraved on the foot of his image in the Church of the Holy Crown, at Vicenza.

and such was the power of his eloquence that even Ezzelino hid his face and wept. Then was heard a cry that rose from that great multitude as from one man. "Peace, peace," they cried, "and mercy!" And then, when they had given vent to their emotion, John spoke again, and blessed them in the name of the Pope, and all swore to peace and unity; and Ezzelino and his brother Alberic were proclaimed citizens of Padua.

And in the evening there were rejoicings—the first that land had seen for many a day—fires and illuminations, music and happy laughter, all the hours of that summer's night, to celebrate "The Festival of Peace." It was of short duration; yet short as it was, and soon disturbed by the unquiet spirits of evil men, there was a harvest of glory won that day that was worth a thousand battlefields of victory. Ezzelino soon added heresy to his other crimes, and while he deluged Lombardy with blood, he let loose on it the poison of false doctrine. The cities of Italy at length banded against him, and in 1259 he was taken prisoner; and refusing to be cured of his wounds or to receive any food, he died a miserable death of despair.

An obscurity hangs over the last days of John of Vicenza. By some he is said to have died in the prisons of Ezzelino; whilst others affirm him to have found a martyr's death among the Cumans. But, however this may be—and the uncertainty of his fate is but one among many examples of the indifference of the Order to historical fame—the acclamations of Italy declared him "Blessed"; a title from time immemorial allowed by the Sovereign Pontiff, though never ratified by any formal process of beatification.

To return, however, to Dominic and his novices. The vocations of which we have spoken were certainly very remarkable, and were often the result of what we should call a mere chance, directed by the providence of God. Thus a certain priest, greatly drawn to the person of Dominic, yet still uncertain how to act, had recourse to a favorite custom of those days, and opening the Bible after prayer beheld the words addressed to the centurion, "Arise, and go with him, nothing doubting, for I have sent him." The same means were adopted by another, Conrad, bishop of Porto, who was a Cistercian monk and entertained grievous and perplexing suspicions as to the character of the Order. He opened his missal and read the words, *"Laudare, benedicere, praedicare";* and embracing the Saint the next time he met him, he exclaimed, "I am all yours: my habit is Cistercian, but in heart I am a Friar Preacher."

Sometimes the sudden vocations of some caused violent opposition from their friends. A young student, just received to the habit, was beset by all his relations and companions, who threatened if he would not return to the world, to carry him off by violence. Dominic's friends advised him to seek the protection of the magistrates. "Trouble not yourselves, my good friends," he replied, "we have no need of magistrates; even now I see more than two hundred angels standing round about the church, and guarding it from our enemies."

These threats of violence were sometimes, however, carried into execution. There was among the novices a youth whose singular gentleness and sweetness of disposition greatly endeared him to Dominic. His name was Thomas of Paglio; and shortly after his reception his relatives forcibly carried him off by night and dragging him to a neighboring vineyard, stripped off his habit and clothed him in his former worldly garb. Dominic, hearing what had happened, immediately betook himself to his only arms—of prayer; and as he prayed, Thomas was seized with a strange and unendurable heat. "I burn, I burn," he cried; "take these clothes from me, and give me back my habit"; and having once more gained possession of his woollen tunic, he made his way back to the convent in spite of all opposition, and at the touch of that white robe of innocence the fiery anguish was felt no more.

The same author who relates this circumstance tells us that other miraculous signs, besides those of the efficacy of his prayers, were noticed as attaching to the person of Dominic.

A student of the university who served his Mass attested that as he kissed his hand, a divine fragrance was perceptible, which had the power of delivering him from grievous temptations with which he was tormented; and that a certain usurer, whom the Saint communicated, felt the Sacred Host burning against his mouth like hot coals, whereupon he was moved to penitence—and making restitution of all his ill-gotten gains, became sincerely converted to God.

CHAPTER 24

Heretics of northern Italy. Foundation of the third order. Last visit to Rome. Meeting with Fulk of Toulouse. Second general chapter. Division of the Order into provinces. Blessed Paul of Hungary. St. Peter Martyr.

The heretics of northern Italy, of whom frequent mention has been already made, were not less violent in their attacks on the rights and property of the Catholics than their brethren of Languedoc. Protected as they were in many cases by the secular princes, who in their constant feuds one with another made use of them as political instruments, even when no way sharers in their opinions, they availed themselves of every opportunity for seizing the lands of the Church, so that the clergy were in many places reduced to the same state of degradation and dependence which had already produced such frightful effects in Languedoc.

It was to oppose this abuse, and to place a barrier against the track of the Manichean heresy, that Dominic founded his third order. Intimately entering into the needs of his age, his quick and sagacious eye perceived that his institute was imperfect so long as it aimed at the salvation of souls only through the ministrations of preaching, or the discipline of convent rule. The world itself was to be sanctified; therefore, out of the world itself should be formed the instruments of sanctification. The "Militia of Jesus Christ," as the new institute was called, ranked under the standard of the Church those of either sex who had received no call to separate themselves from the ordinary life of seculars, and yet desired to shelter it under the skirts of the religious mantle. The first object contemplated in its institution was the defense of ecclesiastical property; but this was a very small part of the work to which, in God's providence, it was afterwards called.

The third orders of Dominic and Francis completed the conquest of the world. They placed the religious habit under the breastplate of warriors and the robes of kings. They were like streams, carrying the fertility of Paradise to many a dry and barren region, so that the wilderness blossomed like a rose. Something of the barrier between the world and the cloister was broken down; and the degrees of heroic sanctity were placed, as it were, within the grasp of thousands, who else, perhaps, had never risen above the ordinary standard.

These third orders have given us a crowd of saints, dearer to us, perhaps, and more familiar than any others, insofar as we feel able to claim their close sympathy with ourselves; and the more so, that they are a perpetual witness to us that no path in life is so busy, or so beset with temptations, but that God's grace may cover it with the very choicest beauty of holiness. As time went on and the circumstances of its first institution had passed away, the Militia of Jesus Christ exchanged its name for that of the "Order of Penance of St. Dominic," and by degrees assumed more and more of the religious character; particularly after St. Catherine of Siena had by her example given new shape to the Order, insofar as regarded its adoption by her own sex; and in her life, and that of the numberless saints who have trodden in her steps, we see the final triumph and vindication of what we may venture to call the primary Dominican idea—namely, that the highest walks of contemplation are not incompatible with the exercises of active charity and the labor for souls; but that a union of both is possible, which more nearly fulfills our conception of the life of Christ than the separated perfection of either.

The circumstances attending the first establishment of this Order are unknown to us: many authors are of opinion that it is to be referred to a much earlier date, and that it was even the first of the three founded by St. Dominic, having been originally instituted in Languedoc for the resistance of the Albigenses. It is very probable that some kind of association had been formed by him among the Catholic confederates and afterwards developed into a more regular shape, when the renewed encroachment of the heretics in Lombardy rendered a similar means of protection desirable; for such a supposition would harmonize very much with St. Dominic's general method of action.

It is certainly not a little remarkable that an uncertainty hangs over the foundation both of this institute, and even of the first regular establishment of his greater Order, which shows how little the thought of human praise or celebrity found its way into the soul of their author—like the silence in the Gospels on the life of Mary, which tells us more of her sublime humility than many words could do—and this humility and simplicity of action forms also, if we mistake not, a large feature in the portraiture of Dominic. It is without doubt, however, that to him must be ascribed the first origin of this form of the religious life; for the third order of St. Francis, which so long divided with its sister institute the favor of Christendom, was not founded until 1224, three years after St. Dominic's death.

The December of 1220 saw Dominic once more in Rome. This, his last visit to a city which had been the scene of so many labors and miracles, is marked by the date of various fresh briefs and privileges granted to his Order by its faithful friend and benefactor, Pope Honorius. The first of these briefs was for remedying some irregularities which had taken place in the ordinations of the brethren; others were addressed to the bishops and prelates of the Church, recommending the Order to their protection in terms of the warmest eulogy; and one, dated April 1221, had reference to the nuns of St. Sixtus, to whom it secured the possessions formerly enjoyed by the community of the Trastevere. This visit to Rome was the occasion of a meeting that must have been full of the tenderest interest to the heart of Dominic.

Fulk of Toulouse was then at the pontifical court; little

more than three years had elapsed since that dispersion of the sixteen brethren of St. Romain, which had taken place in his own presence, and now he witnessed the triumph of an order to which he had been so true a nursing father. Three years had converted the prior of Prouille, the leader of that devoted little band whose destinies, to every eye but his, seemed then so hopeless and obscure, into the master general of a great order whose convents were spread through the length and breadth of Christendom. All things in their respective positions were changed, save Dominic himself; but Fulk could have detected no difference between Dominic the apostle of Languedoc and Dominic the master of the Friars Preachers, save in the adoption of a yet poorer habit and those few silver hairs which, we are told, his long labors, and not his years, had begun to sprinkle over his tonsured head. But the heroic heart, the patient gentle spirit, the simple hearty joyousness of his friend, were still the same; and so, too, was the disinterestedness of his soul, of which Fulk had proof in a transaction whose acts are still preserved.

This was the renunciation, on Dominic's part, of that grant, formerly made by the bishop, of the sixth part of the tenths of his revenues for the support of the Order when it was yet young and friendless. The principle of poverty had since then been more strictly developed in the institute, and Dominic believed he could no longer in conscience accept this revenue—even though given, in the very terms of the grant, as an alms to the poor of Christ. Fulk, on his part, confirmed the donation of the church of Notre-Dame-de-Fangeaux to the religious of Prouille; for it will be observed that the rigid law of poverty which he enforced on the rest of his Order, he relaxed in favor of the communities of women, for whose state he judged a moderate revenue was requisite to be secured.

It were to be wished that more particulars had been left us of the great patriarch's last appearance in the Roman capital. Rome had witnessed the *épopée* of his life; henceforward St. Sixtus and Santa Sabina were to become classic names among his children; and if, as we have reason to believe, a prophetic knowledge had been granted him that the period of his death was not far off, there must have been a peculiar charm in his parting visits to these familiar scenes. As usual, every day saw him at the grating of St. Sixtus, renewing his exhortations to the sisters to keep fast to the holy rule under whose power they had been transformed into the saintly life.

The affection which he so faithfully preserved for these spiritual children is illustrated by one of the miracles related to us by Sister Cecilia as happening at this time. Upon a certain day he stopped at the gate, and without entering asked of the portress how Sister Theodora, Sister Tedrano and Sister Ninfa were. She replied they were all three ill of fever. "Tell them," said Dominic, "from me, that I command them all to be cured"; and at the delivery of the message they all three arose in perfect health.

Dominic's presence was always peculiarly welcomed in Rome, where he was well-known to many of the cardinals and others attached to the Pontifical court; and these vied one with another in the diligence with which they sought his companionship; for as it was well expressed in the bull of his canonization, "none ever spoke to him and went away without feeling the better."

But popularity was the last thing that he sought; and it is to be believed that the celebrity he enjoyed at Rome was one of the principal motives for his formerly removing his residence from thence to Bologna, whither he now returned early in the month of May, to meet the second chapter of the Order, which was about to assemble in that city. On his way he passed through Bolsena, where he was often accustomed to stay, being at such times always hospitably entertained by a certain citizen who, to prove his friendship for his guest, left it as an obligation to his heirs that they should always receive and lodge all the Friars Preachers who should pass through Bolsena in time to come, a condition still faithfully observed at the end of the thirteenth century, as Theodoric of Apoldia narrates. This particular mark of esteem was probably a token of gratitude, for it happened that in one of his visits to this house, Dominic had preserved the vines of his host in the midst of a violent storm which devastated all the surrounding vineyards.

The second chapter of Bologna opened on the 30th of May, 1221. Dominic, at the commencement of their proceedings, addressed the brethren at considerable length, laying before them the state of the Order in the countries wherein it was already established and proposing its still farther extension. It appeared that sixty convents were already founded, and a yet greater number in course of erection. For the more perfect government, therefore, of the Order, it was now divided into eight provinces, and a prior-provincial appointed to each of them; namely, to Spain, Toulouse, France, Lombardy, Rome, Germany, Hungary and England. These two latter countries were yet to be colonized by the Friars Preachers; and the appointment and dispatch of their first missioners formed one of the undertakings of this chapter. Of the foundation of the English province we shall presently speak more at length; that of Hungary was placed under the government of a native of the country named Paul, who had recently been received into the Order by Dominic, and had previously filled the chair of canon law in the university of Bologna.

Immediately after his reception, Paul was dispatched to his new province with four companions, of whom one was blessed Sadoc of Poland, the tale of whose martyrdom, with his forty-eight companions, is among the most interesting incidents recorded in the annals of the Order.* The crown of martyrdom was reserved for Paul also. He received it the following year, together with ninety of his brethren, from the hands of the Cuman Tartars, who infested the borders of Hungary and whose conversion to the Christian Faith had so long formed the cherished daydream of St. Dominic.

---

*See No. 2. of "Catholic Legends," in this series.

It would seem, indeed, as though this nation, whose barbarity exceeded that of any of the savage hordes that still hung round the boundaries of Christian Europe, was destined, if not to be converted by his Order, at least to fill its ranks with an army of martyrs. Another of Paul's earliest companions, blessed Berengarius of Poland, the archbishop of Cracow, was slain by them a few years afterwards, and in 1260 seventy more were sent to join their company; all of whom it is said, were children and disciples of the glorious St. Hyacinth.

The extraordinary manner in which these first founders propagated the Order in the countries whither they were sent may be estimated by the number of these martyrs: the ninety who died in company with blessed Paul must all have been gathered into the ranks of the institute within a year from the period of his departure from Bologna. If this may be taken as anything like a fair proof of the stimulus to religion which everywhere followed on the appearance of the Friars Preachers, it may perhaps dispose us the more readily to believe an incident which is said to have occurred just before the meeting of this second chapter.

Two of the brethren who were travelling towards Bologna were met on the road by a man who joined himself to their company and fell into conversation with them. He inquired the object of their journey, and being informed of the approaching chapter, "What," he asked, "is the business which is likely to be discussed?" "The establishment of our brethren in new countries," replied one of the friars; "England and Hungary are amongst those proposed." "And Greece also," said the stranger, "and Germany, is it not so?" "You say truly," returned the friar; "it is said that we shall shortly be dispersed into all these provinces." Then the stranger uttered a loud cry as of great anguish, and exclaiming, "Your Order is my confusion," he leapt into the air, and so disappeared; and the friars knew that it was the voice of the great enemy of man, who was thus compelled to bear witness to the power which the servants of God exercised against him.

The convents of the Friars Preachers in the new province of Hungary may be said to have been planted in blood, that seed of the Church which has never failed to bring forth the hundredfold. "In blood were they sown," says Marchese, "and in blood did they increase; so that the more they were slain, so much the more numerous did they become, till within a brief space a province was erected of vast extent, including the countries of Moldavia, Transylvania, Croatia, Bosnia and Dalmatia"; and this was afterwards divided into two, the second of which bearing the name of Dalmatia, contained a great number of convents, illustrious for the names of many saints and martyrs who flourished in them.

In his address to the assembled fathers, Dominic gave them an earnest exhortation to the pursuit of sacred learning, that they might be the better fitted for the charge laid on them by their vocation as Preachers. He reminded them that the briefs granted so liberally by the Vicar of Christ recommended them to the favor of the universal Church, inasmuch as they were therein declared to be laborers for God's honor and the salvation of souls, and that this end could never be attained without a diligent application to the divine Scriptures; he therefore enjoined all who should be engaged in the sacred office of preaching to apply without ceasing to the study of theology, and to carry always with them a copy of the Gospels and the seven canonical Epistles.

The letter commonly attributed to St. Dominic, and purporting to be addressed by him to his religious in the province of Poland after the conclusion of the second general chapter, has been questioned by some as of doubtful authenticity. Without venturing to decide the disputed point, we may refer to the peculiar force with which the study of the divine Scriptures is recommended in this letter, as exactly harmonizing with the tone of his address to the chapter: it is given by Malvenda and Bzovius as undoubtedly the work of St. Dominic, nor was its authorship ever called in question until the time of Echard. Touron, in his life of the Saint, has entered into a critical examination of the question and decides that the evidence is all in favor of its authenticity; while the letter itself is, as he says, not unworthy of him. It breathes a noble spirit throughout, exhorting the brethren to a fervent observance of their rule and a life worthy of the angelic ministry with which they were charged. "Let us apply ourselves with energy," he adds in the concluding paragraph, "to the great actions which God demands of us"; a word of heroic exhortation which has rung for centuries in the ears of his children, and led them on to aim at something of that greatness in the paths of holiness which it points out to them as the object of their vocation.

It was probably whilst the chapter was still sitting that Dominic gave the habit to one who was eventually to become one of the brightest ornaments of the Order. Peter of Verona, the son of heretical parents but himself destined to die a martyr in defense of the Faith, was at that time a student in the University of Bologna, and though a mere youth of sixteen, his learning and holiness had already made his name respected among his fellows. Dominic did not live to see the glory of his future career, yet even now there were sufficient indications of it to make him peculiarly dear to the heart of the Saint, who felt himself drawn by a powerful attraction to the youth whose angelic innocence of life had been united, even from infancy, to an extraordinary courage in the profession of the Catholic Faith. "The hammer of the heretics," as he was commonly termed, he died by their hand, writing on the ground in his blood the word *Credo*; and among all the disciples whom St. Dominic left behind him to continue his work, we may single out St. Peter Martyr as the one on whom his mantle may most surely be said to have fallen.

Leaving for awhile the course of St. Dominic's life, we will proceed to say a few words concerning the foundation of the Order in our own island, trusting that the digression, if it be one, may be pardoned on a subject so full of interest to the English reader.

CHAPTER 25

The Order in England. Arrival at Oxford of Gilbert de Fresnoy. Celebrated
Englishmen of the Order. Walter Malclerk, Bacon, and Fishacre. The
Order and the universities. The German province.

Gilbert de Fresnoy was the person appointed by Dominic
to undertake the foundation of the new province of England; the establishment of which was, it is said, resolved
on in compliance with the earnest entreaties of certain distinguished persons of that nation. Previous to the period
of this second chapter, we can find no mention of Brother
Gilbert; but we are told he immediately set out with twelve
companions, travelling in the suite of Peter de Roche, bishop
of Winchester, whose presence at Bologna, on his return
from the Holy Land, may probably have hastened the dispatch of the English mission.

They arrived at Canterbury some time in the month of
June, where the archbishop, Stephen Langton, was then
residing. He received the newcomers with extraordinary kindness, and insisted on Gilbert's addressing a sermon to the
people on that very day. It must have been a somewhat
hard tax on the preacher's powers, the more so as he probably felt the future success of his enterprise, insofar as it depended on the favor of the archbishop, was in no small degree
likely to hang on the good or bad opinion he might form
of his sermon. Happily it was received with universal applause. It was declared to be grave, elegant, and full of wisdom; and Stephen promised both him and his companions
that they should never fail to find in him a friend and a
protector. They proceeded on their journey to London, and
thence to Oxford, where they arrived on the feast of the
Assumption; and having settled in the parish of St. Edward's,

they immediately erected a little oratory dedicated to Our Lady, and opened schools, which from the name of the parish were called St. Edward's schools.

Thus the children of St. Dominic found themselves at length in connection with the three great universities of Europe—Bologna, Paris, and Oxford; although, indeed, it was not until the famous struggle which took place seven years afterwards at Paris that any of their numbers were raised to the professors' chairs. But from the very first, the character they aimed at as a teaching order was universally avowed, as the very letter of their constitutions—and the provisions they assign for the carrying out of their system of study, and receiving degrees—evidently show.

Yet it is worthy of notice that the first occasion on which we find any formal mention of their schools is in the account of those opened at Oxford; for hitherto, at both the other universities, they are rather spoken of as students, than as having yet assumed the office of teachers, except in the pulpits. They continued to reside in the parish of St. Edward's till the king granted them a site of ground outside the walls; but this place proving inconvenient for their purpose, owing to its distance from the city, they betook themselves to prayer that they might find favor in the eyes of the university authorities. Nor were their prayers in vain; for they soon after obtained a settlement in the Jewish quarter in the town, "to the intent," says Wood, "that they might induce the Jews to embrace the Christian Faith, as well by the sanctity of their lives as by preaching the word, in which they excelled."

Shortly after this the canons of St. Frideswide let them some lands at a low rate; and, aided by further benefactions from the countess of Oxford and Walter Malclerk, bishop of Carlisle, they built themselves a house and church, which stood partly in the parish of St. Aldate on ground belonging to the canons before mentioned. The composition entered into between the canons and themselves in regard to this ground still exists, and seems to bear a little hardly on the friars; nevertheless, we are assured they were

in favor with them as with the citizens, "being as accept-
able to the latter for their piety, as they were to the former
for their learning." Forty years afterwards, their houses being
too small to accommodate the immense number of scholars
who flocked to hear them, they removed to an island in
the river, "in the south suburbs, and most delightful for
situation," where they continued to reside until the general
destruction of religious houses in the time of Henry VIII.

The first who taught in the schools of St. Edward was
one John of St. Giles, "a man," says Matthew Paris, "skill-
full in the art of medicine, a great professor of divinity,
and excellently learned and instructing." They were there
greatly cramped for room, but in their island house, we
read, they had larger space; and that the acts of divinity
were given in the church and chapter house, whilst the lectures on philosophy were delivered in the cloister. They became in time the greatest ornaments of the university,
eminent, as it is said, for all the learning of the time.

Of the great men whom they gave to England it would
be impossible to recount all the names; yet some we should
not pass over without a word of notice. Walter Malclerk,
their first benefactor, became afterwards a member of their
community, and resigned his bishopric and every other dignity he possessed to assume their humble habit. His history
is a remarkable one. His noble birth, attractive manners
and extraordinary genius raised him to the highest favor
at the court of Henry III, who, besides elevating him to
the bishopric of Carlisle, made him lord high treasurer of
the kingdom. In this position many years were spent in a
life of brilliant state services; but, as it would seem, the
taint of worldly ambition for a time obscured his better
qualities and his religious character. After a brief period
of disgrace at court, we find him again at the head of affairs in 1234; and when, eleven years later, the king marched
from London against his revolted subjects, he left Walter
Malclerk to govern the kingdom during the period of his
absence in the field.

But God had destined the conclusion of his life to present us with another of those many singular conversions whose stories crowd the annals of the Dominican Order. We are not told what was the immediate cause which wrought the change in his views and desires and disgusted him with the very career which he had hitherto so ardently pursued; but as soon as grace had effectually touched his heart, he resolved on a generous and entire sacrifice; and resigning his bishopric and distributing all he possessed to the poor, he took the habit of the Friars Preachers at Oxford, where he gave himself wholly to a life of penance and religious fervor. This act of heroic renunciation filled all England with surprise, whilst the friars themselves were forced to admire the marvel which had transformed a courtier and a minister of state into the humble novice of a mendicant community. He died two years afterwards, and left behind him several learned works.

Another renowned member of the Order was Robert Bacon, the brother, or as some say, the uncle, of the yet more celebrated Roger Bacon. He joined the friars when an old man, out of the great love he bore St. Dominic. Together with him we must notice his dear and bosom friend, Richard Fishacre, whom Ireland calls "the most learned among the learned." He was a great admirer of Aristotle, whose works he ever carried in his bosom. "He was," says Wood, "renowned both as a philosopher and as a divine, for which reason he was so dear to Bacon that he became his inseparable companion; and as they were most constant associates in life, so neither could they be separated in death. For as the turtledove, bewailing its lost mate, dies, so, Bacon being dead, Fishacre neither could nor would survive." He was the first English preacher who commented on the "Book of Sentences."

Other convents of the Order were soon affiliated to the parent house, the Black Friars in London being one of the earliest of these foundations. Indeed, they seem to have been deservedly popular among the English, who were then, as now, a sermon-loving people; and so great were the crowds that flocked to hear the new preachers that the sermons were generally delivered out of doors; and we find frequent mention of the "portable pulpits" they used, convenient to be set up in the public streets.

From England they soon found their way to Ireland; Father Ronald, an Irishman by birth and one of the first missionaries from Bologna, being sent over there very shortly after the settlement of his companions at Oxford. He died archbishop of Armagh, having lived to see the Order spread through almost every province of the island. The spectacle exhibited in the example of Walter Malclerk was again and again repeated in a long list of eminent men of both countries, who, in the succeeding centuries, laid aside every dignity to become children in the novitiates of the Friars Preachers.

The Franciscans soon followed in the track of their sister order, and an interesting account is given us of their first arrival at Oxford, where they were generously and hospitably received by their Dominican brethren. Two of the Friars Minors, ignorant of the country and perfectly friendless, had first begged at the door of the Benedictine monastery of Abingdon, and being unknown and mistaken for "mimics or disguised persons," were driven away with bad usage. They would have passed the night in the road if a young monk, touched with compassion, had not secretly hid them in a hayloft; and the next morning they pursued their way to Oxford, praying as they went, that "God would dispose some goodwill for them among the men of Oxford. Nor were their prayers in vain; for being come to the city, and going directly to the house of the Dominicans in the Jewry, though they durst scarce hope for it, they were by them entertained with extraordinary care and charity, and having found them as friendly as the Abingdonians had been merciless, they had the benefit of the refectory and dormitory till the eighth day."* This mutual exchange of hospitality forms one of the

---

*Steven's Dugdale, from the MS. of A. Wood.

most beautiful features in the history of the two Orders, and might be illustrated by innumerable examples of a similar kind.

It will be seen that both at Oxford and Paris, and also at Bologna, the Order immediately assumed a position in connection with the universities. In fact, this connection was one of the principal objects contemplated by these foundations in those cities. The constitutions of the Order were drawn up with the view of providing for a regular system of study; and at the same time things were so arranged that the student was still under religious discipline, and study was made only a part of his religious training. They were not cast abroad on the great world of university life to shift for themselves; but the idea was, that in all the great centers of learning there should be a religious house, to which the students of the Order were bound as members of its community during the period of their university course; and so the university and community life were woven together, and the intellectual advantages of the one laid under the restrictions of the other.

The nature of their studies was regulated and limited so as, if not exclusively theological, at least to bear more or less on theology. Merely secular and honorary distinctions and degrees, granted by the university authorities, were not recognized, the Order reserving a system of graduation in its own hands; and so by means of very minute and most sagacious legislation, one of the great Dominican ideas was gradually given an active and practical existence, namely, the Christianizing of the intellect, the cultivation of human science as a handmaid to the science of divine things, and the pursuit of learning under the safeguard of that subjection and spiritual bondage which secured humility. This was the system which, founded by Dominic himself, in the succeeding age produced St. Thomas. We say, founded by St. Dominic himself, for it is in the very year following that of his first visit to the brethren of St. James, before spoken of, that we find that community described by Pope Honorius as "The brethren of the Order of Preachers, studying in the Sacred Page at Paris."

Doubtless it was the peculiar adaptation of this system to the wants of the day which produced the surprising effects we observe in the period immediately succeeding Dominic's death. The learning and the piety of Europe then flowed into the Order of Preachers like a great wave. Blessed Jordan, his successor in the government, is said to have clothed more than a thousand novices with his own hand; and Martene, before quoted, says of him, "There entered under his rule at Paris, into the Order of Preachers, so many masters in theology, doctors in law, bachelors and masters of arts, and such a countless multitude of others, that the whole world stood amazed at the grace which attended their preaching, and at the wonderful things that they did."*

Before resuming the thread of Dominic's personal history, we cannot pass without notice the foundation of the German province, which took place at the same time as those of England and Hungary. The provincial appointed for Germany by the chapter of Bologna was that same Master Conrad who had been gained to the Order in so extraordinary a manner by the progress of Dominic; and when, soon after his arrival in his new government, the people of Cologne demanded a foundation of the friars among them, Henry of Utrecht was chosen as superior of the new house destined to be so celebrated in the Dominican annals. Since his profession at Paris in company with Jordan of Saxony, as related in a former chapter, he had remained in that city, where the charm of his character no less than of his preaching had obtained him universal applause.

But popularity had no power to change or disturb the perfect calm and humility of his soul. "Never was there seen

---

*Those of our readers who may be curious for a more particular account of the Dominican system of study, and its happy blending of the intellectual and monastic training, we may refer to an article in the *Dublin Review* (Sept. 1845), on "the Ancient Irish Dominican Schools"; and another, from a well-known writer, in the *British Critic* (Jan. 1843), on "Dante and the Catholic Philosophy."

in him," says Blessed Jordan, "any trouble, emotion, or sadness; the peace of God and the joy of a good conscience were so painted in his countenance that you needed but to see him to learn how to love God." It is said that when the news of his entrance into the Order reached Utrecht, the canon who had educated him from boyhood, and two other of his friends, were greatly grieved; and before setting out for Paris to persuade him to return, they spent a night in earnest prayer to obtain light from God on the subject. As they prayed, a voice sounded through the church, saying, "It is the Lord who has done this, and He does not change." Relieved from their anxiety, they abandoned their first purpose, and exhorted him instead to a faithful perseverance.

In 1224 the convent of Cologne was at length founded. Henry went there alone; but his talents, and the singular attractiveness of his virtues, soon gathered many about him; his influence over the people was extraordinary. The besetting vice of the nation at that time was blasphemy—one, perhaps, the most difficult to eradicate from the inveterate force of habit: yet such was the power of Henry's eloquence that he inspired the whole city with a horror of every kind of imprecation.

Cologne became in the succeeding century the nursery of the Dominican Order. Within its walls St. Ambrose of Siena and St. Thomas of Aquin studied together under Albert the Great; names to which might be associated a crowd of others who illustrated their age with the splendor of their learning and the saintliness of their lives; and when, in a succeeding age, the violence of heresy laid waste so many a sanctuary and the children of Dominic were foremost to suffer for a cause they had ever been foremost to defend, there were not wanting those who, by the generous sacrifice of their lives, gave the crowning splendor of martyrdom to the glories of Cologne.

CHAPTER 26

Dominic's last missionary journey. His return to Bologna, and illness. His death. Revelations of his glory. His canonization, and the translation of his relics.

The career of Dominic was now fast drawing to a close; but five years had been granted him to reap the harvest of his long solitary labors, and yet, short as the time might seem, it was enough: he had lived to see that little seed, planted in the fields of Languedoc, grown into a mighty tree, whose branches might now be said to cover the earth, and his work was accomplished.

The chapter had broken up in the latter part of May; on the 30th of the same month, Dominic received an unusual mark of honor from the magistrates of Bologna, who by a solemn act admitted him to the rights of a citizen, with the privilege of entering their council and voting on all public questions. Nor did they confine this expression of their gratitude to his person alone, but declared it to be henceforth granted to all his successors in the supreme government of the Order. When we remember that it was through his means that peace had been restored to the city after it had been for years the victim of cruel civil dissensions, we feel that this was but a fitting and natural testimony of affection from the citizens to their deliverer.

In the following month Dominic left Bologna on his last missionary journey. At Venice he met Cardinal Ugolino, and laid the foundation of the great convent of Saints John and Paul; some say that this visit was undertaken with the idea that some opportunity might still present itself which should enable him to pass to the countries of the infidels, a plan he had nearly laid aside. And yet there is little doubt that

222

even before he left Bologna he had received from God an intimation of his approaching release. Blessed Jordan tells us that, being one night in fervent prayer, an unusually powerful emotion overwhelmed him with the desire to be with God; and suddenly a youth of dazzling beauty appeared before him, and calling him by name, said to him, "Dominic, my well-beloved, come to the nuptials, come."

And there seemed after this time a certain change about him, as though he knew the end of all sadness was at hand. As he sat in familiar conversation with some of the students and clergy of the university, he spoke with his usual cheerfulness and sweetness for some time, then, rising to bid them farewell, he said, "You see me now in health, but before the next feast of the Assumption I shall be with God." These words surprised those who heard them; for indeed there were no signs of approaching sickness, or of the failure of that vigorous and manly spirit for which he had been ever distinguished.

Nevertheless, when he returned to Bologna after a few weeks, a marked change was visible. His hair was thinning on his temples, the excessive heat of the summer appeared to render him languid and exhausted; and yet, for all he was evidently suffering, he never relaxed in any of his usual labors. It was the 6th of August: he had travelled from Venice to Bologna on foot as usual, stopping at Milan, and preaching as he went; nay, there was even a more than ordinary zeal observable in his conduct, as if he felt the time was shortening, and desired that the last hour should find him watching and at work.

As he approached Bologna, the extraordinary heat affected him painfully. It was evening when he reached the convent of St. Nicholas; in spite of his fatigue, he remained until past midnight conversing with the procurator and prior, and then proceeded to the church, where he continued in prayer until the hour of matins, notwithstanding their earnest entreaty that for once he would consent to rest during the office. As soon as it was finished, he was obliged to give way to the violence of the fever, the advances of which he had hitherto disregarded: they begged him to allow himself a little repose on a bed, but he gently refused, and desired to be laid on a sacking which was stretched upon the ground. His head was swimming with the pain and heaviness of his malady; but even then he would not spare himself, but desired the novices to be called round him that he might speak to them, for what he felt would be the last time; and all the time his patience and sweetness were never interrupted; nor, in spite of the pallor of death that fast overspread his noble features, was the joy and cheerfulness of their expression for a moment changed.

The brethren were overwhelmed with affliction; and hoping that some relief might be afforded by a change of air, they took him to Santa Maria dei Monti, situated on a hill just outside the city. He himself, however, well knowing that no human skill could avail for his recovery, called the community around him, that he might leave them his last testament. "Have charity in your hearts," he said, "practice humility after the example of Jesus Christ, and make your treasure and riches out of voluntary poverty. You know that to serve God is to reign; but you must serve Him in love, and with a whole heart. It is only by a holy life and by fidelity to your rule, that you can do honor to your profession."

It was thus he continued to speak as he lay on the ground, whilst Fr. Ventura and the other brethren stood weeping around him. "He did not even sigh," says Ventura in his evidence; "I never heard him speak a more excellent and edifying sermon." The rector of Santa Maria made a rather unsuitable interruption to this scene by suggesting that, should the Saint die in that convent, he would certainly not wish to be carried elsewhere for burial. This obliged the brethren to refer the question to himself, and he immediately replied, with some energy, "Look well to it that I am buried nowhere but under the feet of my brethren. Carry me away from here, and let me die in that vineyard;

then no one will be able to oppose my being buried in our own church." And although they almost feared that he would expire on the road, they nevertheless fulfilled his command, and brought him back to St. Nicholas, carrying him through the fields and vineyards, wrapped in a woollen sacking, weeping as they went.

Having no cell of his own, he was taken to that of Brother Moneta, and there laid on his bed. He had already received Extreme Unction at Santa Maria; and after remaining quiet for about an hour, he called the prior to him, saying, "Prepare," (meaning for the recommendation of a departing soul); but as they were about to begin, he added, "You can wait a little"; and it was perhaps during these moments that, according to the revelation made to St. Bridget, the Mother of God, to whom he had ever shown himself so loyal and loving a servant, visibly appeared to him and promised that she would never withdraw her patronage and protection from his Order.

He was now sinking so rapidly that they saw a very short time would rob them of the Father to whom their hearts cleaved with so overflowing a tenderness; all were bathed in tears. Rodolph held his head, and gently wiped the death sweat from his forehead; Ventura bent over him, saying, "Dear Father, you leave us desolate and afflicted; remember us, and pray for us to God." Then the dying Saint summoned his fast-failing strength, and, raising his hands and eyes to Heaven, he said in a clear and distinct voice: "Holy Father, since by Thy mercy I have ever fulfilled Thy will, and have kept and preserved those whom Thou hast given me, now I recommend them to Thee. Do Thou keep them; do Thou preserve them."

Then, turning to his children, he added tenderly, "Do not weep, my children; I shall be more useful to you where I am now going, than I have ever been in this life." One of them again asking him to tell them exactly where he would be buried, he replied in his former words, "Under the feet of my brethren." He seemed then for the first time to perceive that they had laid him on a kind of bed, and obliged them to remove him, and place him on ashes on the floor: the novices left the room, and about twelve of the elder brethren alone remained beside him. He made his general confession to Father Ventura, and when it was finished, he added, addressing himself to the others, "Thanks be to God, whose mercy has preserved me in perfect virginity until this day: if you would keep chastity, guard yourselves from all dangerous conversations, and watch over your own hearts."

But, an instant afterwards, a kind of scruple seemed to seize him; and he turned to Ventura with a touching humility, saying, "Father, I fear lest I have sinned in speaking of this grace before our brethren." The recommendation of his soul now began, and he followed the prayers as well as he could; they could see his lips moving; and as they recited the words, *"Subvenite, Sancti Dei; occurrite, angeli Domini, suscipientes animam ejus, offerentes eam in conspectu Altissimi,"* he stretched his arms to Heaven and expired, being in the 51st year of his age.

His weeping children stood for awhile around the body without venturing to touch the sacred remains; but as it became necessary to prepare for their interment, they began to strip off the tunic in which he died, and which was not his own, but one belonging to Brother Moneta; and having done so, their tears of tenderness flowed afresh, for they discovered an iron chain tightly bound round his waist, and from the scars and marks it had produced, it was evident that it had been worn for many years. Rodolph removed it with the utmost reverence, and it was afterwards delivered to blessed Jordan, his successor in the government of the Order, who kept it as a precious relic.

It was a singular and appropriate circumstance that the funeral obsequies of this great man should be performed by one who had ever during life shown himself his truest and most faithful friend. Cardinal Ugolino Conti came from Venice to Bologna to preside at a ceremony which, in spite of their orphanhood and desolation, his children could scarcely feel a melancholy one. Ugolino claimed this office as his right, and it was he who celebrated the funeral Mass. The people of Bologna, who had shown an extraordinary sympathy with the friars during the last days of Dominic's illness and had made continual prayers for their benefactor's recovery, followed the procession in a dense body.

Patriarchs, bishops, and abbots from all the neighboring country swelled the train. Among them was one who had been a dear and familiar friend of the departed Saint, Albert, prior of the convent of St. Catherine in Bologna, a man of great piety and warm affections. As he followed, sorrowful, and bathed in tears, he observed that the friars chanted the Psalms with a certain joyfulness and calm of spirit; and this had such an effect on him that he too stayed his tears and began to sing with them. And then he began to reflect on the misery of this present state, and the folly of mourning it as an evil, when a holy soul was released from bondage and sent to the presence of his God. With this thought in his heart he went up, in an impulse of devout affection, to the sacred body, and bending over it and conquering his grief, he embraced his dead friend and congratulated him on his blessedness. When he rose, an emotion of wonderful happiness was observable on his countenance. He went up to the prior of St. Nicholas, and taking him by the hand, "Dear Father, rejoice with me," he said; "Master Dominic has even now spoken to me, and assured me that before the year is ended we shall both be re-united in Christ." And the event proved his words, for before the close of the year Albert was with his friend.

Nor was this the only revelation of the blessedness of Dominic which was granted to his friends. At the same hour in which he expired, Father Guallo Romanoni, prior of the convent of Friars Preachers in Brescia, fell asleep, leaning against the bell-tower of his church, and he seemed to see two ladders let down from an opening in the sky above him. At the top of one stood Our Lord, and His blessed Mother was at the summit of the other. Angels were going up and down them, and at their foot was seated one in the habit of the Order, but his face was covered with his hood, after the fashion in which the friars are wont to cover the face of the dead when they are carried out for burial. The ladders were drawn up into Heaven, and he saw the unknown friar received into the company of the angels, surrounded by a dazzling glory, and borne to the very feet of Jesus.

Guallo awoke, not knowing what the vision could signify; and hastening to Bologna, he found that his great patriarch had breathed his last at the very moment in which it had appeared to him, namely, six in the evening; and he judged it as a certain token that the soul of Dominic had been taken up to Heaven. Moreover, on that same day, the 6th of August, Brother Raoul had gone from Rome to Tivoli in company with Tancred, the prior of Santa Sabina, and at the hour of Sext he celebrated Mass and made an earnest memento for his holy founder, whom he knew to be then lying in the extremity of sickness at Bologna. And as he did so, he seemed to see the great road reaching out of that city, and walking along it was the figure of Dominic between two men of venerable aspect, crowned with a golden coronet, and dazzling with light.

Nor was this the last of these visions. A student of the university, warmly attached to the Saint, who had been prevented by business from assisting at his funeral, saw him on the following night in a state of surpassing glory, as it seemed to him, seated in a particular spot in the church of St. Nicholas. The vision was so distinct that, as he gazed on it, he exclaimed, "How, Master Dominic, are you still here?" "Yes," was the reply, "I live, indeed, since God has deigned to grant me an eternal life in Heaven." When he sent to St. Nicholas on the following morning, he found the place of sepulture was the same indicated in his dream.

We shall not attempt the task of transcribing the miracles which rendered the place of his rest glorious; they already fill volumes entirely devoted to the purpose of recording

them. His brethren of Bologna have been severely blamed
by many authors, because, in spite of this accumulation of
prodigies and Divine favors, they allowed the body to remain under the plain flagstone where it had been placed
by the care of Rodolph of Faenza, without any sign of honor
to distinguish it to the eye. And what is more, in spite of
the crowds who flocked thither day and night on pilgrimage,
and whose gratitude for the graces poured out on them with
such abundance was attested by a very forest of waxen im-
ages and other similar votive offerings which they hung over
the spot, no move was made by the authorities of the Order
to obtain the canonization of the Saint.

This conduct has, as we have said, been censured as a
culpable neglect; but we may perhaps be permitted to instance it as an example of that simplicity and modesty which
Dominic left behind him as a heritage to his children. The
answer of one of the friars, when questioned on the subject,
may be taken as a sample of the spirit of the whole body.
"What need for canonization?" he said; "the holiness of Master Dominic is known to God: it matters little if it be declared
publicly by man." A feeling similar to this has been hereditary in the Order, and has been the cause why the early
annals of many of their most illustrious saints are so barren
of details. They never thought of providing for the applause
of man; and brilliant as is the renown of the Dominican
institute in the history of the Church, it may perhaps be
said that its greatest works have never been made manifest.

It was chance, or rather necessity, that at length obliged
the religious of St. Nicholas to undertake the first translation of the sacred relics. The convent had to be enlarged
on account of the ever-increasing size of the community,
and the church stood in need of repair and alteration. The
tomb of Dominic had, therefore, to be disturbed, and to
do so, the Pope's permission was first required. Honorius
III was dead, and his successor in the papal chair was none
other than Ugolino Conti, who had been consecrated Pope
under the name of Gregory IX. He acceded to the request

with joy, sharply reproving the friars for their long negligence. The solemn translation accordingly took place on the 24th of May, 1233, during the Whitsuntide chapter of the Order, then assembled at Bologna under blessed Jordan of Saxony, who had succeeded his great patriarch in the government.

The Pope wished to have attended in person at this ceremony, but, being prevented doing so, deputed the archbishop of Ravenna to represent him, in company with a crowd of other distinguished prelates. Three hundred Friars Preachers from all countries were assembled to assist at this function, not without a secret fear lest the sacred remains should be found to have suffered change; and this doubt as to the result of the translation agitated many of them during the day and night preceding that on which it was appointed to take place, with a painful emotion. Among those who showed the greatest disturbance was one named Brother Nicholas of Giovenazzo; but it pleased God to reassure him, and all who shared his timidity, by a special revelation. For as he prayed, there appeared to him a man of majestic appearance who spoke these words in a clear and joyous tone: *"Hic accipiet benedictionem a Domino, et misericordiam a Deo salutari suo."* And he understood them to signify the blessedness enjoyed by St. Dominic, and to be a pledge of the honor which God would cause to be shown to his relics.

On the 24th of May the ceremony of translation took place. The general, and all the chief fathers of the general chapter then assembled at Bologna, together with the bishops, prelates, and magistrates who had come to be present on the occasion, stood round in silence whilst the grave was opened. Rodolph of Faenza, who still held the office of procurator and who had been so dear a son to the great patriarch, was the first to commence raising the stone. Hardly had he begun to remove the mortar and earth that lay beneath when an extraordinary odor was perceptible, which increased in power and sweetness as they dug deeper, until at length, when the coffin appeared and was raised to the surface of the grave, the whole church was filled with the perfume, as though from the burning of some precious and costly gums. The bystanders knelt on the pavement, shedding tears of emotion as the lid was raised, when there were once more exposed to their eyes, unchanged, and with the same look of sweetness and majesty they had ever worn in life, the features of their glorious father.

Cantipratano, in his second book, *De Apibus*, relates a singular circumstance which has been repeated by Malvenda. He says that among the fathers present at the ceremony was John of Vicenza, whose singular zeal and sanctity had always rendered him specially dear to St. Dominic. As he stood by the body, he made way to give place to William, bishop of Modena; but immediately the sacred remains were seen to turn in the direction in which he stood. His humility moved him to change his place again, and the same thing was observed; and it seemed as though, on this the first day when the public honors of the Church were about to be paid to the holy patriarch, he was willing by this token to show that he counted his chiefest glory to be less in such honors than in the sanctity of his children.

It was blessed Jordan who raised the body of the beloved father from the coffin, and reverently laid it in a new case. Eight days afterwards, this was once more opened to satisfy the devotion of some nobles and others who had been present on the previous occasion; then it was that Jordan, taking the sacred head between his hands, kissed it, while tears of tenderness flowed from his eyes; and, so holding it in his arms, he desired all the fathers of the chapter to approach and gaze at it for the last time: one after another they came, and kissed the features that still smiled on them like a father; all were conscious of the same extraordinary odor; it remained on the hands and clothes of all who touched, or came near the body; nor was this the case merely at the time of the translation. Flaminius, who lived 300 years afterwards, thus writes in 1527: "This divine odor of which we have spoken, adheres to the relics even to this present day."

We shall not pause to give a detail of those abundant miracles which every day shed fresh glory round the sepulcher of St. Dominic. They were scarcely needed, one may say, as attestations of his sanctity; it seemed the universal feeling, both of prelates and people, that his canonization should be no longer deferred. The bull to that effect was published in the July of 1234; and it was the singular happiness of Pope Gregory IX, who had been bound in such close ties of friendship to the founders of the two Orders of the Friars Minors and Friars Preachers, that both should be raised to the altars of the Church by his means, and during his pontificate. His well-known expression with regard to Dominic has been preserved to us by Stefano Salanco: "I have no more doubt of the sanctity of this man, than I have of that of St. Peter or St. Paul."

Three festivals have been consecrated to the memory of St. Dominic: the 4th of August, on which his death is celebrated (instead of the 6th, already occupied by the feast of the Transfiguration); the 24th of May, in memory of the translation of his relics; and lastly, the 15th of September, in honor of the miraculous picture of Suriano. An obscurity rests over the origin of this picture; or perhaps we should rather say that the Church, whilst granting the festival and bearing her willing testimony to the extraordinary Divine favors shown to the devotion of the pilgrims of Suriano, has been silent as to the history of the painting itself. It first appeared in the convent in the year 1530 and did not attract much popular regard until the beginning of the following century, when the miracles and conversions wrought at Suriano made it a place of pilgrimage to the whole world. After a number of briefs granted by successive pontiffs, and a severe examination of the facts, Benedict XIII at length appointed the 15th of September to be observed through the whole Order, in commemoration of the graces received before this remarkable picture.

A second translation of the relics of St. Dominic took place in 1267; but the beautiful sculptures which now adorn his place of burial, and which are probably the first, both in design and execution, among similar works of art, were not placed over his tomb until 1473, being the *chef-d'oeuvre* of Nicholas de Bari.

CHAPTER 27

Dominic's writings. His supposed defense of the Immaculate Conception. His portraits by Fra Angelico, and in the verses of Dante, observations on the Order.

"We should have wished," says Polidori, in the concluding chapter of his life, "to have been able to put before the eyes of our readers all that St. Dominic ever wrote in defense of the Catholic religion, for the instruction of his disciples, in order that they might collect from these writings yet greater and more copious illustrations of his virtues. But there remains to us nothing, except the constitutions of his Order (added to the rule of St. Austin), the sentence of reconciliation to the Church of Pontio Rogerio, and the faculty granted to Raymond William of Altaripa, to entertain the heretic William Uguccione in his house. It is, however, certain that he wrote many letters to his brethren, especially exhorting them to the study of the Sacred Scriptures, but none of these now remain; that addressed to the Polish friars, and bearing his name, not being genuine."

We have already spoken of the letter here alluded to, and as may be remembered, have mentioned that many of the best and most cautious writers have taken a more favorable view of its claims to authenticity. We shall not, therefore, again enter on the question in this place. The commentaries of St. Dominic on the Epistles of St. Paul were still extant in the time of Giovanni Colonna; and when we remember how those Epistles formed the constant and favorite reading of the Saint, we shall know how to regret the loss of their exposition from the hand of one who followed so closely in the footsteps of St. Paul, and seemed in a special manner to have borne his mantle and received his spirit.

The lectures he gave in the apostolic palace on these sai.. Epistles, together with the conferences given at Bologna, on the Psalms and the canonical Epistles and on the Gospel of St. Matthew, are also referred to by Lusitano as still existing in his day; but all have since been lost, and it is the misfortune of the Order and of the Church that, with the exceptions mentioned above, nothing of the writings of this great man now remains.

There is one book, the mention of which occurs in one of the most striking anecdotes of his life, and which, could it be restored to us, would naturally be held in peculiar veneration, not merely for the sake of its author, but also for that token of the Divine approbation which gave to its doctrines and contents even more than the authority of a saint. We refer to the book written by Dominic in confutation of the Albigensian heresies, and which, thrice cast into the fire, remained uninjured, and was even flung out of the burning heap by the flames which refused to touch it. Although this book is lost to us, together with the other writings of St. Dominic, there exists a tradition concerning its contents which is of particular interest to us at this time; and which, without passing any judgment as to its authenticity, we will give, as it is to be found alluded to by several writers.

The following extract is from a letter of Father Alessandro Santo Canale, of the Society of Jesus, published in a collection of letters on the Immaculate Conception at Palermo in the year 1742. He says, "All the regular orders, following the inclination of the Holy Church their mother, have always shown a courageous zeal in defense of the Immaculate Conception. And I say *all*; because one of the most earnest in favor of the Immaculate Conception has been the most learned and most holy Dominican Order, even from its very first beginning—I mean even from the time of the great patriarch St. Dominic, in the dispute which he held with the Albigenses at Toulouse, with so much glory to the Church and to himself. Almost from the time of St. Dominic

down to the present day, there has been preserved in the
public archives of Barcelona a very ancient tablet, whereon
is described the famous dispute of the Saint with the Albigenses and the triumph of the truth, confirmed by the
miracle of the fire into which, at the request of the heretics,
the Saint having thrown his book, when that of the Albigenses
was destroyed, his remained uninjured." Of which book this
inscription thus speaks: "Against these errors St. Dominic
wrote a book on the Flesh of Christ. And the Albigenses,
rising up furiously against the said blessed Dominic, said
that the Virgin was conceived in Original Sin. And blessed
Dominic replied even as it is contained in his book, that
what they said was not true; because the Virgin Mary was
she of whom the Holy Ghost says by Solomon, 'Thou art
all fair, my beloved, and there is no stain in thee.'"

In this book of St. Dominic's on the Flesh of Christ, chap.
17, there are, among other passages, the following words,
quoted from the Acts of St. Andrew: "Even as the first Adam
was made of virgin earth, which had never been cursed,
so also was it fitting for the second Adam to be made in
like manner."* It would seem, therefore, that the book was
still extant at the time of this inscription, and that the above
passages were quoted from it. Nor is it any way surprising,
or difficult for us to believe, that Dominic, educated in the
schools of Palencia, should have been a firm and undoubt-
ing defender of that doctrine which was, so to speak, the
heritage of Spanish theologians.

Two men have been given to the world, each of them
foremost in the ranks of genius, who have in different ways
left us the living portrait of St. Dominic. The first is his

---

*"According to creditable opinion," says Monseigneur Parisis, "St. Dominic pro-
fessed in very express terms his belief in the Immaculate Conception. It is even
said that he committed it to writing in a certain book, which the heretics required him to cast into the flames, &c. . . It contained (it is said) in the following
terms the precious text of the Acts of the Martyrdom of St. Andrew." And he
proceeds to quote the words given above.—*Démonstration de l'Immaculée Conception de la B. Vierge Marie, Mère de Dieu.*

own son Angelico, who, steeped in the spirit of his Order, drew its founder, not indeed according to the material likeness of flesh and blood—for *that* he had not seen—but according to that truer portraiture which is the type of the spiritual man. The idea of St. Dominic as it came before the eye of Angelico in hours of prayer and mystic contemplation has been left us on a thousand frescoed walls, in every attitude and under every variety. Amidst them all we see it is the same idea, the same man; he is there in his joyousness, his majestic beauty, and his life of prayer. Always noble, always simple, with the bright star upon his forehead and the lily in his hand, he stands among a crowd of saints and angels, beneath the Redeemer's Cross or by the side of the Madonna's starry throne, and everywhere we recognize in him our old familiar friend; him who drew all men to him by his winning courtesy and from whose brow there went out that mystic splendor which attracted all who gazed upon it.

The other painter is a poet; *the* poet of Italy and of the middle ages. If Dante drew his inspiration from the fount of human imagination, it was to the Order of St. Dominic that he owed the religious character in which it has been clothed. The poetry of Dante is to poetry what the paintings of Angelico are to art; and indeed the new impulse his writings gave to the early Christian artists exhibits the close harmony that exists between their works and his. And if he might thus claim brotherhood with the Angelic painter, to the Angelic doctor he was bound by yet stricter ties. His theology is that of St. Thomas; and to understand the *Divina Commedia*, we must first read the *Summa*. Thus we may understand how it is that when he comes to draw the portrait of "the holy athlete for the Christian Faith," as he terms St. Dominic, his words flow forth with such a power of vivid and inspired delineation.

Do we not feel that someone greater than the herd of common men is drawing near us, when the great master prepares us for his coming by those few low tones of sweetest

harmony which he draws from his lyre when he speaks of
the founder of the Friars Preachers. "There," he says, "where
the gentle breeze whispers and waves among the young
flowers that blossom over the fields of Europe—not far from
that shore where break the waves behind which the big sun
sinks at eventide, is the fortunate Calaroga; and there was
born the loyal lover of the Christian Faith, the holy athlete,
gentle to his friends and terrible to the enemies of truth.
They called him Dominic; and he was the ambassador and
the friend of Christ; and his first love was for the first counsel that Jesus gave. His nurse found him often lying on the
ground, as though he had said, 'It was for this I came.' It
was because of love for the Divine truth, and not for the
world, that he became a great doctor in a short time; and
he came before the throne of Peter, not to seek dispensa-
tions, or tithes, or the best benefices, or the patrimony of
the poor; but only for freedom to combat against the errors
of the world by the word of God. Then, armed with his
doctrine and his mighty will, he went forth to his apostolic
ministry, even as some mountain torrent precipitates itself
from its rocky height. And the impetuosity of that great
flood, throwing itself on the heresies that stemmed its way,
flowed on far and wide, and broke into many a stream that
watered the garden of the Church."

We must apologize to our readers for giving the glorious
poetry of Dante in weak and ineffective prose; yet perhaps
less weak and less ineffective than the attempt to render
it into such verse as a translator can give. We have but
reminded them of the passage, that they may turn to it in
the original; for a sketch of the character of St. Dominic
seems incomplete without an allusion, at least, to the writer
who has perhaps drawn him best.

We should be departing from the plan we have proposed
to ourselves, if we detained our readers with any summary
and critical examination of the character of St. Dominic's
virtues which is usual in lives of more pretension, and written with a different object to this. But we have sought only

to place this great Saint before our readers in a popular
light, trusting that he might speak to them himself in the
story of his life; and that something of that charm of gracious joyousness on which his old biographers are so eloquent, might win them to a closer study of one whose Order
has been termed so emphatically, "The Order of Truth";
and whose spirit is, even in our own day, as young and
vigorous as ever.

If there be one saint who has greater claims than another
on the love and veneration of the Church, struggling as she
is in our own country against the high tide of heresy, it
is St. Dominic. And if we would learn the way to fight her
battles, we can scarcely do better than sit at the feet of
one who knew so well how to be at the same time the enemy
of heresy and the lover of souls. That wonderful intelligence,
which was able to unite so rigid a discipline with the flexi-
bility which is to be found in what his great daughter St.
Catherine calls "the free and joyous spirit of his Order,"*
had it been engaged in prescribing for the wants of England in our own day, could scarcely have devised a fitter
rule for those who would labor in her cause.

The austerity of St. Dominic was for himself and his own
children; but wherever there was the question of saving souls,
we find only the gay sweet manner that men called magic,
because they could not resist it; the familiarity that mixed
with the people, and would let them cut his very habit to
pieces sooner than drive them from his side; the tenderness
that never wept but for the sufferings or the sins of others,
and which, as the Castilians said, made even penance itself
seem easy, when it was preached to them by Master Dominic.

All labor came alike to him, and the rule that at other
times laid such an iron grasp upon its subjects, relaxed in
a moment when the work of God was to be done. Then,
too, how wonderful it is to find, along with all this popularity
and preaching, the theological spirit never separated from

*"La sua religione, tutta larga, tutta gioconda."—*Treatise on Obedience*, chap. 158.

any part of his design, building up every word on the foundation of Catholic truth, and aiming yet more at instruction than either eloquence or exhortation. The Friars Preachers were pre-eminently to be Friars Teachers; and from the mysteries of the Rosary up to the *Summa* of St. Thomas, we may see the same principle of making a solid knowledge of Christian truth the groundwork of Christian devotion. Thus the most popular order was at the same time the most learned; and whilst their portable pulpits were erected in the streets of London and Oxford, and surrounded by the sermon-loving English crowds of the thirteenth century, the men who filled them and knew how to win the ear and rouse the conscience of their rude and ignorant audience, were the same who filled the chairs of the university with so brilliant a renown that they may be said to have commenced a new era in theological studies.

This mixed character, which is so distinctive a feature of the Dominican rule, gives it peculiar capabilities in a country crowded with population, and crying aloud to be taught. It has its sermons and Rosaries for the poor, and its theology for the learned; for sin and suffering of all kinds and in all shapes, there is the tenderness of that most gentle and fatherly heart of its great founder, who, when he sold his books for his starving countrymen and was ready to sell his own life also, left to his children in those two actions the rule of charity which he would have them follow as their guide.

Of all the founders of religious orders, it may be said that they live again in the history of their institutes; but with St. Dominic this perpetual presence among his followers in all ages was the last legacy of his dying lips. And we can scarcely close this notice of his life with fitter words than those which the Church places on our own, when she teaches us to invoke him:

"Thou didst promise that after death thou wouldst be helpful to thy brethren. Fulfill, O Father, what thou hast said, and assist us by thy prayers."

If you have enjoyed this book, consider making your next selection from among the following . . .

Prices guaranteed through December 31, 1989.

At your bookdealer or direct from the publisher.

Prices guaranteed through December 31, 1989.